C000235525

A TANKIE'S TRAVELS

4th Edition

Published in 2008 by

Woodfield Publishing Ltd
West Sussex, England
www.woodfieldpublishing.co.uk

Copyright © 2008 Jock Watt

All rights reserved

The right of Jock Watt to be identified as author of this work has been
asserted in accordance with the Copyright, Designs and Patents Act
1988

Apart from any use permitted under UK copyright law, this
publication may only be reproduced, stored, or transmitted, in any
form, or by any means, with prior permission in writing of the
publishers or, in the case of reprographic production, in accordance
with the terms of licences issued by the Copyright Licensing Agency.

Every effort has been made to fulfil requirements with regard to
reproducing copyright material. The author and publisher will be glad
to rectify any omissions at the earliest opportunity.

Cataloguing in Publication Data is available from the British Library

ISBN 978-1-84683-197-3

Printed and bound in England

Typesetting & page design: Nic Pastorius
Cover design: Klaus Schaffer

Source document:
A Tankie's Travels (4th Edn).ppp

A TANKIE'S TRAVELS

A TANK COMMANDER'S
EXPERIENCES WITH
THE 3RD ROYAL TANK REGIMENT
IN GREECE & NORTH AFRICA
DURING WORLD WAR TWO

BY

JOCK WATT

woodfieldpublishing.co.uk
Publishing Ltd
WOODFIELD
independent book publishers

Woodfield Publishing Ltd

West Sussex ~ England

tel 01243 821234 ~ **e/m** info@woodfieldpublishing.co.uk

Interesting and informative books on a variety of subjects

For full details of all our published titles, visit our website at
www.woodfieldpublishing.co.uk

This book is dedicated to all the
soldiers, comrades and friends
who fought alongside me
and to the memory of
the many who lost their lives.

Royal Tank Regiment Officer's Cap Badge

CONTENTS

INTRODUCTION

A S A CHILD, GROWING UP in Fraserburgh, a Scottish fishing town just north of Aberdeen, I was obsessed by mechanical things and at every opportunity took them apart, often with disastrous results. At the age of fourteen, I started my engineering career, involved in the repair and maintenance of ships, transport vehicles and farm equipment. This was my utopia and I loved every minute of it.

During the three-month herring fishing season, the town was a throbbing hive of industry, but for the rest of the year it almost died. So, like my three older brothers before me, I moved south in search of fame and fortune.

It was in 1937, at the age of 18, that I enlisted in the Royal Tank Corps (RTC), an organisation which I believed was steeped in engineering. I survived the months of square-bashing, technical training, gunnery and all other courses necessary to become a fully trained 'tankie' and was posted to 3rd Battalion of the RTC at Lydd in Kent. My engineering background proved invaluable and I sailed through with flying colours to early promotion.

I enjoyed my regimented way of life and involvement in tank engineering until Hitler decided he did not have enough space and invaded Poland. I and my colleagues were at our new barracks in Warminster when we heard the grim words of Mr Chamberlain, "...we are at War with Germany", but although more rigorous training was ordered, the full significance of his words was not really understood. We moved around the country and, at each venue, enjoyed the new pattern of life.

A false sense of security, created by many months of inactivity, while opposing armies just watched each other, without firing a shot, was shattered by the enemy's sudden attack and drive across Belgium. We of the 3rd Royal Tank Regiment, comfortably relaxing in England, were hurriedly dispatched to Europe and landed at Calais, ill-prepared for the sequence of events that followed. It was a short-lived, traumatic experience, ending back on the shores of England, defeated, depressed and frightened.

Re-equipped and dispatched to the Middle East to take part in the Desert War, our initiation into the hostile environment of grit, stones, sagebrush and sun was brief. Once again, events dictated a sudden change of scenery and we were urgently dispatched to the mountainous region of northern Greece, this time to confront the German Army driving south through Yugo-slavia. But we were massively outnumbered and outgunned, and in just a few weeks we were once again back on the seashore, defeated and depressed, but this time cut off by the enemy with an empty sea behind us.

In a small motor boat, liberated from a local fisherman, our motley crew sailed the coastline during the hours of darkness to Crete. But it was 'out of the frying pan into the fire', for the island was preparing for imminent invasion and, once again with our backs to the sea, we had to liberate a ship and sail to Alexandria.

The battles in the desert war that followed were long, tiring and very frightening; trying to survive in a hostile land, with the constant fear that the odds of remaining alive were decreasing with every passing day.

It ended at Tunis and we sailed back to England, three years from the day we had left.

D-Day, for me, was spent in hospital, suffering from jaundice. The Regiment had gone without me and I followed their path in a replacement unit, training new tank crews to replace the heavy casualties they suffered.

I re-joined my old comrades, what was left of them, when hostilities ended and suffered with them the trauma of changing from years of nervous tension to a life of relative tranquillity.

With the change from soldier to civilian came the revelation that the country I had served remained only in my memories...

The author, in Royal Tank Corps uniform.

~ CHAPTER 1 ~

IN THE BEGINNING...

O N THE 2ND SEPTEMBER 1939 a revolt in the House of Commons over the suspicion of possibly another Munich fiasco, when promises by Hitler proved to be worthless, left the Prime Minister, Mr Neville Chamberlain, with no option but to send instructions to the British Ambassador in Berlin to issue an ultimatum to Hitler at 0900 hours the following morning: "If German Troops did not end all aggressive action against Poland, and begin to withdraw from Polish Territory by 1100 hours that day, then Britain and Germany would be at War."

We, in the 3rd Battalion of the Royal Tank Regiment, billeted in the Barracks at Warminster, were ordered to assemble in the canteen to hear a very special announcement by the Prime Minister. What a bind that was! It was Sunday, our only day of relaxation and I had planned other things. I listened to the statement on the radio, spoken by a sad, depressing voice, but like many others failed to understand just what those words really meant. My feelings at that moment were difficult to describe; was it nervousness at the prospect of an exciting adventure, or dreaded fear of the unknown? Whatever the truth, the events that followed completely changed my life forever.

It was in 1937 on my 18th birthday that I enlisted in the Royal Tank Corps, in the hopes of continuing my career in engineering. I, like my three brothers before me, could envisage no future in that small fishing town on the north coast of Scotland; we all left to seek a better way of life. The problems did not lie in our home or family life. I grew up in a very happy environment. With the seashore a few hundred yards away and the countryside just over the back garden fence, I had the best of both worlds. A heather-covered hill, about five miles to the south-west, looked down upon the town and harbour, jutting out into the North Sea in this north-east corner of Aberdeenshire. At the end of a long breakwater, sheltering the harbour, the rocks changed to clean golden sands that formed a five-mile crescent around the bay, backed by tall sand dunes covered in long, waving grasses. The blue sea, with its white horses and the contrasting colours of the grasses, presented a continuous, fascinating spectacle of colour and movement.

To the west of the town, a flat, rocky coastline held an abundance of sea life, a perfect feeding ground for masses of different sea birds, sharing their utopia with seals, bobbing about in the water or sleeping on the rocks. As a child all this was my world, the school where I learned of the things that occupied the sea, or flew in the air. Here, I could sit quietly, lulled into dreams of fantasy by the lapping of water on the rocks, the gentle movement of the seaweeds and the birds calling in the background.

The harbour, with its many basins, was another source of adventurous entertainment, whether sailing around it, from the fish-market to the parking areas or catching coley from the quayside with a hook, line and sinker. Generally messing about in boats, on the water or in the shipyards, was like opening the door of an Aladdin's cave. In the winter, a long spell of snow and ice provided the alternatives, sledging down roads almost free of traffic, or skidding down frozen sand dunes on a sheet of corrugated iron. A bucket of water thrown down a sloping pavement produced a long slide in twenty minutes, providing hours of exciting pleasure and exercise for us kids but, for adults struggling up the hill after a long, weary day, it was an unnecessary hazard and an end to our fun was soon administered with a packet of salt.

Between the months of June and August, the herring fishing season transformed the town into a throbbing hive of industry. Up to three hundred drifters would cram into the harbour, each unloading their catches daily, five days a week, juggling for space to tie up, discharge, and get back to sea again. Lorries, horses and carts, barrels, boxes and fish occupied and congested every square yard of quay, all being jostled and moved as if there would be no tomorrow. Indeed, for every day's catch there could be no tomorrow; all fish had to be cleaned, packed and stored before the ships returned next day; working round the clock was common practice.

Almost as suddenly as it all started, the herring moved south, the ships and crews followed, and so did the men and women from the West Coast and Islands, who had traditionally followed the shoals for centuries. The whole town's fishing industry went with them and, but for a few small engineering establishments, the town died.

I did not intend to die with it.

~ CHAPTER 2 ~

A SOLDIER'S LIFE

THE ARMY TOOK MY MIND to pieces, rearranged it into another pattern and made it easily adaptable to whatever circumstances they dictated. In just a few months I became a military machine.

In the beginning, whilst still in civilian clothes, being *asked* to do something gradually changed to being *told* and, from the moment you changed into uniform, you were *ordered*. This was a bitter pill to swallow in the presence of a large group of strange young men.

It took only 48 hours to plunge us into the thick of it; hair cut (a real carve-up that was), Blanco your webbing, polish the brasses – Blanco the webbing again you idiot, you got Brasso all over it! – spit and polish your boots until you see your face in them and, when all your kit is spick and span, lay it out on your bed for inspection. Blankets neatly folded with all spare clothes and equipment laid out in a specified order and, on the towel at the bottom, the implements, knife, fork, spoon, razor, comb, toothbrush, lather brush, button stick, housewife. My god, how well I must have been brainwashed! I can still remember it all after 60 years.

The days were long and the training hard. We ate every crumb of food presented to us and the quality was not important, we were hungry and the body needed it, even prepared to fight for it if necessary. Each table was set out with twelve men's rations; that is, twelve pieces of butter on a plate and the same for jam and bread. You sat down at the table and immediately grabbed your portions; it was dog eat dog, in fact you were hungry enough to eat a horse, so good table manners were a little neglected.

On one particular day I had my butter and bread and the jam plate was in front of me with only one portion on it. The soldier sitting opposite reached out and pulled the plate towards him. I grabbed it back and he started to whimper about it being unfair he had no jam. I asked him if he wanted it and he whimpered 'yes', so I gave it to him, complete with plate, right onto his big fat nose. Perhaps I was a little heavy-handed. He went backwards over the form and skidded along the polished floor on his back. It was not my lucky day; he finished up at the feet of the Orderly Sergeant. That cost me seven days jankers, doing all the lousy jobs they could think of. I scoured pots and pans in the Officers' Mess after dinner until about 10pm and reported to the Guard Room every time that damned bugle blew. It taught me a lesson I never forgot, to keep my temper under control.

The last meal of the day was a mug of cocoa and maybe a slice of bread, that is if you had enough energy left to drag that weary body to the dining room. Then came the hard, springless army bed with its three 'biscuit' mattress, as solid as a rock, but as the bugle called for lights out it caressed your body like a mountain of feathers.

But almost as the notes faded, the sound of reveille and the screaming voice of the orderly corporal heralded another day...

In an instant the barrack room was alive with thirty men stripping beds, folding blankets, washing and shaving, all hell-bent on being prepared for the first order of the day: "Outside for PT!" Come rain, fog, sleet or snow, we punished our bodies like men possessed, with the pride of soldiers that we were – or was it fear of that screaming voice?

Every minute of every day was programmed to meet the demands of training to be a proficient soldier in tank warfare.

The mechanics of light and medium tanks plus many other types of road transport were taught in great detail. All were trained and tested in driving and maintenance and the ability to handle the tank armament on a mock-up machine, which pitched and twisted to simulate movement.

Gunnery was taught at another camp, so, towards the end of our training, we marched the six miles to Lulworth, with all our equipment packed on our back. It was a day of warm sunshine and, in full marching order, the sweat poured from our bodies, but after the past weeks of physical and mental exercise we took it all in our stride.

Gunnery was a completely new world to me and I tackled it with such enthusiasm that it almost cost me my life. We learned about telescopic sights, used to align the barrel of the gun with the target, and the intricate mechanisms of shells and their explosive propellant. Vickers water-cooled machine guns were a mass of mind-boggling components, but we learned to strip and rebuild them with speed and efficiency, even blindfolded and in the dark.

Firing with live ammunition on the ranges was another new and exciting adventure. The large anti-tank gun, which also fired explosive shells, went off with a deafening bang and rocked the tank back on its tracks. We all competed against each other at loading and firing as fast as possible, with the main object of hitting a target, either stationary or moving. Combined with this was firing the machine gun mounted alongside the big gun. What a fascinating sight to see a string of tracer bullets streaking through the air towards the far hillside!

Never in my life had I experienced such a feeling of power as I now did, sitting with my eye pressed against the telescope, my finger on the trigger, in complete command of this mighty gun. One gentle squeeze and a shell hurled from the barrel towards the target, the red glow of it's tracer almost too fast to follow. The breach automatically opened, throwing out an empty shell-case, followed by the red glow of unburned gasses. Almost immediately, a new shell was slid into the gun and the breach closed with an ominous clang. Smoke filled the turret with a pungent smell of burned cordite, it penetrated clothes and lungs and left a never-to-be-forgotten imprint on the mind.

Initial training in the handling of machine guns and our personal weapon, the .45 revolver, was carried out on a thirty-yard range. A long, shed-type building held a number of mock-up gun mountings, facing target frames set in the hillside at thirty yards distance. We all took it in turns mounting the gun, feeding in the ammunition belts, firing at and changing targets. All carried out in an atmosphere of voices screaming in your ear, feet hammering on the floorboards and the rattle of machine gun fire.

With tension stretched to the limit, the brain struggled to anticipate the next order. It was my turn to dash up the range and change targets when firing stopped and I stood poised, waiting for the command. A voice screamed and I took off like a gazelle, hell-bent on achieving the fastest target change ever, but half way up the range I stopped dead in my tracks, with alarm bells ringing in my head. Things were not quite right. I could still hear the rattle of machine guns and I was running into the target area. I turned and ran back, to be met by a very irate sergeant threatening to take the skin off my back and using words I had never heard before. There was no doubt about it, I had committed a court martial offence and would probably be discharged from the army in shame. It was rather strange, then, that I heard nothing more about it. Perhaps when he calmed down he realised that it was he who could be charged with neglect of duty.

I was lucky to get away with that one, although the rest of the squad pulled my leg about it for days, but one of them was not so lucky. We were stripping the guns in our hut and some idiot had brought a live round back from the range, which he pushed into the breach and the gun fired. The bullet passed through the wooden walls of three huts full of men and thankfully missed them all. We never saw him again. Rumours voiced his fate as everything from discharge to hanging.

Back at the base depot, training continued for a few more weeks, with the now familiar mixture of parades, drill, map-reading, spud-bashing and floor-polishing. We were even allowed a pass to leave camp, a luxury indeed, or would have been if there had been somewhere to go and money to spend. Apart from a walk out onto the moors which surrounded the camp, or a stroll two miles to the nearest village, there was nothing but the NAAFI or a train to Poole or Bournemouth, but that would cost a quarter of your weekly wage...

Now fully trained and passed out on the barrack square, we were posted to regular regiments; I went to the third battalion of the Royal Tank Corps – and a much more acceptable and stable lifestyle.

Although training was more extensive and much harder, a limited social life was available. Mind you, there was not a lot you could do on a wage of two shillings a day. We were paid ten shillings a week, the other four shillings being kept 'in credit' to cover the cost of your boot repairs, etc. Yes that's right, they made you wear out the boots marching up and down a barrack square, then took back the money they had given you to replace the worn out soles!

The game of orders and discipline was very cleverly played from top to bottom, right down through all the ranks to the poor bloody private. It couldn't go any further, could it? For any mistake you made, in the opinion of any superior, a public bawling-out was the order of the day, in front of anybody and everybody. At first, the embarrassment was unbearable – you wished for the earth to swallow you up – but gradually the bombardment changed the feeling to one of guilt – you had let your mates down, the squadron and the regiment, in fact, you were responsible for the collapse of the whole bloody Army!

One classic example was barrack-room and kit inspection, a weekly charade, with not a speck of dust to be seen on the gleaming, polished floor and equipment displayed on your bed with immaculate precision. It should be; you had spent hours the previous night laying it out and slept on the floor. Imagine the disillusionment, then, after sweating for an hour to buff up a brilliant shine on a floor, of being bawled out for footprints made on it by the inspecting officer.

The evil hour arrives and you find yourself standing stiffly to attention, eyes glued to a tiny spot on the far wall, heart beating faster as the thump of the sergeant major's boots comes nearer, praying that you will not be the target for today. The footsteps stop and you gasp for breath. Is he looking at my bed or the one before? Oh God, please let him walk past! A sudden scream in my ear leaves me trembling like a jelly.

"You 'orrible little man! Outside on parade, in full marching order, in half an hour!"

With that, his metre stick, which he has slid under the blanket with all my kit on it, is whipped up, sending my hours of patient work flying into the air.

That charade resulted in everyone in the room being confined to barracks for the day and it was *my* fault – not a very popular position to be in. Of course, there was nothing wrong with the layout of my equipment, it just happened to be my turn to carry the can for another brainwashing lesson in discipline. At the next inspection, someone else would be picked on and I would feel relieved and pleased that my standard must have improved. They had won the battle. I felt proud to be a soldier amongst those men and would never let them down again. That was lesson number one, but I was yet to discover just how important a part pride would play in forging the dictates of my life.

Lesson number two followed quite quickly. That bellowing bastard of a sergeant major had me standing stiffly to attention in his office, gave me a damned good talking to, then promoted me to lance corporal. What a shock that was, the man was actually human! I was thrilled to bits and strutted around like a turkey cock with two tails. It even meant a small pay rise. My elation was short lived, however. It took just a few hours for the truth to sink in that he had done me no favour. I now had to carry the can for the mistakes of others, my mates, or should I say my ex-mates, because according to them I was now a bigger bastard than the sergeant major. That was not very fair; he lived in the remote comfort of married quarters, whilst I had to rough-it in the barrack room along with them and, whilst I could only vent my frustration on a handful of men, he took it out on the whole bloody squadron!

Happily the lads' aggressive attitude towards me was soon replaced by a common respect for each other's ability. We were all taught specific tasks as gunners, drivers, wireless operators, etc, to qualify as a member of a tank crew. As such, we were part of a team completely dependant upon each other, that was the spirit in which we had been trained – "*esprit de corps*" – a regard for honour and the interests of the body of men to which one belonged. I was most certainly growing up fast.

Being located on the most southern tip of Kent, with the English Channel almost a stone's throw south of the barracks and farmland to the north, we shared a sympathetic bond of isolationism with the residents of Lydd, just outside the camp gates. This village, with almost as many pubs as houses (I seem to remember a number like thirteen) was our usual escape from the irrepressible military atmosphere of the barracks and, although sometimes supplemented by the pub at Camber, a few miles away, or a night out in Hastings via the Regimental bus, it was still our haven in times of need.

An occasional dance in the gym attracted sufficient girls from surrounding areas to make it a night to remember and I, being a student of the art, never missed a dance. Most other leisure hours were spent in the gym, occupied with boxing, fencing and other physical activities and, with the daily routine of tank maintenance, training and, of course, guard duties, there was little time for the luxury of boredom.

Like almost everyone, anywhere, life became a habit of living.

Stationed at the southern end of England with my home six hundred miles away in the north of Scotland, a short weekend pass home was not practical and a longer spell of leave also had it's limitations, due to my low salary and high travel costs. There was a Tank Regiment at Catterick, which would have reduced the distance to my home by half, but one of the three wise men had posted me to Lydd, and probably with the same stroke of his pen sent those from Kent to Catterick. It was a cruel world, but that was what I had signed up for...

From the seashore and shingle of Lydd in Kent, we moved to a brand new barracks at Warminster in Wiltshire, a beautiful setting on the edge of Salisbury Plain, comfortable accommodation, excellent food and greatly improved social amenities. What more could one ask for? To take part in tactical exercises with other Army units on this vast plain was a new experience for us. Driving across the old Artillery Range, with its mass of overlapping shell holes, was dangerous and exciting, although throwing a track off while sliding sideways into a hole resulted in hours of dirty, cursing, hard labour in all weathers.

The town of Warminster and the surrounding villages had much to offer in the form of entertainment and we took full advantage of those new stomping grounds. For a small group of us, Friday was the day we searched the local newspapers for activities outside the town, our aim being to get away from our comrades in arms and break new ground. Perhaps we were fearful of the competition but, whatever the reason, our social life in the villages was fantastic.

Sadly, this utopia was short-lived. It was here, in the NAAFI canteen, that our new-found dream life came to an end. War was declared. Our beautiful barracks was turned into an Infantry Depot and we were moved out into tents in a muddy field. This was our RSM's dream. He walked across from the married quarters, stood on nice clean duckboards and screamed at us for having muddy boots. But even his dream world was soon to be shattered when we moved into billets at Fordingbridge, a delightful country town on the River Avon, at the edge of the New Forest.

~ CHAPTER 3 ~

FRANCE, FEAR & FAILURE

NOW WHAT ABOUT THAT WAR...? Apart from moving a few regiments across the channel to sit quietly and glare at the enemy, nothing appeared to be happening. Dragging on through winter and spring, it was referred to by all as the 'Phoney War'. Rumour had it that the war had begun, but this time the news did not come from the girls in the local laundry, so we just laughed it off. I never ceased to be amazed by these girls; they always seemed to know where we were going long before we did. Where the hell did they get their information from? They were seldom wrong.

The rumours became a reality and everyone was caught with their trousers down. What a dreadful waste of time and money building those massive defensive walls between France and Germany. The German Army simply crossed the borders of Holland and Belgium, where no walls existed, and drove west to the sea. It took just 18 days to inflict a devastating defeat on the allied Armies. Everyone was left gasping in disbelief.

Probably the greatest shock to allied commanders, some still deeply committed to the static trench warfare of World War I, was the *blitzkrieg* tactic used by the Germans. Fast-moving armoured columns preceded by dive-bombers and sometimes paratroops dropped from the sky, created terror and panic amongst soldiers and civilians alike. People abandoned their homes and fled west to escape the invaders and in doing so they blocked the roads and prevented the Allied forces from moving to counter the German offensive.

In the meantime, the official announcement of the situation brought back that sick feeling in the pit of the stomach; a dreaded fear of the unknown. I found only one cure for fear, deep involvement in mental and physical activities and, in the few days that followed, we certainly had plenty of that. We worked from dawn to dusk, packing up and preparing the tanks and other vehicles for shipment to France. Thinking back on those days, I have never ceased to be amazed at the speed and efficiency with which those tasks were carried out, everyone without question carrying out his orders.

At this time I was a corporal and driver of the CO's staff car. I never did understand why they trusted me to drive the Colonel, 'a real cushy job' according to my mates, but I was not so sure. From then on, everything happened so fast my memory is vague. Our tanks were loaded at Southampton and a few days later we embarked on a ship at Dover, our destination Calais. Once again our underground intelligence service (the Fordingbridge Laundry) had told us correctly when, where and how.

Our ship tied up at the quay and we were ordered to stay on board. I struggled to a spot where I could get a clear view of the town – and what a shock that was – my first frightening look at the devastation of war. A dark pall of smoke, sent up by buildings on fire, hung low over the town. Ships lay dead in the water and broken glass from a deserted hotel on the quayside covered the roadway. It crunched and cracked underfoot as a mixed group of dejected Allied soldiers, hoping to embark on our ship for the sanctuary of England, came towards us.

Already feeling uncomfortably dirty, unshaven and weary from 24 hours of travelling, this scene did little to encourage my enthusiasm for war. Added to this, the ship with our tanks aboard had not arrived, and nobody seemed to know what the hell was going on. What a bloody shambles! We were eventually instructed to vacate the ship, which was urgently needed for a trainload of casualties arriving on the quayside, and disperse amongst the sand dunes.

Lying amongst the dunes, looking up at a lovely blue sky, my mind wandered back to the miles of dunes at home, where we had played as children. What wonderful days they had been: seagulls strutting up and down at the water's edge, the wind blowing off the sea, rustling the long dune grasses as we hid amongst them, playing 'cowboys and indians'. We used to crawl amongst the grass, jump up, shout 'bang!' and then roll over and get up again, completely unhurt.

Sadly, this was not the same sort of game...

Suddenly, the drone of planes overhead, the scream of bombs and the deafening crash of explosions left me clawing at the sand. This was for real, my first encounter with the reality of war. I was shaking with fear and felt ashamed that others may see it on my face.

Still, it was amazing how quickly peace and normality returned, as the drone of the planes faded. Everyone wandered around, chatting and laughing at events so far in a show of bravado, hiding our true feelings of frustration and fear. But all was not doom and gloom. We had one good laugh when two of our group went on the scrounge around the hotel. They found the wine cellar and returned loaded with beautifully-shaped small bottles. What a fantastic find and what a joke; it was only soda water.

The tank ship eventually arrived but had a deck cargo of cans of petrol – a nice situation with the next air-raid expected any minute. It was all hands on deck to unload this bomb of leaking cans before an unfriendly enemy ignited it for us and, with no power available for the dockside cranes, the ship's derricks had to be used to unload the tanks. We prepared them for battle, and what a monstrous task that was, everything having been heavily greased for sea travel. Thankfully, I was called back to my duty as car driver. The last time I saw our tanks was on the outskirts of Calais as they went off to meet the enemy on the road to Boulogne.

Our transport supply column followed the tanks and parked amongst the houses on the outskirts of the town. I remained with them and watched a never-ending trail of refugees, stretching to the far horizon, moving slowly past us towards the centre of town. Men, women and children, rhythmically moving one foot in front of the other, plodding towards some unknown destination, eyes downcast in an expression of sadness and shame, their worldly goods perched across bent backs. The very fortunate had a horse and cart, but for many the horse had gone and the family now took its place. The less fortunate had just a small bundle dangling at the end of a weary arm.

We had another air-raid and the scream of bombs sent us scurrying for cover. I dived under a lorry, but there was little space left; not an ideal situation to find I was rubbing noses with a sergeant, who was whimpering and shaking with fear. In contrast to the refugees, who appeared to have heard nothing, or perhaps just didn't care any more, the pathetic state of this massive six-foot-plus man was depressing. He did nothing to help me maintain my outward appearance of bravado, even though my heart was pounding louder than the bomb blasts. I feel sad when I remember this sergeant as the man who had trained the Regiment's Tug-of-War teams, with military precision, to a condition where they challenged all-comers and beat most. We were very proud of our athletic achievements, but who could have predicted that this soldier, who gave so many so much to be proud of, would become such a spectacle of pity. He later committed suicide with a rifle.

I was glad when an order came for me to leave the staff car and return to Calais with the remains of our supply column. The shells started to scream overhead and we took cover in some dugouts in a park, but there was no letup in the shelling, the barrage just moved from one part of town to another. One shell went through the church spire and left a large hole in the centre.

The days dragged on with little time between salvos of shells for sleep and the lack of positive activity did nothing to quell the fear and frustration. At last, a positive order came through to move to the docks for evacuation. Thank God for that! I was beginning to feel quite helpless.

We moved off in small groups but had covered just a few hundred yards when shells came crashing around us. I dropped to the pavement and rolled into the gutter, the kerb offering the only cover available. The house beside me came crashing down, throwing up a large cloud of choking dust with a pungent smell of soot. Debris pelted my body. I got up, shook off the muck and looked around. There was no one to be seen. I was all alone, and that was more frightening than the shellfire.

Most of the buildings around me were just piles of rubble but there, reflecting my image, was a large, plate-glass window. How in the name of hell had that survived? As a child I had always been fascinated by the image of windows shattering, broken by the actors in comedy films, and now, here before me, was a God-given opportunity to achieve a childish ambition. I picked up a brick and hurled it at the window. What an anti-climax; it just cracked and fell apart. I felt nothing. How ridic-ulous for a grown man to indulge in a childish fantasy in such an atmosphere of death and destruction.

I continued my lone journey to the docks, with frequent delays, diving for cover from screaming shells, the thought that I could be left behind hurrying me on. The nearer I got to the dock area, the more depressing became the scene. How could the mighty British Army, with its long history of victorious wars, be reduced to this pathetic state of defeat in just a few days? The streets became progressively more congested with abandoned vehicles, some burning, others disarmed by hand-grenades. The road and pavements were littered with personal equipment, obviously hurriedly discarded in a mad rush to get away. The whole scene was like an ill-kept junkyard.

At the end of the street, the docks spread out before me. I stopped and gasped, my heart dropped into my boots and I could have cried. The scene was almost indescribable. Dock installations blown up, lorries and other equipment dumped in the harbour, adding to the remains of ships sunk or disabled by bombing. An uneasy stillness hung in the air, even the sound of gunfire seemed to have receded into the distance; it was as if the death-blow had been delivered and the dead left in peace.

Movement of some soldiers towards a breakwater brought back the reality of my predicament. I had to get away, so I hurriedly joined them. An old coaster was tied up at the quayside, the only vessel in the harbour with smoke pouring from its funnel. We clambered aboard as if our lives depended upon it, which, indeed they did. The hatch cover was off the single hold and a wall ladder led down into the depths. I saw a seething mass of bodies packed onto the bottom floor and decided that was not for me. I stayed on deck.

With a sigh of relief, we cast-off almost immediately and sailed south, parallel to the coast. German troops were running along the beach towards Calais and shells started exploding in the air above us. I began to doubt the wisdom of my decision to stay on deck. I panicked and searched for a place to hide. Lagged steam pipes to the forward winch were attached to the side of the hatch. Thank God I was skinny, I crammed my body underneath. By the grace of God or just good luck, the German gunners, probably firing at such short range with open sights, failed to hit us with a single shot.

The trip across the Channel was uneventful and, as we slowly approached the white cliffs of Dover, voices were heard from the bowels of the ship where an uneasy silence had prevailed since the shelling stopped. No one was allowed to leave the ship for some considerable time, after all, we were a mixed group of many nationalities and security had to be maintained. For a short time no one seemed to mind, thankful that we had escaped from Calais and that those dreadful pangs of fear had gone. A quiet calmness settled over the crowd, now packed on deck, but gradually the pangs of hunger took over. It was hard to remember when we had last eaten. Everyone stirred anxiously when a load of boxes of tinned food were dumped on the quay. That was the last straw. A mad rush over the side and the boxes were torn apart. I reached for a tin of beans and a bayonet just missed the back of my hand. I decided that the leftovers would satisfy me.

Then by rail to a camp somewhere in England and a lovely hot meal, with strict instructions not to discuss our adventures. The camp was full of new recruits and any hint of the chaos across the water could alarm these virgin soldiers. Eventually it was back to Fordingbridge, where the Regiment was regrouped and re-equipped, ready for the next stage of events. It was a tearful return for some, with joy from their womenfolk to see husbands and sweethearts safely home, but for many there was sadness and grief at the loss of those who had given their lives or were destined to spend many years behind barbed wire as Prisoners of War.

But for those who were lucky enough to return, there was to be no respite; they would soon have to do it all over again...

~ CHAPTER 4 ~

A Voyage Overseas

OUR RETURN VISIT TO FORDINGBRIDGE was short-lived; we were moved again to Bottisham Park, near Cambridge, but the memories of the previous winter in billets lingered on. Mac and I, both car drivers, were billeted on the third floor of a very old house, standing in parkland at the edge of town. With the exception of an old couple on the ground floor and us on the third, this large house was completely deserted.

Our room was like an attic, with broken windows and no furniture. Our bedrolls and other equipment occupied the bare wooden floor. There was no heat or light and the icy wind blew across that room as if there were no walls either. The Hood Arms Hotel supplied our main needs for survival; a beer and a couple of glasses of rum and peppermint drugged us to sleep and kept our body temperature up throughout the night. Well... that was our excuse.

I usually slept undisturbed, but one night Mac woke me, wandering around the room, probably still under the influence. Either he had a weak bladder or perhaps he had consumed more beer than I, in any event, he wanted to go to the loo, but that amenity was on the ground floor. Being of a considerate nature and not wishing to disturb the other residents, I watched him stagger to the broken window and discharge his duty like the proud soldier he was. I was fearful that this act may disturb those below, but I need not have worried; instead he probably awakened the whole town. Directly beneath our window was a shed with a corrugated iron roof. The noise was like an ack-ack barrage! Someone must have complained, for we were moved a few days later – into the ground-floor lounge of a bank manager's house – fantastic!

In contrast, our next home, at Bottisham, near Cambridge, was a tent in the park – cold, wet, overcrowded and too near for comfort to a two-inch water standpipe, used for filling our water trucks. The constant spillage from over-filling soon turned the area into a quagmire so, with the attitude of "if you can't beat them join them", we used the pipe as a shower. A high hedge about a hundred yards away screened us from the road, at least that is what we thought until, unknown to us and soon to be enlightened, the local Chivers Marmalade factory collected its employees from around the villages in an open-top double-deck bus. One morning whilst larking under the shower as usual, we were shocked and embarrassed when a bus with two girls on the top deck, eyes popping out, moved slowly down the road. Well, to be truthful, we were not really embarrassed, in fact we enjoyed every bloody minute of it and reacted like the gentlemen we were!

From that day on, the top deck was full, regardless of the weather. I could imagine the problem we gave that poor driver, trying to negotiate those country lanes with an overloaded top deck. Of course we carried on with our stage show and gave the girls a treat, probably our only contribution to the war effort at that time, since we had no tanks and very little even to defend ourselves with. Our losses at Calais were gradually restored by replacements from the Depot and other tank units and many of us survivors were promoted to replace our lost non-commissioned officers. I was promoted sergeant and joined a tank troop.

We collected a new consignment of A13 Cruiser tanks and began retraining as a regiment. This brought renewed mental and physical activity into our life and helped erase the deep depression that had lingered on after our flight from France. The feeling of having been defeated and forced to run for home put an enormous dent in our personal pride. It was something that no one talked about although everyone must have felt it; I know I did.

Time and events sped on to a day when, with little warning, the colour of our tanks was changed from green to sand and our kit to khaki drill. No imagination was required to guess where we were going. We loaded our tanks on the *Clan Lamont* and embarked on the liner *Stirling Castle* at Liverpool. It was a sad farewell to England, we had no idea how long it would take to reach our destination, but had no illusions about the potential dangers that awaited us in the Atlantic Ocean.

At first, the problems of adapting to life on a cramped ship left little time to worry about what might be; that was until we hit a spell of rough water, then we did have a problem. Seasickness took priority over many other duties. Brave soldiers, defeated by the roll of a ship, lay around in their own mess, apparently unable to muster enough energy to reach the upper decks. Under the circumstances, we had no option but to enforce military discipline by shouting orders and bullying until all the mess was cleaned up and the offenders chased to the upper decks to be buffeted by the wind. The change was remarkable; even their sense of humour returned. One soldier laughingly suggested that the other had a weak stomach. "Not me," was the answer. "I can throw up further than any of you!" The philosophy of 'being cruel to be kind' worked and the battle against seasickness was quickly won.

Cramped for space and with very limited organised activity or entertainment, the main enemy was boredom. Playing card games for fun, but more often for money, was a popular occupation, but much of the time was spent just lazing around, chatting and writing letters. Of course, there was plenty of time to just dream of the past. It is remarkable how vivid details of pleasant events in life can quickly be brought to mind and relived; an exercise I frequently put into effect as a relief from boredom.

When we sailed from Liverpool there were no friends or relatives waving farewell; the sobs and tears had already been shed in the villages around Kettering (perhaps some even sighed with relief!) but as the land faded into the skyline, pleasant memories lingered. The town of Hitchin came to mind with a pleasant sigh; it had been the playground of airmen from a nearby airfield for many years and the locals had welcomed us like a breath of fresh air. The friendliness and generosity of the people of Hitchin was a new experience to us; we had lapped it up and enjoyed every minute of it. Our tanks, parked in the centre of the town, were accepted by the residents as willingly as their offer of billets were by the troops. Usually, those big steel monsters, tearing up roads and destroying grass verges, are cursed by all and banished to the muddy fields of the countryside.

Hitchin, to us, was paradise, living next door to perhaps a pub or a café or dancing in the Hermitage Ballroom and not requiring a pass to walk out of our respective front doors. Probably the most memorable contribution to our Utopia was the girls, who were delightful and a number of marriages resulted. But wherever there are girls there is trouble, especially when the Air Force and Army are in competition for them and, inevitably, a number of battles did occur. We bore no malice, of course, but we usually won.

Movement to a muddy field at Deene, near Corby, was a bitter blow in contrast to billets in a town. Here, in tents, just a few hundred yards from a lake, with the limitations of open-air cooking and a ten-mile journey in the back of a lorry to the nearest town of Kettering, it was not exactly paradise. But, like the good soldiers we were, we made the best of a bad lot ... and cursed every bloody minute of it!

Two unusual incidents occurred here. Part of a broken-down, rotten fence around the field perimeter was used by the cooks to fuel their fires and, after we had left, the Regiment received a bill for a new fence, with a suggestion that it be deducted from our pay; this was probably the greatest contribution the estate owners made to the War Effort. The other incident was a sudden awakening in the middle of the night by millions of tiny frogs, about a quarter of an inch long, crawling all over us. They were in our beds, on our faces and squelched under our feet. Where the hell did they come from? It was suggested that they rained from the sky. I am not so sure about that.

Kettering, a very pleasant country town, was our usual venue for a night out, but with a very limited local bus service, the Regimental transport controlled our social life. There was plenty of entertainment to get ones teeth into, with bars, dance halls and, if you were lucky enough to get a day off, the pleasures of Wicksteeds Park (a useful place for courting at night, as well). My memories of Kettering are probably more intimate than most, for it was here that I formed my first serious relationship with a girlfriend. We eventually married and set up home here at the end of the war.

Although our Regiment had said 'hello' and 'cheerio' to many towns and villages throughout the country, for me this was the saddest, sailing off to the unknown wondering if I would ever return.

The first sighting of land brought back some form of normality after days of limitless horizons of sea; it was Freetown, Sierra Leone, on the west coast of Africa. Anchored in the bay, the air was hot, humid and rich with the smell of rotting vegetation. On the distant shore we watched the Palm Trees waving in the wind; it was a pleasant tranquil scene and thoughts of war could not have been further from my mind. Quite suddenly, the wind increased and rain came tumbling down in a torrent such as I had never seen; the sky and sea were as one. It ended as suddenly as it had begun.

We sailed on in our cruise ship, staring day after day at the vast expanse of the Atlantic Ocean, occupied, we hoped, by nothing but the ships of our convoy; it was a frustrating and very boring experience. The Army did their best to keep us mentally and physically occupied, but with such limited space and facilities they could only scratch the surface. The fun formalities observed on crossing the Equator gave a welcome break to the daily routine of boat drill exercises and lectures and to see the shining stars of the Southern Cross for the first time was something new. At night the sea churned up by the ship cutting through the water produced a phosphorescent glow in a continuous display of changing pictures and patterns. This, and the shoals of flying fish shooting up out of the waves and racing alongside the ship, occupied much of my solitary peaceful hours, but the initial excitement of a new adventure had long since faded.

At the southern end of Africa, Table Mountain stood out against the skyline like a massive loaf of bread and beneath it the city of Cape Town covered the land between mountain and sea. We had heard that troop ships frequently refuelled here and local residents generously entertained the troops during their stay, but sadly our high hopes took a dive as we sailed on around the Cape and said farewell to a beautiful dream. What a shame. With a pocketful of money I had won during a lucky gambling streak, I had been all set to burn up the town; now my booze-up and hangover would have to wait.

During the next few days word got around that troops were no longer welcome in Cape Town. The rumour was that an Australian troopship had docked there, a brewers wagon had been unloaded in the streets and a drunken mob had torn the town apart. So for us it was 'back to the card table' to kill a few more boring gambling days, but for me it was also a catastrophe; my luck changed and I was soon broke again. Ah well, easy come easy go! A day later it really hit me below the belt when we docked at Durban, with the opportunity to go ashore, but all my money was gone.

Shore leave was organised and as the troops spewed off the ship onto the quayside, a fleet of private cars picked them up and drove off with a load of smiling faces. The residents of this city, determined to make our stay a memorable one, pulled out all the stops and they most certainly succeeded. Just to put your feet on solid ground after that long, boring journey was a heart-warming experience.

For some reason or other, Mac and I were a bit slow in getting off the ship. All the cars had gone and the quayside was almost deserted. We were debating our predicament when a large saloon car came screaming down the quay, skidded to a halt beside us, and a gentleman jumped out, apologising for being so late. He was manager of a bank and took us to his Country Club for the day; in the evening he handed us over to a hostess who had arranged a dance for the troops, complete with partners and a live Big Band. What a fantastic day that was! The misery of that long, boring sea journey was banished and we felt almost human beings again.

However, the elation and feeling of goodwill towards my fellow man was short-lived. I and four others were transferred to the tank ship, under orders to carry out maintenance on the vehicles during the remainder of the sea voyage. The ship was docked at the coaling quay, where everything was covered in a thick layer of dust and, although we had a few more days ashore without the escorts, the dirty, depressing atmosphere of our new home dampened our enthusiasm for living it up.

Back at sea, the wind and spray cleaned the ship and brightened our outlook on life. Being the sergeant in charge, I had a cabin to myself, and very comfortable it was too. I was also fortunate in that I dined in the ship's Officers Mess and by comparison with the troopship this was luxury indded, with every meal a banquet. How about five courses each for breakfast, lunch and dinner and to wake up from an afternoon nap to tea and toast? The rest of my crew shared a large cabin, but still enjoyed excellent catering facilities and certainly fared much better than on the troopship.

The luxury of good food was somewhat balanced by the unenviable tasks we had to perform down in the bowels of that ship; our improved standard of living was well earned by hard work. The main objective was to remove all batteries from the tanks, drag them up on deck and recharge them for 24 hours. Sounds simple doesn't it? Unfortunately, loose cargo had been loaded between, and on top of, the vehicles and this had to be manhandled in the limited space available to allow access to the battery cover plates. Add to this the sweltering heat in a hold sealed to the outside atmosphere in equatorial temperatures and the reward of those gourmet meals was fully justified.

Other disturbing events came to light during our struggles below deck. Many packing cases were easily moved because they had nothing in them; they had been emptied at the port of loading. Even medical supplies had been looted with most of the cases labelled 'Medicinal Brandy' and many others empty. So much for our fellow man, or should I say 'the enemy within'.

We sailed through the Suez Canal, with our fist sighting of the desert sands and the unusual experience of observing the curvature of the Earth when looking down the canal with the flat desert on either side. We anchored for a short stay at Port Said. We were surrounded by docks and the buildings of this large city where crowds of people could be seen moving around amongst carts drawn by bullocks or mules, some loaded with veiled women and others with sugar cane or green vegetation. This was indeed a new experience. The temperature was in the 90s, the air hot and humid, and the sound of unusual wailing music and the strange aroma of spicy food, mixed with the smell of vegetation and the stench of horse dung drifted from the shore. Such was our introduction to the 'Land of the Pharaohs'.

I stood with my back to the rail, chatting to a ship's officer, when a voice somewhere behind me called out, in a very broad Scottish accent, "Hello Jock, would you like some fruit?" I looked down at the water and there, in what was termed a 'Bum Boat', was an Egyptian, surrounded by a variety of fruit. "I am Jock McGregor fae Ayberdeen," he shouted, as he threw up a line. His Aberdeen accent was broader than mine. A basket of fruit was hauled up and I exchange it for money. He accepted what I put in the basket and the fresh fruit was very welcome.

We docked at Alexandria and I felt for sure that this was our destination. What a strange new world this was! Leaning on the ship's rail, under a lovely blue sky, the sun warm on my face and weird music drifting in the air, I watched Egyptian dockers, in clothes that resembled nightgowns, running with loads on their back between stacks on the quayside and a warehouse. The pace of their movement was regulated by a foreman-type character, carrying a long cane with a large knob at one end; this was obviously his symbol of office and he used it to beat time on a box. The dockers chanted to the rhythm and this was the timing for each man to grab his load and run. However, the cane did have another function; it was also used most effectively to beat any who failed to pick up their load on time.

This foreman was responsible for the movement of goods, but if he was too slow they gave his cane to someone else. Those poor miserable souls worked from dawn to dusk for just a few piastres a day. What a hell of a way to live.

It was a cruel world indeed, here I was, at the gateway to a new adventure, yet unable to leave the ship. I could imagine everyone in the Regiment, with the exception of our small tank party, living it up in the bars and cafés of Alexandria. How was I to know that they had been dumped in a hellhole ten miles out in the desert?

~ CHAPTER 5 ~

THE HELLHOLE OF AMIRIYA

WITH A SIGH OF RELIEF, the last vehicle was unloaded. We packed our gear and drove west out of the city, along the coast road, with the sea on one side and the desert on the other, then turned south onto the Cairo Desert Road and into an area covered with tents. Surely this was not our new home? It was. I vowed never again to complain about billets. This was it, a few palm trees on the seaward side of the camp and the rest just sand littered with stones for as far as the eye could see. What a blow to my dream of golden sands with waving palms around an oasis pool; damn those old romantic films of the desert, they had certainly fooled me.

There was a bonus, though, we were allowed passes into Alexandria and that was well worth the hassle of being thrown about in the back of a lorry on that road full of potholes. Only one other hurdle marred our journey on the way, passing through an area near the docks called Mex, with its large tanneries belching out the most dreadful stink. A procedure was adopted which involved drawing in a deep breath at a given signal and holding it as long as humanly possible. Returning late at night was not so bad when a gentle breeze off the sea reduced the smell to a tolerable level and a good soaking of beer, for re-hydration purposes of course, helped dull the senses.

Alexandria, with its miles of promenade, sandy beaches and hotels, gave the impression of an expensive holiday resort. Located at the eastern end was Stanley Bay, with its many tiers of chalets, a popular playground for the locals. Further to the east stood the Army barracks of Mustaffa. Within the city, behind the promenade, was the more popular soldiers' stomping ground. Here were the bars, nightclubs, cafés with dance floors, the Navy's Fleet Club and, of course, a hunting ground for girls. The Fleet Club was very popular, especially with the squaddies, who only had an odd pound to spend on beer, which was duty free and there was always a chance to win a line on Housey-Housey, which was a nightly event. On one visit, three of us won almost forty pounds on a full house, a small fortune. But it didn't do us any good; we went across the street to a nightclub and blew it all on food and drink, resulting in a very expensive bad stomach and a thick head, but what the hell, it helped dull the pain of returning to Amiriya.

There were occasions when we missed the truck back to camp and a group of us would hire a taxi, which we always had to pay for before the driver started the journey. The Egyptians were a very trusting race; they always made a call before leaving the city and left their money with someone else. Mind you, I could understand it when dealing with a lot of boozed-up barbary soldiers like us.

However, they were not quite the honest, upright citizens that they pretended to be; we were about halfway home when the engine stopped, the driver got out, lifted the bonnet, tinkered with the engine, and declared it was bust. That was it, but we could not have our money back because he had cleverly left it back in Alexandria. We had no choice but to get out and walk; however we had covered only a few hundred yards when we heard the engine start, the vehicle turn round and go belting back into town.

They say you pay for your learning and we certainly did, but at a later date we had our revenge. Strangely enough, we happened upon the same taxi driver again, who we recognised, but he failed to recognise us, which was a big mistake. He went through the same ritual with well-practiced precision; again the engine was declared 'no good', but this time we helped him by making sure; someone put a hand under the dashboard, grabbed the loom and pulled all the wiring out. We walked back to camp singing our heads off; there was no sound of a running engine to disturb us.

Reluctantly we accepted the inevitable and settled down to a daily routine, but worse was yet to come. Without warning the wind started to blow, picked up the dust and within minutes the sun was blacked out. The whole area became shrouded in a thick fog, not moisture, but blinding, gritty dust, which penetrated into every nook and cranny. It crunched between the teeth at meal times and left a thick layer in the bottom of your mug. This was our first experience of a dust storm; it was hell and lasted for days.

Eventually our Cruisers were loaded on to a train and we chugged along a single track to the railhead at Mersa Matruh. It was with great pleasure that we wished Amiriya a fond farewell and settled down to a relaxing journey into the unknown. It was a barren excursion with no railway stations as we knew them, just a hut by the railway line with a name on it and not a sign of a town or village anywhere. It was difficult to imagine this was it, 'The Desert'. Surely there must be something over that far ridge? But if there was, I never saw it.

We did stop part way along the track, where a number of large cooking Dixies discharged ladles of hot stew; just like mother used to make with everything including the kitchen sink. It was a real gourmet treat and our introduction to the skills of desert eating; balance the Dixie on your knee, eat with a spoon in the right hand and wave off the flies with the left, that way you get a fair share, including fresh meat.

The news of Wavell's victories in Cyrenaica did much to boost our morale and hopes were high as we rumbled along this iron road. With the sparkling blue sea on one side, rolling sand dunes on the other and the warm sun on your skin, it was easy to drift off into a dream world with thoughts of England and those left behind. But the constant jolting and the vision of that vast expanse of the unknown passing before the eyes brought back the reality that you were here, in a never-ending terrain of sand and stones. Where in the hell can you hide in a battlefield like this when the enemy can see ten miles with the naked eye? A very frightening thought indeed.

Well, this was it, our new world of grit, stones and sagebrush. There was no scenic beauty to admire and yet some compelling force to keep looking was always present; somehow this vast, barren, silent land cried out for the veil to be raised and it's mysteries revealed. Throughout my years in this barren land I never lost the urge to keep looking, I always felt that over the next ridge I would find what I searched for, but I found only one of two things – fear or relief.

We really had no choice, the last bus had gone and so had Xmas 1940, without leaving even a memory.

~ CHAPTER 6 ~

AN EXCURSION TO GREECE

A T MERSA MATRUH OUR CRUISERS were offloaded in an atmosphere charged with excitement and expectation. Here was the starting point of what we had come to Egypt to do; but sadly it was not to be. Events in Europe changed our destiny and we swapped our beautiful new Cruisers for a bunch of worn out old A10s and headed back down the line to Alexandria. What a blow that was to our egos, to be rejected by a victorious Army just when our moral courage was at its highest. Ah well, it is an ill wind that does not blow someone good and that other Regiment certainly got the best of this deal.

From then on events happened so fast it was difficult to keep the memory in focus with the pace of them. Almost overnight I found myself in a small group dumped on the quayside with three trucks in Piraes Harbour and driving north through Greece to a mountainous area on the borders of Yugoslavia. Under the command of a one-eyed Major nicknamed in Arabic *"Wahid Shufty"* meaning 'One Look', we constituted an 'advance and recce party' with the task of mapping the area and preparing for the eventual arrival of the Regiment.

It is interesting that I met this mystical Major in England, just after Dunkirk, at Guilsborough Hall near Northampton. He was responsible for the organisation and running of a special school on a different aspect of warfare and his number two i/c was a Captain Stirling, who later became associated with the Long Range Desert Group. We were taught explosives, demolition, the use of enemy weapons, sabotage and collecting information on troop movements. Many exercises were carried out against the Home Guard, penetrating roadblocks and other security systems and spying on the movements of any British Forces in the area. In many ways it was quite a madhouse; we knew it as "Major Carey's Cosy Coaches" and I believe that the Long Range Desert Group and other similar bodies, started right there at Guilsborough.

At first, because we were trained, professional soldiers competing against the Home Guard we considered these exercises a huge joke, but our smug superiority backfired on many occasions. They gave us a lot more trouble than we had bargained for. On one exercise, two of our patrols were ordered to mine the banks of a local reservoir, but we failed to reach our objective. Casually walking down the edge of an apparently deserted road a voice from a ditch called out a challenge, we dived into the ditch on the other side and practically fell on top of the other half of the Home Guard patrol. At the local Police Station we were detained under suspicion, given a meal of sausages, mash and onions and kept in overnight until Major Carey identified us the next day.

We were lucky to be released so quickly, because Carey was noted for his odd sense of humour. On another occasion one of our sergeants, dressed in a borrowed Home Guard uniform, was collecting information in Northampton; he was not recognised by the local HG as 'one of theirs' so they arrested him. His claim to be one of Carey's group was initially denied by the major, who, after leaving him in gaol for three days, eventually contacted the Police and had him released.

It was on October 28th 1940 that the Albanian and Italian Forces invaded Greece. The Greek government, having trained its young men by conscription in the forces over many years, called the nation to arms and, by 8th November had halted the invaders and captured 5,000 Italian prisoners. What a fantastic feat by soldiers equipped with old-fashioned WW1 weapons, mules carrying artillery and much of their supplies moved by bullock-cart! Just six days later the Greek Army pushed the invaders back over the border, driving on to capture Koritsa and the port of Sarande. In six weeks the Greek Army had defeated the Italian IX Army and occupied a large area of Albania.

And what were *we* doing whilst all this was going on? Well, our Air Force was involved in limited support but our Army was up to its neck fighting in the Wavell desert campaign. Our first links with the Greek campaign were forged in April 1939, when the British government guaranteed the independence of Greece, but though much was said, little or nothing was done. The failure of Albania and Italy to occupy Greece boosted the morale of the unoccupied Balkan states and prompted Hitler to take over the campaign. He assembled six divisions, originally ear-marked for the invasion of Russia, and invaded Bulgaria. This movement compelled the British Government to honour their commitment to Greece and, on 24th February 1941, the cabinet agreed to send a military force.

We were welcomed by the Greek people almost as liberators with wine, waving hands and smiling faces. This was quite a contrast to our arrival in Calais, with its shattered buildings, broken glass crunching underfoot and faces with expressions of fear and anxiety. Our journey north on poor roads through valleys and over mountains, was both hazardous and cold, with snow on the high ground and often rain in the lowlands. But this was a new adventure in a strange new land, with anticipation of something exciting and unknown driving us on to those mountains in the north.

Our destination was at the north end of the Florina Valley, a small village called Amyntaon, lying beneath the mountains that separated Greece from Yugoslavia. It was a pleasant, tranquil scene, this tiny hamlet at the end of the railway, the centre of a farming community, squeezing a meagre existence from the land. Sadly, we knew a change was about to take place; tanks would churn up these orderly rows of ploughing and the whole valley could be transformed into a bloody battlefield.

I don't think these people had any illusions about what the future had in store for them because, just a few miles to the west, the Albanians had invaded their land and they, the Greeks, had beaten the living daylights out of them. Those battles were still ranging, but with a difference, they were now knocking hell out of the Italians, who had come to the aid of Albania – and they were using captured Italian equipment to do it. What a fantastic fighting spirit those Greek soldiers had.

Above the village and through a pass in the mountains the road wound its way into Yugoslavia. This was the Monastir Gap, which apparently we were expected to defend. The surrounding hills were barren and strewn with boulders and rough tracks provided the only access to the area. Carrying out a recce was not easy; any maps available were pretty useless and the only sign of life was sheep and goats. We were on the mountain above the road through the pass into Yugoslavia and Carey sent me to a lone herdsman to see if he could help us. I approached this old man and asked if he understood English. He looked up with a smile and said, "No, but I can speak American." I felt quite an idiot. He had lived in the USA for twenty years, returned to buy a flock of sheep and live peacefully amongst his mountains. I felt sad that his dream world was about to be blown apart.

The trainload of tanks arrived on flats which were just the width of the tracks and looked as if they were about to fall apart. Unloading was precarious, but apart from tearing a few planks from the decking, there was no serious mishap and we parked in the hedges around the fields. The train had no accommodation for the tank crews who, throughout the long journey from Athens, had to survive the snow and freezing conditions wrapped up on the backs of the tanks. We parked along the hedgerows of a field, the only area available and camouflaged against the possibility of spotter planes.

It was essential to hide our presence but it was an added obstacle and hindered our frantic efforts to get these old A10's battleworthy. Soon it became apparent that someone had neglected to inform the Quarter Master in Egypt that we had exchanged our nice new A13s for these clapped-out A10s. All spares supplied to us were for A13s. What a bloody shambles! And the battle had not even started yet. Ah well, what's new?

Spring must have been in the air; tiny baby turtles were crawling about on the soil and at daylight the farmer herded his family to the fields to work. This was very interesting, the whole family, with the exception of the farmer, carried implements and they all worked whilst he leaned on the gate and shouted orders. I remember thinking: 'what a fantastic man's world this must be,' and made a mental note of how I should raise my own family in the future.

Life in the village remained very much a mystery to us. We had little time available for social contact, but furtive glances gave me the impression that, being not of their clan, we were not welcome in their glen. The baker was friendly enough, but of course that was business, and the very dark brown loaves of bread were a welcome change from our issue biscuits. Compared to our standard of living these people were very poor. When I offered a one thousand drachma note to pay for my bread, the baker had to collect money from other people in the village to give me my change. Our empty four-gallon petrol cans were very popular; they could be exchanged for six eggs or twelve drachmas and within a few days could be seen in use as water and food containers. All this brought back memories of my childhood, when we were poor to the extent that nothing could be wasted. But it was a happy life nonetheless.

As was expected, the German Army invaded Yugoslavia from Bulgaria. We were ordered to move up into the hills and parked amongst the trees. In contrast to the dry warmth of the desert, where we laid our bedroll on the ground and slept, here on the hillside it was cold and damp, so a bivouac was erected on one side of the tank to contain the warmth and keep out the rain and mosquitoes. It was constructed quickly and simply; the tank sheet was attached to the mudguard, dropped down to ground level, along the ground for about six feet, and back up to the mudguard. It was dry and reasonably comfy with four of us keeping each other warm.

As the sun went down, mosquitoes appeared from nowhere, hell-bent on sucking us dry, probably in exchange for malaria. This gave us two choices: bleed to death or suffocate in cigarette smoke. We chose the latter. With the ends dropped down to seal our tent like an envelope, we smoked like mad until the atmosphere was almost unbearable. We didn't like it, but neither did the mosquitoes.

The unsettled weather caught us out when a deluge during the night sent a torrent of water rushing down the pathway supporting our tent. It did not pass underneath but rushed straight through, taking everything with it that was loose. How were we to know that this nice, solid base supporting our tent was a dried-up waterway? Another lesson learnt.

By this time the truth had dawned on us that we were here to fight a war and we waited nervously for the onslaught we knew was inevitable. The latest information was that the Germans had invaded Yugoslavia with five Panzer Divisions, which included about 500 tanks, supported by bomber and fighter planes, did little to boost our enthusiasm for a fight. To put it mildly, our position was precarious, dumped in the north of a barren, mountainous country, with poor road facilities and our only escape route hundreds of miles to the south.

As usual, being tankies, we had to fend for ourselves when it came to the cooking, the laundry and all the other necessities of life. The Quartermaster supplied the means and we did the rest. Just waiting for the enemy to come gave us time to think of food, so how about 'spotted dick' for pudding? We had the flour, baking powder and fruit, a large Dixie to boil it in and I had a spare vest. Since it would take a couple of hours, two petrol fires were organised in a ditch, a couple of yards apart. In went the petrol and the pot was soon boiling, but the petrol was soon burned up and we switched to the other fire all ready to light up. I decided to top-up the first fire, ready for re-use and, standing with my back to the burning second fire, poured petrol onto the hot soil. What an idiot! The vapour passed along the ditch to the lit fire and ignited. Flames shot up in front of me, lit the petrol in the can and I threw it aside; net result, burning trees, which took half an hour to put out. I had a red face, but we did have our 'spotted dick'!

We knew that our presence represented nothing more than a gesture to the Greek government that Britain would give whatever assistance was available; unfortunately, we were it. Not exactly an army, just two tank regiments, 3rd Bn RTR, with our fifty old A10's, each armed with a two-pounder anti-tank gun and a BSA machine-gun and the 4th Hussars, with MkV1b light tanks, armed with two machine-guns. Two infantry brigades, one Australian and one New Zealand, supported by artillery and other services completed Britain's contribution to the defence of Greece. As for air support, all I ever saw was six old Gloster Gladiators, which lasted just a few days against the far superior Messerschmitt 109s. Those Gladiator pilots were not brave, that word is inadequate to describe their actions; they knowingly sacrificed themselves, against tremendous odds, trying to protect us. Any commendation would be an insult to their gallantry.

The Greek Army were already deeply committed, with most of their forces involved on the Albanian border. There was a division deployed in the next valley, but since it was their home ground, they were reluctant to move to a more strategic position. Just like the clans in Scotland, many years in the past, they were prepared to die to defend their own piece of land but not that of the tribe next door. From what I saw, their equipment was of low quality; mountain artillery being dragged up a winding path, loaded on mules. I watched a column of bullock-carts loaded with supplies moving slowly up the mountain road; it reminded me of a long train of camels I had seen moving slowly across the desert. I wondered if the supplies ever reached their destination.

The Regiment, supported by the 4th Hussars plus some anti-tank guns, artillery and a machine gun troop, were dispersed in the valley below the pass to defend the road from Yugoslavia. At first, because Yugoslavia was not yet committed, access for our patrols into their territory was denied, but within days, our armoured car recce troop probed north of the border, to be met by German motorcycle troops. Now we knew for sure that our holiday in Greece was over. On our right, stretching into the plains of Salonica, was the Australian Division and on their right the New Zealanders. On our left, the Greek Army were up to their neck in it with the Italians.

Our defences on the north side of the pass collapsed and the enemy forces poured through on to the Florina Plain. 'B' and 'C' squadrons of 3 RTR took up defensive positions on the Sotei Ridge, just below the pass and hammered the enemy as they spread out across the plain. They inflicted heavy casualties on the infantry, who apparently marched forward as if on a parade ground, and took a heavy toll of the panzers that followed. We, in 'A' squadron, in company with 4th Hussars, took up defensive positions on the next ridge, to the south at Plotenais. At first it was a very frustrating task trying to identify friend from foe amongst thousands of refugees, intermingled with Greek and Yugoslav soldiers.

After days of battle, what was left of 'B' and 'C' squadrons retreated through our line to reform and protect HQ. Tank losses had been high, but not from enemy activity; the majority of our losses were broken-down vehicles that could not be repaired due to the absence of spares. This was hostile tank country, which limited manoeuvrability for fear of shedding a track and the AEC diesel bus engines modified to drive these 16-ton vehicles, were sadly underpowered. Not a happy situation on a narrow mountain road to throw off a track and that was likely to happen if you reached 20 mph.

The long columns of refugees fleeing before the enemy added to the confusion. On one occasion we spent the whole night on a rearguard at the roadside, checking for infiltrators. It was two days since we had slept and we drank gallons of tea to keep awake by the need to 'spend a penny'. Just as we had seen in France, but under worse conditions, these poor wretches dragged their feet through mud and slush in a biting, wintry wind, on roads churned up by tank tracks. Many Yugoslav soldiers, wrapped in heavy overcoats and blankets, some with horses carrying equipment and others just aimlessly staggering under heavy packs, were amongst the refugees.

We had been warned about fifth columnists, but to identify friend from foe, at night, with just a torch and flickering firelight, was practically impossible. However, we soon recognised that fires burning amongst the trees near where we parked were not always the result of explosions, but lit by pro-Nazis to indicate our position to the Luftwaffe.

About 60 km south of Florina, we in 'A' Squadron, with what was left of our tanks, eventually took up a hull-down position overlooking the village of Plotenais. With only the top half of my body protruding above the ridge I was able to observe without the tank being seen. Unfortunately, much of the road leading south towards us was obscured by the ridge and I, as troop sergeant, was ordered to take up a forward position in front of the hills, to cover parts of the road hidden from our other tanks. I ordered the driver to advance down the road towards the village to a point where all of the road could be observed. A small depression at the roadside was ideal; we parked there in the shadow of the hill and waited for a reaction from the enemy, who must have observed our movement.

I had a clear view all the way to the village at the crossroads about a mile to the north and, about half way between me and the village, the road passed over a wooden bridge, which spanned a deep, wide waterway. I remember thinking that the ditch would be a good tank obstacle, if only the bridge had been blown. Of course, it could have been mined, but I had no knowledge of that. I had an excellent view in front of me, about 2,000 yards all the way to the village and the road coming from the north along which we had travelled. My view to the left was completely blocked by the hillside, but that was covered by our tanks on the ridge behind.

It was a very frightening situation again, sitting out here on our own in full view of the enemy. I could not see any, but they would certainly have seen me as I drove down the road to take up my position. All was quiet, there was no movement in or around the village and no one talked. We waited, quietly and nervously, for what we felt just had to come. The strain from peering through binoculars sent the blood pounding in my head and distorted my vision, but I was there as the eyes of the squadron and could not afford a moment's relaxation.

Suddenly there was movement, a motorcycle combination left the village and came down the road towards me. Where the hell did he come from? I had seen nothing enter the village.

Had he been there all the time or had I nodded off? I reported the movement and watched the two-man crew in their combination drive slowly towards the bridge. An aerial was sticking up from the rear of the sidecar and a machine gun was mounted on the front.

Our guns were loaded and ready. We had to stop him reaching that bridge and reporting its condition, but to open fire too soon and miss him would be just as disastrous. He was about 100 yards from the bridge when I gave the order to fire. The tanks behind me opened up at the same time and we blasted the machine off the road into the ditch. I searched with my binoculars for the occupants, but nothing moved. My gunner was ready to give a burst of machine gun fire, but no target appeared.

Nothing else moved in the village. That must have been a single recce unit. I wondered what he had reported, if anything, before we put him out of action. The morning drifted into the afternoon and I began to hope, unashamedly, that nothing more would appear. How wonderful it would be to quietly creep away in the dark and have a good night's sleep. My God, I felt so tired. Crunching a few hard biscuits with jam and cheese on and swilled down with water, our only meal that day, helped to keep the mind and body active, but concentration on the job in hand was not easy. I had been informed that, on the forward slope of the hill to my right, an infantry regiment was dug in, but I could observe no movement and wondered about the validity of my information.

My prayers went unheeded. An enemy column appeared along the road from the east into the village and it presented a most depressing sight. There was everything in that column: tanks, artillery, infantry ... the lot. The artillery pulled off the road into a field, dropped the gun trails and ammunition limbers and prepared for action. They appeared so close through the binoculars I felt I could reach out and touch them, and that was just a bit too bloody close for me!

I held my breath and waited for the first salvo. We were in such an exposed position I felt sure it would land on my doorstep. The guns flashed and I lowered my body down into the turret and waited. The explosions were loud, but I felt no impact on the tank. I popped my head up and had a look. The infantry on the hillside to my right were catching most of it, but some went over the top into the hills behind. Something kept tapping on the outside of the hull. The driver shouted "come in" but it was not funny. We had been spotted and someone was ripping our paint off with machine gun bullets.

The battle hotted up and our infantry got the worst of the shelling. Two light tanks came down the road towards us but they did not get very far. We burned up the leading one and the crew baled out into the ditch. The other turned round and belted back towards the village. I could see the tracer from our two-pounder shells disappearing into the back of its turret. That crew could not have survived.

A radio signal to return behind the hill was acknowledged with pleasure and relief. We turned back onto the road and drove like the bats out of hell towards our sanctuary, very much aware that our soft backside was exposed to the enemy guns. This time we were lucky, they did not take advantage of the easy target we presented.

The gunfire gradually lessened and an uneasy calm took its place; it was almost as if both sides were getting their breath back. This was interrupted by a voice on the radio reporting that a man was walking down the road we had just driven up; he was dressed in civilian clothes and walked towards the enemy as if immune to the noise and clamour around him. This was a very delicate and dangerous situation; he had observed the disposition of our forces and was a threat to our security.

A more urgent situation took over the airwaves. Information was coming through that a column of enemy tanks had skirted our left flank and, at any moment, would threaten our rear. Once again, I was ordered forward to observe the area in front of our position, so down the road we clattered towards the enemy. There, lying across the road in front of us, was the body of a civilian. He appeared to have been caught in the machine gun crossfire, which had continued throughout the afternoon. The road, at this point, had steep banks at either side, so we had no option but to drive over him. I felt sick as the tank lurched a bit to one side. My God, what a dreadful way to end one's life, poor devil, he probably just wanted to go home.

We pulled off the road back at our position of observation and from then on life became rather hectic. Machine gun bullets rattled on the outside of our tank and salvos of shells screamed overhead, but fortunately nothing heavier came our way. Our infantry on the hillside were engaged with German infantry, who had penetrated across the open ground, but there was little I could do or report in the fading light.

Behind me in the hills, the sound of gunfire escalated and continuous flashing lit up the sky. What the hell was going on back there? There was a constant stream of radio chatter, but it merely added to the confusion. Fear of being left behind in what appeared to be a chaotic situation surged through my body. My crewmates were also getting rather anxious, sitting in semi-darkness, listening to the noise of battle but unable to see what the hell was going on. Although sick with fear myself, I had to hide my emotions and tell them there was no problem. At last, an order to pull back came through loud and clear and I heard a sigh of relief from the crew as I ordered, "start up, turn round and get back down that bloody road ... but for God's sake don't shed a track!" I need not have warned Davey about the tracks, he was an excellent driver and we had come a long way together, but there was no one between us and the enemy and I shuddered at the thought of being left behind in a broken-down tank.

We were held up on the road and it was getting dark; infantry were coming off the hillside and piling into their lorries and Brengun carriers and, none too soon for me, the column eventually headed south. At the tail end of the column, we drove towards the area where a battle appeared to be raging and round a bend in the road the driver stopped. We stared in horror at what lay before us; the way ahead was an inferno with the flashing of guns and the flames of burning vehicles creating an image of a Devil's Cauldron.

The enemy had bypassed our position and was trying to close the trap. All hell had descended on that valley. The air was alive with a constant stream of tracer flying from both sides. This was our only way out and we pressed forward, almost pushing the infantry Brens and lorries before us. I was reminded of the poem, 'Into the valley of death rode the six hundred'. We were not quite so many, but it did look like a valley of death. At least we did have armour protection; those poor bloody infantry had nothing, they just huddled close together and hoped for the best.

The enemy guns appeared to be on the hills at both sides of the road and our tanks must have engaged them; there were many fires up there on the hillsides. A couple of our tanks and other vehicles were burning at the roadside and, as we drove past, fearful of being ignited by the flames. I could feel the intense heat on my face. What a perfect target we were against the light of those flames. We just held our breath and kept going, but not one vehicle in our small convoy was hit. How the hell we managed to travel the length of that valley with tracer flying all around us and survive, will always be a mystery. At that moment, I knew someone was watching over me.

Throughout the night, our little convoy crawled slowly south; there was no choice, the roads were choked with traffic. Broken down vehicles littered the roadside. Many were tipped over the side in an attempt to keep the traffic flowing, they may even have crashed onto another road further down the hill, but no one seemed to care in this atmosphere of self-preservation. Lights at the roadside eventually waved me off; it was a staging area and thankfully my Regiment was there; that is, what was left of them.

It had been a night of near panic and I had no desire to see another like it. For the first time in my life I had felt like giving up and was ashamed at the thought.

~ CHAPTER 7 ~

A CHAOTIC RETREAT

THE DAYS THAT FOLLOWED WERE confused, a repetition of rearguard action and withdrawal without, on some occasions, contact with the enemy. Confusing pieces of information failed to give a picture of the disposition of other troops; wireless silence had been ordered without alternative means of contacting our supply column and that created a constant fear of running out of fuel and ammunition. Although full advantage was taken of every spare minute to rest, we were very tired and found it extremely difficult to concentrate on the job in hand. Much time was spent maintaining those lousy tanks, but they were all we had and we made the best of it. Our survival depended upon them.

This was tank country at its worst, steep mountain passes with S-bends on single-lane roads and deep ravines with narrow wooden bridges, usually made from railway sleepers. Quite a hair raising experience negotiating a bridge the same width as the tracks, watching it swing under the weight with one eye on that torrent of water far below. Negotiating roads strewn with discarded equipment, burned-out and broken-down vehicles, dead horses, body parts and other war debris hanging on trees was a grotesque nightmare come alive. Add to that the constant harassment by aircraft machine gunning and bombing and you have a reasonable image of hell on earth.

We were trapped on such a pass amongst a convoy of mixed transport when the planes came screaming in. The convoy stopped, troops baled out and scrambled under their vehicles.

On a narrow mountain road with a high cliff on one side and a sheer drop on the other, there was nowhere to hide. What a sad, pathetic sight, to see grown men clawing at the ground in fear and frustration, some screaming to relieve the pressure. How fortunate I was, I hid my fear behind the rattling of our guns whilst many others just blasted away with whatever weapons they had to hand.

In a tank, with earphones on and concentrating on directing the driver, I heard little else above the sound of the engine and clatter of the tracks on the road. We relied upon the activity of others on the road to give an indication of imminent air attack; troops clambering off the back of trucks, even before they had stopped, indicated aircraft diving.

I dropped down into the turret, ordered the driver to close his flap and the gunner to stand by. It was remarkable how concentration of the mind on some other task, such as aiming and firing at an enemy plane, obscured the dangers directed towards you. It was the deathly silence which followed that brought the fear; the sudden realisation that those whistling sounds which faintly penetrated all else, were bullets aimed at you. Had death knocked gently on my door?

Near Grevena, almost 150km from where we started in the mountains of the Florina Valley, the road wound down the side of a steep cliff, across a deep ravine and up the other side. What a tragic sight, a long snake of vehicles crawling along, nose to tail, almost close enough to be pushing each other. It appeared that a breakdown on the other side had stopped the column and the bridge was crammed solid. Some men had left their vehicles and were heading for the bridge, with the obvious intention of crossing on foot. How ridiculous! They couldn't possibly get past the lorries. My worry was all the weight sitting on that flimsy structure. Lose that bridge and we would all be in a mess.

I suppose it was inevitable, we had not seen them for about an hour; down they came, screaming towards us with guns blazing. Everyone opened up with whatever weapon they had and the noise echoing in that ravine was deafening. The planes were so close that a handful of rocks may have been more effective. I held my breath, waiting for the crunch of bombs that could destroy the bridge and our hopes of getting out of this godforsaken land. Idiot! Of course he wouldn't bomb the bridge; he needed it himself. A lorry just ahead started to burn, but somehow others were squeezing past on that narrow road, oblivious of the flames trying to engulf them.

As the sound of planes faded, the noise of moving lorries once again echoed across the ravine. That air raid must have jolted someone into action. A few stragglers had come up behind me, they were Royal Engineers with orders to blow bridges when all had passed. I let them pass and followed down to the bridge. I waited till the last one had cleared the other side. It looked strong enough to take our tank's weight, but it had taken quite a hiding from all that transport. We had to cross; there was no choice. We drove across with part of the tracks hanging over the edge. A dreadful fear gripped me as each track plate clonked onto the sleepers; I guided the driver on the intercom every inch of the way with furtive glances at the swirling mass of water far below.

At the top on the other side of the ravine I called a halt. We would wait until the engineers, left at the bridge to lay explosive charges, had passed through us. An enemy patrol arrived on the other side and stopped to survey the scene, it was the usual motorcycle combination and a couple of armoured cars. The arrogant sods got out of their trucks and strutted around, full of victor's confidence, but not for long, we sent them diving for cover with a few quick bursts of machine gun fire and left a few rolling on the ground. It was but a few minutes later when our

Royal Engineers came roaring round the bend in their truck and we followed them. I never did find out if they blew that bridge.

Eventually I came to believe we were the only tank left in this part of the country. The radio was dead and there was no one to communicate with. I had lost contact with my troop officer some days previously and another officer named Bob Crisp had joined me when his tank failed. He brought with him a REME captain, presumably to ensure the efficient running of our only means of transport, but he played no part in the maintenance of the vehicle. My driver Davey and I were more than capable of handling any problem that lousy tank could throw at us. Crisp was a very aggressive character, well known for his brave deeds, but we were not all brave men and his actions were not always agreeable.

We struggled south amidst a depressive confusion of derelict vehicles and equipment. The roadside was littered with the devastation of war I had seen before at Calais and to see it again brought back that sickening feeling of defeat. Our task was to cover the rear of the retreating columns, but I knew from the bombing and machine gun fire to the north that there were many stragglers yet to come. At times, when possible, we drove across the fields to evade the concentrations of bombing and strafing, rejoining the road to cross bridges. Sometimes, driving up a roadside bank, we gained extra elevation for our turret guns, giving more effective fire against the dive-bombers. We had no idea how much damage we inflicted, but it certainly made them fly higher and that gave us a morale boost.

A cat and mouse game was played with the German recce groups for days, doing whatever we could to disrupt and delay their advance, but our efforts were merely a fly tickling the enemy's nose. We knew, from odd pieces of info passed on by MPs at some road junctions, that the defences on the Aliakmon

River had collapsed and withdrawal to the next defensive line was in progress. At one point, turning off the road to allow a few remaining trucks to pass, we shed a track and damaged the plates beyond repair. Almost within minutes the planes came screaming at us again, hell bent on wiping the few remaining vehicles from that stretch of road.

With no gun to fire and the sudden realisation that I had no armour protection, I lay trembling on the ground with fear, hardly daring to breathe lest the movements of my body indicated my presence to the enemy. My whole body was rigid, waiting for the inevitable shock of impact, wondering if the scream and explosion of the next bomb was the one meant for me. Suddenly it was all over again and, as the sound of the planes faded, I stood up casually, dusted myself down and hoped that no one had noticed my mental anguish. A near miss by a bomb added the final blow to our beleaguered A10; we were fortunate that no one was injured, we had all dived for cover.

An eerie silence remained, almost unbearable after days of clanking tracks and revving engines. The road was empty, our rearguard duty finished, we were alone. Nothing moved except the flicker of flames from a few burning vehicles. 'Where the hell do we go from here?' I thought. 'This could be the end of the war for us.' We were still a long way from Athens with no means of getting there. In the absence of any form of communication I wondered just how long it would be before an enemy patrol came down this road. With the turret damaged, there was nothing we could do to stop him. Our situation was bad, but we were not ready to give up our freedom just yet; there just had to be an answer to our predicament.

We unloaded our gear, including the BSA machine gun and a few boxes of ammo and checked the vehicles nearby for a possible runner. One truck, loaded with a variety of food worthy of any Officers Mess, appeared to be unmarked except for a few bullet holes in the radiator. We checked it with water and it leaked like a sieve, but the engine seemed to be OK. A search in the back produced a selection of possible radiator repair components: soap to bung up the holes on the outside and eggs to put in the water. The whites of the eggs cooked as the engine warmed up and helped to plug the holes on the inside; a useful tip I learned when about fourteen years old.

With the machine gun mounted between the stays at the rear of the truck, more as a morale booster than a viable means of defence, we drove south with hope restored and, of course, numerous stops to keep the radiator topped up. By comparison with the previous week, the days that followed were sheer heaven. Bob Crisp was particularly pleased; he found a box of his favourite food, tinned Asparagus. We all dined extremely well, gorging on rich food, originally intended for some Officer's Mess but now liberated to provide our first hot meals since the Germans entered Greece.

We eventually caught up with the tail end of a transport column and moved south towards Athens, in the hope that our rear was being protected by the remains of the infantry divisions further north. Supplies of fuel and food were no problem, we just took whatever was required from the many dumps along the way, assisted by the Military Police waiting to burn it all up when the last stragglers had passed. The alcohol stores would have made a lovely bonfire, but that would have been a sad waste. Being a Scot, I could not allow such sacrilege, so I liberated whatever we required.

It was on the airfield south of Athens that we finally joined up with part of the Regiment. There were no tanks, just a few lorries like ours, with machine guns saved from the lost tanks mounted in the back. We believed that plans were being made for our evacuation but in many ways chaos prevailed and our knowledge of the state of this war was almost nil. What's new?

However we were here in Athens, to us an unknown city, so what better than to use what little time we had left to invade the place? It was rumoured that enemy units had already arrived, but what the hell, after what we had been through the reward was worthy of the risk. Someone knew their way around and took us to what I thought was a services club. It had a large entrance hall with tables, comfortable settees, a bar, and lots of lovely girls in long evening dresses. A long, wide stairway curved up to the floors above. The girls were very attentive, fetching our drinks and generally tending to our comfort, but I must have been very naïve. It took me half an hour to realise I was in a brothel.

A few of us decided it was not our scene and a helpful taxi driver took us to a nightclub. It had a name like Barbarinas, with access down narrow, dingy stairs and, at the bottom, opened out into a large room, packed with tables and chairs. The ceiling was low and a thick veil of smoke shrouded the occupants, like ghostly figures in a fog. The scene was like a movie of mystery and intrigue. There was plenty of drink and music was coming from somewhere in that fog. They cleared a table for us and we had all that was necessary to drown our sorrows of defeat. A few girls joined us, but there was a language problem and communication was difficult. However, Boris came to the rescue with his excellent knowledge of Arabic, although I had a feeling he conned us a bit on the cost of drinks; I wonder what his cut was?

We had a real rave up there, determined to create at least one night of memories in this land, which had given us so much to regret. The toilet facilities were a real eye opener, a row of gents urinals along one wall and a row of cabinets with doors along the other; how about spending a penny whilst a female attendant brushed down the back of your jacket and at the same time girls wandered in and out of the cabinets behind you? When ready to leave two of our party were missing, they had nodded off sitting in the loo with the door locked and not even threats and verbal abuse could dislodge them, but they had to be got out and drastic measures were called for. These continental type toilets with a hole in the floor and footprints in the concrete, had water running continuously underneath; a newspaper on fire dropped into a hole upstream of our targets brought screams of agony from behind the closed doors, followed by the sudden appearance of two bodies with their trousers down. We were a rotten lot!

Back at the airport, the evacuation of what remained of 3 RTR had been ordered and groups were loaded into trucks for transportation to ports south of the Corinth canal; well, not all of us. Small groups were formed, with a couple of trucks and a few machine guns, and ordered north to positions on the outskirts of Athens; yes, as usual, I was included. Our role was that of anti-paratroop patrols, defending the main roads into Athens with troops of B, C, and HQ squadrons in positions on the outskirts of the city and we, from A Squadron, across the road about twenty miles north at Malakasa. Our role was to help keep the road clear for the withdrawal of the infantry further north, mainly Australian and New Zealand forces.

My memories of events at that stage are rather vague, but I do remember someone had picked up a German submachine gun and was examining the mechanism when it fired, sending a bullet through the chest of one of the troop. The name Henna comes to mind as the man who was shot, but I have no memory of the final outcome of that accident.

It was at that time that the Greek Government capitulated and the order came to evacuate the country urgently so, with great relief and much uncertainty, we piled aboard our truck and drove towards Athens and the Corinth Canal, 150 miles to the south.

We joined the mad rush driving south to the ports, frustrated by abandoned vehicles and discarded equipment and harassed by enemy planes with complete control of the skies. A few miles from Corinth everything stopped and information quickly spread that paratroops had landed south of the canal and the bridge had been blown. Well, that was it, nothing left but to walk, so our small party, carrying what light arms and other equipment that was necessary, headed for the eastern end of the canal. At a small village, fishermen rowed us across the canal entrance and once again we headed south.

Luck was on our side, we found an abandoned truck, liberated some petrol and, on advice from Military Police still directing traffic, drove south towards Naplion, the port of Argos where evacuation was in progress. We made no contact with the paratroops but did pick up a few stragglers who had been captured by them, disarmed and released.

On the outskirts of the town we were stopped by an MP who informed us that evacuation had stopped at that port due to the high loss of ships from bombing. A large black cloud hung over the harbour area, where apparently a ship had been bombed and sunk across the entrance, preventing other ships from entering. I have often wondered what became of that MP, left behind with the unenviable task of assisting others to escape with little hope for himself.

Why did we always seem to be at the tail end of everything? On advice from the MP we burned our vehicle and set off across the hills to a beach at the village of Tolo, just a few kilometres over the hill. It was suggested that ships may pick up personnel from that beach after dark so, with a feeling of hope in our hearts, we dragged our weary feet eastwards as the light faded until darkness called a halt to our progress. We lay down among the trees and slept, undisturbed but for the grumbling of our empty stomachs.

Tremors on the ground brought me back to life. I opened my eyes and looked up at the trees. The sun was shining and tiny droplets hanging from the foliage sparkled like diamonds. At that instant the war did not exist, it was like waking up in another world. What a beautiful moment that was. The sound of planes and the scream of a bomb jolted me back to reality. We grabbed our gear and moved off in a hurry, the beach was just over the next ridge. What a terrible shock, a long stretch of sand around a bay with a few cottages at the far end and a turquoise blue sea, completely empty. Where the hell were all the ships? My heart sank into my boots. This was the end of the line, there was nowhere else to go. Unlike Calais or Dunkirk, there was no flotilla just across the Channel, waiting to come to our rescue. As one Kiwi put it, "We are on our own, mate. The hatchet men are in front and the sharks are behind."

An officer approached and asked if we could handle an anti-tank gun. It was in the trees at the edge of a grit road; a two-pounder with only six rounds of ammo. That was the total defence for the beach. It was an impossible task to attempt a defence of that beach with the small groups of stragglers who aimlessly wandered amongst the trees. In the absence of my Troop Officer – God knows where he was – I was responsible for the Troop and as good soldiers we had to get away. The sound of planes returning for another attempt to drive us into the sea sent everyone in the open diving for cover amongst the trees.

I felt shocked and numb as the reality of the situation became clear. It was less than two months since we had stepped ashore as saviours of the Greek Empire and now, we were back at the water's edge, having achieved little and suffered a disastrous defeat – driven six hundred miles by superior forces from the borders of Yugoslavia to the city of Athens, a journey equal to that from John O'Groats to Bristol, but with a difference. It was six hundred miles of mountainous land with narrow, poor-quality roads, obstructed by war debris and bombarded almost continuously during daylight by enemy planes. The constant uncertainty of supplies of fuel, ammo, food and water, physical punishment in the turret of a moving tank and the pressure of battle with little time for sleep, reduced the body almost to the limit of human endurance. But motivation by personal pride and the natural instinct of survival kept a light glowing at the end of the tunnel and we went for it.

It was many months later, as the many stories of survivors and official pieces of information painted the tragic picture, that the utter shambles of that Greek fiasco became clear. Of the many thousands driven down through the Peloponnesus to ports of evacuation, a large percentage were transported to freedom but many were left on the beaches to fend for themselves. At Kalamata, the most southerly port, the loss of ships was too great a sacrifice and the evacuation, for all but a few who fended for themselves, was stopped. At that port, soldiers armed only with small arms, defeated the first enemy advance party to arrive but finally surrendered to their superior forces. Approximately ten thousand were captured and marched off to spend four years in POW camps.

~ CHAPTER 8 ~

GETTING OUT OF GREECE

J OCK STEWART AND I GATHERED our motley crew of stragglers together. There were only about ten of us and we had
no desire to stay on this bloody island. Planes appeared
overhead, searching for ships, but there were none, so they got
rid of their frustrations and their bombs on us instead. That
was the last straw, we definitely had to get away and walking on
the water was not our scene, but where could we find an answer
amongst this crowd of sad dejected men, aimlessly wandering
around with an expression of hopelessness on every face.

A collection of small houses lay at the southern end of the
beach and, pulled up on the sand, were a few fishing boats. We
took one of them and hauled it along the shore to the spot
where our crew eagerly awaited. It was a small motor boat, about
fifteen feet long, with a small hold at the front and a hatch over
the single-cylinder engine at the rear. Our gear, along with all
the food and water we could lay our hands on, was loaded on
board and we shoved off with no predetermined plan of where
we were headed or how we could achieve it; we just wanted to
get off that beach, with its atmosphere of chaos and defeat.

Having spent most of my younger days involved with boats
and engineering, I took over the engine and Jock became ship's
captain. It was a single cylinder paraffin injector-type with a
drip-feed oiler and this was familiar ground to me, coming from
a small fishing town. I quickly checked it over, wrapped a cord
around the flywheel and pulled. It started first time and with a
big sigh of relief we headed out to sea. What a wonderful

moment that was, to feel the throb of the engine vibrating through the boat; it was like a heart pumping new blood into our veins. But our joy was short-lived; just about two hundred yards off shore, near a small island standing in the bay, the engine stopped and everyone looked at me. It was my fault, of course, but I had done nothing, the bloody thing just stopped. We tied up near the rock and found a cave, crowded with women and children. They probably came from the village on shore and eyed us with suspicion, but we had our own problems.

It took some little time to calmly assess the situation and identify the problem. Of course, bloody fool that I was, I should have noticed it right from the start! There was no water pumping through the engine to keep it cool and there, staring me in the face, was the drive pulley on the engine and the platform for the pump, but no pump. I groped about in the filthy water of the bilges and there it was, a handful of components. It took some time, but I eventually got it back together. It is remarkable how in times of need the brain comes to the rescue with an answer, especially since the knowledge had lain dormant for so many years. I was about fourteen years old when I last handled one of those pumps.

During my struggle with the pump I was distracted by a voice shouting 'Heave!' It was Boris again, who always seemed to appear in times of need, but this time he was no help to us. He had his own problems, with eight men in a boat rowing out to sea and, like ourselves, hell bent on getting off that dreadful beach. He just waved and shouted "see you in Crete Jock!" almost as if they were rowing up the Thames on a picnic. He arrived at Suda Bay three weeks later, having rowed over two hundred miles to the island of Crete, we must have passed him in the night unnoticed.

Another party passed us at the rock, hell bent on escape, there were just two men sitting on a door, each with a piece of board as a paddle, heading south towards a distant shoreline. I remember thinking at the time, 'how bloody ridiculous can you get', then pride surged up inside me as I realised they were also British and that we are a nation of survivors.

The pump was finally reassembled and, with a deep sigh of relief, we chugged across the bay towards the southern coast of the Gulf of Argos. We kept a lookout but saw nothing of the two on the door. Aircraft continued to be active but they left us alone, they vented their wrath on those we had left behind. It was almost dark when we reached that southern shore and we felt very pleased with ourselves. Only that morning it had been all doom and gloom, but now we were free again, spurred on by the thought that if Boris thought he could do it in a rowing boat then we had to have a go. A small cove looked deserted and peaceful, so we tied up the boat, arranged a guard, and within minutes the sound of deep breathing was all that disturbed the stillness of the night.

Up with the dawn, a few hard biscuits and a cup of cocoa, yes we were brave enough at that time to light a fire and set sail once again but our bravery was short-lived. We were happily chugging along in brilliant sunshine when a flight of planes came screaming across the sea towards us. We turned in to the cliffs, jumped ashore and scrambled amongst the rocks for shelter. They raced overhead with guns chattering and bombs exploding as we clung to the cliff face in terror, bodies tense, waiting for that thud in the back from one of those whistling pieces of metal. Almost as quickly as they had appeared they were gone again and, apart from stones and grit falling from above, nothing came our way.

The next cruel blow was only seconds away. In the frantic panic of self-preservation no one had thought to tie up the boat. Now there it was, a hundred yards off shore, wallowing in the gentle swell and drifting out to sea. Two of the crew swam out and towed it back. By God, that was a close one! The thought of losing that boat and all that we possessed brought me out in a cold sweat. What a stupid mistake! Just a few hours on our way to freedom and we had become complacent. I vowed that must never happen again.

A study of our silk map, recovered from the waistband of my tunic, showed that the target had been a narrow road on the cliff top just above us.[1] It was the road to Monemvasia, a port on the southeast coast, where evacuation was probably taking place and the planes were bombing the transport. The map showed that, after following the coast for about forty miles, the road turned in towards the mountains and only touched the coast again at Monemvasia, almost two hundred miles south. The area between the road and the sea appeared to be sparsely inhabited; a situation very much in our favour, since it would be many days before the enemy occupied that part of the Peloponnesus. We were very much aware that contact with the local inhabitants would be necessary to obtain fuel, food and water, but we were also aware of the many fifth columnists in this land, who would readily signal our position to the enemy and the planes would come to help us on our way to the bottom.

All things considered, it was decided that our only chance of survival was to sail at night and hide in the daylight. Although there was always some light reflected on the water, sailing at night was a hazardous experience and rocks had a habit of creeping up on you. Evasive action kept us continually on our toes but there was one definite advantage, the lights of small hamlets on the shore guided us to our sources of food and fuel. We had no choice but to steal, our survival depended upon it,

---

[1] The map was only one of a number of items of an escape kit located in my tunic. Two buttons places on top of each other formed a magnetic compass and the collar and cuffs contained wire files, cord and other useful articles.

and we knew these people could not risk helping us because Nazi sympathizers were everywhere.

In this mountainous country, the majority of the coastal hamlets were not connected to main roads; a network of tracks wound through the valleys and we hoped that it would take some time for the enemy to reach these isolated areas. At one such hamlet, it was still daylight when we risked going ashore. The owner of a small store stood out on the road whilst we helped ourselves inside; he showed his neighbours he was not assisting the British and we left a handful of money on his table. Our biggest problem was engine oil and there appeared to be none in that village, so we emptied the oil lamps in their tiny church, God forgive us.

I spent many hours sitting on the engine hatch, shaking paraffin and grease together in a can to make oil. I knew the engine would not be very happy with it, but then neither was I, with my aching arms and back. How that poor engine tolerated the abuse I gave it I will never understand, the rubbish I poured into that drip oiler made even me feel sick, but it was slippery stuff and the old girl just kept chugging along. Mind you, she did give us a few worrying moments. It was the only engine I ever handled that would run backwards on occasions when starting up, and that only became obvious when the clutch was engaged to drive forward. We had to stop it running, restart, and try again. It usually sailed in the right direction at the second attempt.

There were many small coves along the coast, sometimes a beach but generally high cliffs and rocks, but as daylight slowly crept in, we usually managed to camouflage our boat before settling down for a well-earned rest. One day, we sailed into a sheltered cove as daylight approached; it looked perfect as a hideaway until suddenly a noise amongst the rocks had us scrambling for our guns, ready to blast anything that moved.

This was the worst time of day for us, after a long night peering through the darkness searching for the unknown, nervous tension was at its peak. What a relief to be challenged by an English voice. We cautiously answered and half a dozen soldiers came crawling from amongst the rocks. They, like us, had escaped from the beach, but in a rowing boat. No, it was not Boris and his merry men; God only knows where they had got to. We could easily have passed them in the dark. We pooled our food and resources – they had better stocks than us – and in return we agreed to give them a tow. On this beach we were lucky, there was a well just under the cliff and we were desperate for drinking water. It was brackish, with all sorts of rubbish floating on the top, but it was cool and not too bad with cocoa added. No problem with the milk curdling, we had none.

The extra load in the rowing boat did not slow us down, our speed was already limited by the rock formations of the coastline and on at least one occasion we were grateful for its presence. Sailing along happily across what appeared to be a clear stretch of water a sudden crash threw me forward over the hatch cover. We had hit a reef of rocks and a second jolt quickly followed as the rowing boat hit our stern. Pandemonium followed, with everyone scrambling to disentangle from the gear and salvage what had fallen overboard, but sadly some of our heavy equipment sank without a trace. What a bloody shambles! Stuck hard and fast on the rocks, trying to restart the poor old engine with a bump on my head where it had struck the hatch cover throbbing like mad, I hesitated to wonder what sort of a mess we had got ourselves into this time. Eventually, with the rowing boat pulling at the stern, the engine churning up water in reverse and as much weight as possible aft, we gradually eased off the rocks. My God, that was a relief, but now for the moment of truth; had we punched a hole in the hull? There was nothing we could do but sit patiently and watch the water level in the bilges. This water, which was frequently pumped out by hand, was swilling around under the duckboards at my feet. In the darkness I monitored the level with my hand. It did not rise. My God, how lucky can you be? We sailed on at a reduced speed, with the thought that next time we may not be so bloody lucky.

The next couple of days were relatively uneventful, but our food and water stocks were very low. A glow in the sky was puzzling us until we rounded a headland and there, along the shore, a series of fires were burning. Our first reaction was to quietly creep away into the darkness, but the thought of possible supplies dictated our course of action. As we sailed slowly nearer to the shore, the fires were identified as the flickering flames of burned-out lorries. This must have been a recent evacuation area, probably during the past few days, and we had just missed it. Jock carried out a recce with a number of our crew while the rest of us spent some very anxious moments listening to exploding ammunition and wondering what the devil was going on. We were ready, if necessary, to quickly shove off again, even without those ashore if the situation demanded. They were not long gone and returned empty-handed. It was a very dangerous situation and with the possibility of enemy troops hovering around, we decided to get the hell out of it.

As we neared the southern tip of the peninsula, the nights got much colder and some of the men went below deck under the forward hatch cover for warmth. Next morning they emerged, covered in bites. The boat was alive with bloodsucking bugs and they certainly had their fill that night. I was lucky to be sitting near the engine, surrounded by paraffin fumes; they certainly don't like that. Still, the thought did occur to me that if we ever struck a rock and got holed, there were probably enough bugs down there to float us ashore!

We all had a few anxious moments that night when a shape quite close to us on the skyline turned out to be a submarine.

It was probably just charging its batteries and we had no desire to discover whether it was friend or foe, we just naively chugged on into the night without a care in the world. What a joke! We all sat there, stiff as boards, waiting for the glare a searchlight and the rattle of a machine gun. Thinking about it later, I guessed it must have been one of ours, expecting to see fishing boats or escapees. An enemy submarine surely would have checked our identity.

Our decision to move at night and hide during the day had paid off. We had seen many planes searching the sea whilst we lay hidden, but now, a moment of decision had arrived. The south end of the mainland had been reached, before us was the open sea and, in the distance, an island that would guide us towards Crete. In the dark, with the sky overcast, it would be easy to sail straight past and end up floundering in the Mediterranean. We had not come all this way just to be lost at sea. But the dangers in daylight would be enormous; to be caught in midstream would be a catastrophe. We had endured so much to get this far, but it was agreed the risk had to be taken.

As we sailed towards the rising sun, I sat by the engine, shaking up my mixture of paraffin and grease. All ears were tuned for the drone of engines and all eyes nervously searched the sky. The tense atmosphere was gradually easing when suddenly the engine stopped. The silence was deafening. It was unbelievable that, after all our efforts to get here, we were now wallowing in the swell of the open sea in brilliant sunshine. This was panic stations at its worst and my thoughts turned to a vision of diving planes, torpedo boats and, all around, a shark-infested sea.

God, what a mess!

Of course, as usual, it was all my fault; the urgent need to reach that island had prompted me to speed the poor old girl up a bit. I suspected the lubrication had been inadequate for the task and decided that a short cooling down period might get us under way again. However, circumstances gave us a longer period than I had anticipated. Jock gave me a mouthful of abuse then hit me overboard into the water. I was not surprised, we had all been under intense pressure for some weeks. He was actually a very good friend of mine but this was not the first time we had mixed it.

Thankfully, the engine restarted at the first try and we sailed on towards the island. I remember very clearly having the thought that once again, someone was watching over me.

Around a headland at the west end of this island of Kathira was a beautiful beach of golden sands and a small cluster of farm buildings overlooking the bay. All was quiet as we slowly approached the beach. We feared the Germans may have got there before us, but reassurance came quickly as the farmer and his children ran to the water's edge to greet us. This was such a relief, because throughout this entire journey, groping our way slowly down the coast of Greece, we were completely ignorant of the enemy's location. Now we knew he was definitely not here. The burden of responsibility for the men, whilst trying to hide our fear that around the next headland we would run slap into an ambush, had reduced Jock and I to nervous wrecks. However, our fears were hidden behind our many futile arguments over nothing.

They were very friendly people and, although communication was confined to sign language, we understood each other remarkably well. The idyllic setting and way of life of this family really impressed me; it fitted in with my thoughts of how I would wish to live once this bloody war had ended. With smiles from a very lovely daughter and signs from the parents that they wished me to stay, I was very tempted to tell that motley crew to get lost, but being a blithering idiot and a conscientious soldier, I reluctantly declined their generous offerings.

I have often wondered about the wisdom of that decision. If I had stayed on that island, what then? But, alas, word 'if' has no place in the past.

Their food stocks were very low but they treated us to a meal and supplied enough fuel for the rest of our journey. We paid them with all the money we had left and, with a few tears and waving hands, sailed south east on the last but one stage of our journey to Crete.

Once again, we took a chance in daylight, with clear blue skies and warm sunshine. This time there was no other choice, because the next island, Andikithira, was about twenty five miles away and too small to show above the horizon. My pocket prismatic compass pointed us in the right direction, but we were sailing deeper into the Mediterranean and had no knowledge of the sea currents or where they may take us.

Nevertheless, we reached the island as the light was fading and tied up amongst the rocks to eat the last of meagre rations, a large tin of plums. We had one plum each and a spoonful of juice. A drink of cold water satisfied the thirst; there was no means of heating it and no tea or coffee to put in it either, but it didn't matter any more... we were nearly home.

Next morning our spirits soared. There, on the far horizon, reaching to the sky, were the mountains of Crete. We had not gone far when fishermen hailed us. They soon identified us as British soldiers and recognised the predicament we were in. A line was attached to the bows of our boat and they towed us home. The harbour at Kolimbari was the most beautiful haven I have ever seen, and the quayside the most solid piece of earth I have ever stood on. People crowded around us, shaking our hands and helping with our equipment, or what was left of it. As we were ushered along the only main street I was in a daze and my reflection in a shop window showed the image of a dirty, scruffy, ill-kept tramp. What a shock that was, to see myself as others saw me. Then I understood how the fishermen had recognised us and our predicament. It was almost two weeks since we had crossed the Corinth Canal and, apart from dousing in seawater, personal cleanliness had been sadly neglected. A barber's shop drew me like a magnet. I dived straight in and had the lot: shampoo, haircut and shave and walked away feeling like a new man... but still stinking like a polecat!

Across the street, in a large house, someone made a room available for us. There was very little furniture, just a pile of blankets and a table loaded with food. Was this all a cruel dream? There were whole roast chickens, steaming fresh bread and flagons of wine; a banquet fit for a king. We ate like the hungry animals we were, swilled the wine straight from the flagons and then slept. If it was a dream, we didn't want to wake up. How long we slept, I don't remember, but I do remember that apart from my stinking body and clothes, I was a new man and well prepared for the Army lorry that transported us to Suda Bay, where a number of survivors from the Regiment were concentrated. However, I was not prepared for the brief and unemotional welcome I received from one of our majors.

"Glad to see you sergeant. Take your men up to that tent and draw a rifle and fifty rounds each."

That's right, out of the frying pan into the bloody fire!

We had travelled through hell, from snow in the mountains to the sunshine of southern Greece and suffered a nightmare of groping in the dark on the rocky coast of the Peloponnesus, with the constant fear of enemy attack. Surely some unknown force had not calmed the sea and guided us through all these hazards just to dump us back on the infantry trail once again. God, what a way to live!

~ CHAPTER 9 ~

DECAMPING FROM CRETE

ABOUT A WEEK LATER, A commotion drew my attention to the roadway, where a group of stragglers had just arrived. It was Boris and his crew. He was busy telling the commander that Jock Watt and Jock Stewart were on their way. I stepped out from behind a tree and asked what took him so long. I don't think he spoke to me for a week after that! I had to take my hat off to him; they had spent about two weeks rowing for dear life across the Mediterranean and they looked in better shape than I did.

During the next few days there were many tales told of various soldiers exploits while escaping the enemy, and news came later of many others. Two of our company, Heddich and Kershaw, captured somewhere on the mainland, had escaped from a train passing through Yugoslavia, en route to a prisoner of war camp. They travelled for months through Greece and Turkey to get back to Egypt and the Regiment. Tragically, one of them died in action within weeks of returning.

A chance meeting almost fifty years later told of an event during the Greek fiasco in which I was involved but completely unaware of. A nostalgic journey to Crete brought back many memories, but the return flight was delayed and I landed too late for my coach back home. At 5am I waited at the airport bus station for a coach that would take me back home. A man and his good lady stood nearby. We talked of places visited to while away the time and discovered that we had both been in the north of Greece; in fact, it eventually emerged that I was his

Our route through Greece

Our route from Greece to Crete and Alex.

troop sergeant on that Recce with Major Carey. He told me his name and I remembered him as a tank driver in Greece, but could not remember him in Egypt, and when I told him this he remarked that it was not surprising since he had never reached there.

He went on to relate the events that led up to 'T' beach and how I had gone off with Jock to find some means of escape. Apparently, he went back to the anti-tank gun to collect his gear and returned to the beach to discover we had gone. He could see us about a mile offshore, sailing south. His comment at this point was loud and clear: "You bastard! You left me on the beach!" I had a feeling he was going to lay one on me, but he just stood there, grinning, thank God. He and another tankie called Forsythe were captured by the paratroops but later escaped on a number of occasions and joined forces with the Greek partisans, carrying out acts of sabotage. They remained there through much of the war and finally escaped back to Turkey.

Activity around Suda Bay became more intense by the hour. A brigade of marines had arrived and the Navy were removing equipment from H.M.S. *York*, lying beached on the north shore. An Italian two-man submarine had entered the bay undetected and torpedoed her whilst she lay at anchor. Our major complained to the area commander that it was criminal to use trained tank crews as infantry when they were urgently needed in Africa. I believe his answer was: "If you can get off this bloody island, you can go."

So we went. After a search of the coves around the bay we found it; an old, single-hold, steam coaster, just waiting to be nicked. Unfortunately, it was occupied by the owner, who was the captain, his wife, the engineer and a small piglet tied up on deck. There was no need to commandeer the vessel, the captain readily agreed to sail us to Alexandria. He probably wanted to get away as much as we did, and the Army would pay the bill. We loaded our gear, all the food that could be begged, borrowed or stolen, strapped the machine guns to the rigging and sailed around the west end of Crete before turning east towards Egypt. We had been lumbered with some enemy airmen shot down over Crete and we kept a very wary eye on them.

Our living quarter was the deck and we slept rolled up in blankets with some equipment for a pillow. Food was very scarce and limited to half a tin of bully-beef and a few biscuits each day, not a gourmet's delight but a good, solid, constipating diet. The first couple of days were a bit nerve-wracking, expecting planes to appear any minute, boots loose ready to kick off if we finished up in the water. But, as I have said before, someone was watching over me and we sailed to Alexandria on a calm blue sea.

Well, it was not quite that simple. To start with, we ran out of coal very early in the journey and had to systematically burn the ship to raise steam. Each day a party was detailed to go below, smash up the superstructure and feed it into the fire. It could be said we were burning our boats, but we kept afloat all the way to Alexandria. We were not seamen, but did an excellent job keeping that firebox stuffed with wood at a very dangerous level. This error only became obvious when a friendly submarine surfaced alongside and ordered us to stop under threat of their guns. Someone realised that to stop the engine suddenly would have sent the steam pressure soaring and blown up the boiler. A signal to this effect was urgently dispatched and they eventually sent a boarding party to check us out.

We had a visit from a few enemy planes. They raked us with machine gun fire but did no damage and our guns were fired back at them but had no effect either. But it did make us feel better being able to throw something back. It was all hands on deck one morning ready to abandon ship when the ominous shape of an unidentified naval craft appeared on the horizon, cruising towards, us belching out smoke. There was nothing we could do. One shell well-placed and this rusty old hulk would be gone ... and there was only one small lifeboat. Once again, the dreaded pangs of fear churned in the stomach. This was a grim situation, with a mass of sea all around and probably sharks down there as well. I was just beginning to accept the inevitable when a shout from the bridge brought a big sigh of relief; it was 'one of ours'. What a lovely feeling to have that beautiful grey ship sailing alongside as our personal escort. It stayed on station for a few days until we were well clear of enemy activity, then sped off towards the east. I seem to remember that ship had been damaged in action off the coast of Africa and was heading home for repairs, it just happened to bump into us on the way. I think it was called the *Grimsby*.

Our welcome at Alexandria was fantastic. We felt like visiting royalty, with sirens blasting and small craft buzzing around us like flies. Waiting transport whisked us off to Mustaffa barracks for a good meal, a lovely soak in a bath and a change of clothes.

Our next priority was to head for town with a thirst many weeks old and a pocketful of money, thanks to a regulation which allowed us to claim for the costs involved in evacuating ourselves. We made out a bill for a boat, food, fuel and bribery. The payout was a small fortune. We collected about forty pounds each and blew practically all of it on celebrating our safe return to Egypt.

CHAPTER 10

OUT OF THE FRYING PAN

I T TOOK A FEW DAYS to recover from the most expensive celebration and hangover I have ever experienced, but after the fear and uncertainty of the past weeks it was worth every penny. How wonderful it was to be back in the world of bars, bints and the Fleet Club; with a little imagination, even a stroll down the brothel area of Sister Street was like a saunter through Hyde Park on a Sunday morning and the stench of Mex Tanneries was sweeter than all the roses. I could even have been persuaded to accept Amiriya as a seaside holiday resort; how wonderful it was just to be alive.

We were moved by train to a camp on the outskirts of Cairo. It was a few miles west of the Sweet Water Canal and about five miles south of the Pyramids. The name Beni Yusef was to remain planted in our memory for many years to come. Here in this godforsaken hole, next to a desolate-looking cemetery amongst the sand dunes, we were destined to become a fighting Regiment once again and plunge back into that world of the unknown.

During our brief escapade in Greece, the Desert War had continued and the situation drastically changed. The intervention of the German Army to once again get the Italians out of trouble after their defeat in Cyrenaica, turned General Wavell's victorious drive across the desert into a depressing retreat. As we were running from the Germans in Greece, our Army was doing the same in the desert. Someone must have told Rommel that 3 RTR had left the country, so he grasped the opportunity and ordered the attack. Well, we were back again; that should give him some sleepless nights!

From what information we could glean since our return it appeared that Rommel was stuck with the problem of Tobruk, cut off by him but occupied by our forces. He had reached the Egyptian frontier but could proceed no further; the long supply lines from Benghazi restricted his movements. For months, the Australians and other units trapped with them had repulsed every attempt by the enemy to remove this stumbling block, but they were there to stay in that hellhole and even dedicated a song to their flea-infested dugouts in Tobruk.

Whilst the enemy were hurling themselves against Tobruk, we were sitting comfortably on the sands of Beni Yusef Camp, settling down to a daily routine of training and learning the problems of new equipment. We also had to learn to live with new replacements, many of whom came from prestigious cavalry regiments and initially felt downgraded to be in a common tank regiment. Perhaps they believed that a regiment which had confronted the enemy twice, lost all its equipment and half of its personnel on each occasion, did not come up to their stand-ard of historic glory. However, even the most dogmatic soon realised that we had learned much from our experiences and had given the enemy a lot to remember.

It was not all toil and trouble; a half-hour drive down the road in the back of a lorry and we were in Cairo. This was a new world to us, vast crowds of men, dressed in nightgowns and women all in black, all breathing garlic over you, and taxis, lorries, tramcars, buses, horse-drawn gharrys and bullock-carts, all jostling for a piece of roadway. The noise was deafening; tramcar wheels rattling and screeching on the rails in competi-tion with the continuous blast of vehicle horns, all with a mad urge to get there first. In the background, wailing Egyptian music emitted from every doorway and added the final touch of character to this oriental scene.

With an international community such as the population of Cairo, the aroma of a thousand national dishes saturated the atmosphere and changed what started out as a gourmet delight into an unbearable stink. In addition to struggling through the crowds, progress was restricted by a constant stream of street vendors, conmen and shoeshine boys. They were the worst; if you refused a shine, liquid polish would be splashed on your shoes as you walked and you then had to pay to have it removed.

Many of these street urchins, uneducated and unable to even write their name, could fluently converse in four or five languages. They were excellent guides and negotiated the price on your behalf for anything you wished to purchase, from a ride in a taxi to a meal in a restaurant. One, who I used on a number of occasions, bullied a street vendor into making me a leather suitcase, sitting on the pavement outside a restaurant whilst I ate my lunch and watched him through the window; it cost three pounds and lasted fifty years.

There was another side to Cairo, of course, a history going back many thousands of years, with artefacts displayed in the museums and many areas and buildings steeped in history. The Health and Science Museum was a special attraction; it showed a fascinating display of tropical diseases and their effects. What a gruesome way to spend an afternoon that was! I vowed never to touch drink or women again.

Well... I did keep the vow for at least an hour, but that experience left a nasty taste in my mouth and I needed a drink to get rid of it, and after a few beers the girls once again looked beautiful and perfectly harmless...

In the centre of the city, on the river Nile, was the island of Gazeira, with its promenades, gardens and luxurious riverboats. It was well known as a rich people's playground, with sports fields, bars, restaurants and whatever else money could buy. The mosques, with their beautiful mosaics and minarets, towered up into the sky, sending down the call to worship as if from the heavens above. On the outskirts of the city, at Mena, stood the famous Pyramids and Sphinx, those gigantic monuments to the pharaoh kings whose exact means of construction continued to confound the experts.

Large buildings and blocks of flats occupied much of the city, but on the desert to the south, a large shanty-town housed a mass of people living in dirt and squalor. I was driven through it once, in a horse-drawn gharry, and had no desire to return.

Improvements were in hand, however, and work on large blocks of flats was in progress from dawn to dusk, with hundreds of men and women winding their way up a dangerous-looking walkway, constructed of bamboo poles tied together with rope, to deposit their load at the top and return down the other side. Everything was carried on the back or the head, be it bricks, mortar, or whatever and the whole scene was reminiscent of a colony of foraging ants doggedly following each other. During a discussion with a local official, whose family I had met and with whom I spent many enjoyable evenings, I asked why so many people had to work so hard when so much modern machinery was available. His answer was simply. "what would we do with all the people?"

For me, I think the most fascinating thing was the Egyptian way of life. In the city, people lived and worked much the same as in other parts of the world, but because of the warm climate, many tasks were left until the cool of the evening. Service in hotels, cafés, bars and restaurants was generally available 24 hours a day and laundry left outside a bedroom door at any time of night would be washed, starched and ready to wear in the morning. It was all there to be enjoyed, and we lapped up what little we could afford.

During the hottest hours of the day, nothing moved on the land, but in the cool of the evening the farmers appeared and worked throughout the night. Water drawn from a well by hand was tipped into a trench and flowed around the fields for many hundreds of yards. Crops were harvested by hand, cut with a sickle and the grains beaten from the straw with a weight wielded at the end of a thong. A wooden beam, dragged across the heap of grain, cracked the husks, and tossing in the air during a gentle breeze blew the chaff to one side; no machinery, just manpower, as their forefathers had done for thousands of years.

Our route to camp was along a narrow road, with the Sweet Water Canal on one side and, at one point, a few huts on the other. These were about twelve feet square, with a large gap for a door, a smaller one for a window and one in the roof for a chimney. The floor appeared to be soil, baked hard, and a piece of sacking hung over the doorway. At night, practically everything was housed within that room, the family, chickens, dog, and possibly the donkey also. In the canal there were children swimming, a man washing down a cow and a boy spending a penny; a little further along a woman was washing clothes and another was filling a jug with drinking water. A passing camel made a mess on the road and children fought over it; when dry it was used as fuel for the fire. What a way to live.

We were eventually fitted out with new tanks, supplied to us by our American Allies, and at first sight they were quite a shock. Being accustomed to the low, sleek profile of our Crusaders, the tall, lumpy looking Stuart tanks, nicknamed 'Honeys', looked like something from the dark ages. My introduction to these monsters was with a small group sent to try them out in the desert on the outskirts of Cairo.

We took up residence in the barracks and prepared to enjoy the luxury of living in a building. How wrong we were. It was a nerve-racking experience of sleepless nights and lousy food, but the real monsters were tiny brown things as thick as paper that would blow up to the size of a ladybird and they were already in residence. The barracks had been built during World War One, with cavity walls filled with straw to keep out the heat, but these also provided a perfect breeding ground for millions of bloodsucking bugs. Switch off the lights and out they would come; walk across the floor in the dark and they crunched under your feet. They came down the inside of the mosquito nets from the knot at the top. Those bloody parasites were everywhere and so were the bumps on your body where they fed. My Royal Scottish blood was their favourite diet, I stuck it for a couple of nights then took my mattress out on to the barrack square; it was good to have a long sleep but I never repeated the exercise, someone informed me the area was alive with rats at night.

Saturday was debugging day. The metal beds were taken outside, dismantled and bumped on the concrete. Out they tumbled from the joints and popped in the heat of the sun. With paraffin poured into the joints, the beds were reassembled and stood on the floor, with each of the legs immersed in an empty cigarette tin full of paraffin. It had no effect on the little bastards, they just dive-bombed from the ceiling. Cracks in the walls were torched with a blowlamp and refilled with thick whitewash. The smell and sound of them popping was sickening and the effect of our labours short lived; within days the cracks had opened and out they marched.

The 'Honeys' had a shorter base and were much taller than our Crusader tanks. I could just imagine enemy gunners picking on them as an easy target outlined against the skyline like a damned great monument and that was frightening. Power was supplied by a seven-cylinder air-cooled radial engine. How the hell could that thing work efficiently in the heat of the desert? It ran on high-octane aircraft fuel and we carried over one hundred gallons of the stuff, not nice to have around when angry men are firing shells at you. A look inside made me feel worse. Unlike ours, the turret base did not rotate and a drive shaft cover over a foot high and six inches wide occupied the centre of the floor. Just imagine the gunner traversing the turret quickly with the commander and loader running round inside, all jumping the hurdle. It was also a difficult turret to rotate; it was moved by turning a large hand wheel, which reminded me of a chaff cutter I had used on a farm. In comparison, our turrets were traversed by hydraulic power, which moved the turret swiftly and precisely with the twist of a lever. I could envisage many problems with that damned great wheel.

A large number of modifications were carried out to satisfy our requirements, replacing many items we considered a luxury with racks for extra ammunition. A sling seat was added for the commander. When the situation allowed, he could sit suspended, with half his body sticking out of the turret instead of having to grope with his feet to find a foothold whilst suspended on his elbows. All unnecessary tools were slung out. On each tank there were tools for a complete engine overhaul. What a waste. Imagine sitting in the desert trying to take an engine to pieces with a lot of angry men hell bent on stopping you. There were many more tools and fittings we considered unnecessary and we discarded them all, including four thermos flasks, neatly clipped to brackets on the wall; the net result of all this was to increase the ammunition capacity by about fifty percent.

The armour and armament was similar to our Cruisers but the 37mm main armament did have a slight edge on our Cru-saders. There were HE (high explosive) shells available for the Honey. In addition to three 0.3 machine guns, a 0.5 ack-ack gun was mounted just behind the commander's cupola on top of the turret, but apart from providing a useful hand grip when getting out of the turret, this gun turned out to be a useless commodity when required in a hurry. A long fabric belt loaded with the ammo was stored in a box attached to the gun mounting. On a number of occasions during an air raid, I swung the gun into action, snatched the belt to pull a round into the breech … and almost fell overboard due to the unexpected lightness of the belt. In the dry, hot atmosphere and with the constant vibrations of the tank, the ammo had slipped out of the belt and was rattling around loose in the bottom of the box; of course, by the time the belt was refilled the aircraft had gone.

We also had doubts about the ability of the tracks to survive the sandy and rocky terrain of the desert. Each plate was a rubber pad, moulded on a metal insert twice the size of a Cruiser plate and connected by one-inch diameter pins, although these were definitely an improvement on Cruiser track pins, which were only half that size and needed constant replacement. The air filters mounted at the rear end of the hull were certainly not located with the desert in mind; they collected the dust thrown up by the tracks and needed daily attention.

Despite the shortcomings of our new vehicles, like the good soldiers we were, we shouldered our burden and set off across the desert to confront the enemy...

~ CHAPTER 11 ~

THE RELIEF OF TOBRUK

I T WAS NOW THE MONTH of July and Tobruk had been cut off since April: time, thought the powers-that-be to break them out of there. General Wavell had been removed and posted to India after his failure to prevent Rommel retaking Cyrenaica and General Von Auchinleck was brought from India to take his place. Churchill, as usual, was demanding action and plans were put in place to strengthen our forces for an offensive operation to relieve Tobruk and defeat the enemy. It was known that Rommel was fast building up his forces to take Tobruk and drive east into Egypt, so the race was on. But who would strike first?

Our approach march to the Egyptian frontier was carried out discreetly and well camouflaged. This was my first real look at the desert from the turret of a tank and there were no romantic rolling dunes of golden sands, just dust, rocks, stones and large areas of sagebrush. The dust and stones had settled around the base of each bush, creating a solid mound about a foot high, which reduced our speed considerably and slowed the supply vehicles to a crawl. Any attempt at driving a loaded lorry fast amongst the mounds resulted in broken springs and lots of leaking petrol cans.

Generally devoid of cover, with just an occasional gentle hollow, the simplest means of defence from air attack was to space out – and there was plenty of space for that. A division on the move, with vehicles spread out a hundred yards apart, covered the desert to the far horizons. To look back at this vast military spectacle and to be a part of it, brought a lump to my throat and sent a surge of pride through my body. However, in my position of 'advance patrol', looking ahead, the feeling was somewhat different; one of fear, wondering what was hiding out there, waiting for us.

We were part of 30 Corps, advancing towards the southern part of the Egyptian border, whilst 13 Corps covered the northern and coastal areas. Our regiment, 3rd RTR, was part of the 4th Armoured Brigade, the original Desert Rats, along with 5th RTR and 8th Hussars, all three being battled-scarred regiments. Our orders were to cross the frontier about twenty miles south of the coast, attack and destroy the enemy, and relieve Tobruk.

Now what could be simpler than that?

Information indicated that we had a few more tanks than the enemy. Our 37mm guns, firing a 2lb shell, could knock him out at 800 yards, but his 50mm guns, firing a 4lb shell could knock us out at 1,200 yards.

Ah well, what was new? We had been through it all before.

Advancing in battle formation prior to contact with the enemy would generally involve a squadron of 16 tanks acting as advance guard. The remaining two squadrons and HQ troop followed, and at the rear came the "B" Echelon supply transport. This was part of an "A" Echelon, which was our main supply column, stationed much further to the rear. Even during battle, the "B" Echelon was always in the vicinity, ready to supply petrol and ammo on an urgent basis. How about driving a lorry with 700 gallons of high octane fuel in the back contained in leaking 4-gallon flimsy cans, or a load of high explosive ammunition, often sitting in a hollow within range of enemy guns and vulnerable to air attack. They were the brave ones. At least we had the protection of armour plate and knew from the chatter on our radios what was going on. Those poor devils just sat there under the control of an officer, with only one radio in the column, waiting to be told when and where to move.

We advanced on our centre line through most of the day, with eyes strained against the brilliant sunshine on the far horizon, but as time moved on, with no sign of the enemy, tension eased and confidence returned. Then came the inevitable; an enemy column was reported northeast of our position and we were ordered to change direction and attack it. The sun was low on the horizon and setting fast as we made contact and, after a brief exchange of shots with no casualties that I could see, we closed in to leaguer for the night. It had been a satisfying day, my first in action since Greece and Crete. I had been apprehensive about it, but, as usual, the task of commanding a tank had left little time for nerves.

In this open, flat terrain, darkness was our only true hiding place, but even that depended upon strict procedures being maintained. No radio transmission during approach to the selected area and no lights or fires. Even the glow of a cigarette could be seen with binoculars. A radio switched to transmit could be detected by direction finding equipment and your location pinpointed to a few yards. To avoid discovery by patrols, the Regiment's leaguer occupied the smallest space possible. The three sides of a square were formed by the tank squadrons, each tank facing outwards and the end closed by HQ Troop. The soft vehicles of the infantry, artillery and supply Echelon occupied the centre area.

The end of day ritual was completed with speed and precision and only then could you put your head down and sleep, but even that was limited by guard duty. Fuel tanks had to be topped up, ammo loaded and stored, guns cleaned, mechanical defects repaired by our fitters, and radio frequency reset. Rations were issued to each tank, there was no cookhouse, we had to cook for ourselves, if and when there was time, all carried out in the dark or, in exceptional cases, with a masked light.

It was standard practice to spread out into the desert half an hour before sunrise; this avoided being caught with your trousers down at first light. Our location could have been discovered during the night and a gloating enemy could be waiting to see the whites of our eyes before blasting us to hell. What a perfect target, a 300-yard-square box packed with vehicles. Depending on the situation, a quick breakfast may be possible, but more often than not it was a case of eating on the move. Trying to drink a mug of hot tea in a tank bouncing all over the desert was not funny, especially for the operator sitting just below.

As normal procedure we started to move out in the dark and, by the time the sun tipped the horizon, we were spread out across the desert. Almost immediately, orders in my earphones told of an enemy concentration northwest of our position and we were ordered to engage. We had moved only a few miles when we were halted by anti-tank guns dug in and well hidden, with tanks on the ridge behind, well out of range of our 37mm pop guns. Within minutes, a couple of our tanks were burning and we kept discreetly hull-down whilst our artillery dealt with the a/t guns. The order was to advance, however, and the best we could do was to try and keep the a/t gunner's heads down with machine gun fire whilst trying to get closer to the tanks behind them.

It was not our day. I could hear someone on my right reporting another 100 enemy tanks approaching from the northeast and just prayed there was another regiment available to take them on. At least they would not have an a/t barrier to contend with. All day the battle raged on, with casualties on both sides. Having engaged targets at every opportunity, ammunition was getting low, and so was the sun on the horizon, partly obscured by a thick pall of smoke and dust drifting across the battlefield.

As light faded, we crept away in the darkness to the sanctuary of our leaguer, leaving behind a skyline of flickering flames and the stench of burning rubber, flesh and cordite. For me, this was a very depressing introduction to war in the desert, very different from Greece, where casualties were mostly obscured by hills and trees. Here, it was all laid out on a flat piece of ground, just like a bloody cemetery, with burned-out tanks for gravestones.

There was no respite next morning; as we moved out the enemy was already on our doorstep, coming at us from the east, out of the sun. A running battle continued, with the enemy forcing us south. We lost some tanks, but the enemy, taking forceful chances, lost more. Blinded by the shimmering heat around midday, the battle stopped for a couple of hours; it was impossible to continue under conditions where nothing could be recognised through a haze of twisted, distorted shapes. It was a heaven-sent opportunity to replenish our supplies, brew up and eat, but the strain of battle, lack of sleep and the physical punishment of bouncing around in a tank, could be seen on every face. As visibility improved, the battle continued, with the enemy pushing us still further back towards Egypt until the light faded, when both sides retired to lick their wounds and count their losses. We had lost many tanks that day and a lot of our friends too.

Next day found us under pressure again, but during the night other formations had been moved in to the area to help us and the battle raged on with much ferocity. However, it soon became evident that pressure was easing and reports indicated the enemy was pulling back towards the northwest. Information filtered through that another arm of our Army, advancing north-west had captured Sidi Rezegh airfield, thereby cutting Rommel's supply route to his forces along the coast, so he was withdrawing his force to open it up again. We were ordered to follow up his retreat and destroy as much of his armour as possible. This was not an easy task, since his rearguard tactic of using an a/t gun screen was difficult to dislodge and could cost us dearly without the opportunity to attack his tanks.

It was late afternoon when an order to change direction and speed up turned us north towards Sidi Rezegh airfield, but there was no indication of what was in store. A large, black cloud filled the sky above a distant ridge. We reached the top as the light was fading and the source of the cloud was revealed. My God, what a shock. Beneath the escarpment a large plain spread out before us and the scene was one of utter chaos. There were hundreds of vehicles, tanks, guns and burned out aircraft, spread out in utter confusion amongst the smoke of shell-bursts and gunfire. Incredibly, men seemed to be wandering around, digging trenches and manhandling artillery, doing what was required of them as if on an exercise on Salisbury Plain. I found it impossible to determine who was friend or foe. It was the most terrifying spectacle I had ever seen. I closed my eyes with a wish, but it was still there when I opened them again.

My heart was thumping all over my body and voices were screaming in my earphones. We were ordered down the escarpment trail to join in the action and my stomach sank into my boots as I struggled to keep the tremor from my voice when reporting the scene to my squadron commander. Amongst the debris around me at the edge of the escarpment, within a few feet of the tank, were the bodies of two soldiers, lying one on top of the other in the form of a cross, just as they had fallen. A white, enamel mug was hanging from the webbing of the soldier on top. How strange to remember such an unimportant detail, when the grotesque tragedy of death was all around.

Down on the airfield, as the view became clearer it revealed a scene even more chaotic and depressing. My god, what a mess we had got ourselves into! Bodies lay everywhere and obstruction by battle debris slowed our progress to a crawl, just at a time when speed was vital to get to our target. But where the hell *was* our target? Vehicles were milling about all over the area, with troops of tanks suddenly appearing out of the smoke and dust. It was an impossible situation, open fire on one of these vague, fleeting targets and you could be blasting your own CO to hell.

We stopped to assess the situation but that was a mistake; fire descended upon us from all directions and the noise of screaming shells, explosions, the chatter of machine guns, and the whistle of fragments flying through the air was unbearable. I kept my body as low as possible in the turret and the urgent need to think and act suppressed the fear rising within me. Like everyone else, I must get on with the job I had to do.

A violent explosion rocked the tank and a large crater appeared alongside, big enough to hide the tank in. What in the hell was that? Another missile was screaming through the air and landed just in front of us. Added to the usual artillery, anti-tank and machine gun fire, we were now being targeted by 210mm shells. Someone decided that that was enough and gave the order 'get to hell out of here!' That sounded great in my earphones, but where the hell were we? A cloud of smoke and dust hung over the area such that the tanks around me were drifting in and out of view in the billowing smog, and with infantry on the ground all around, movement was not an easy option.

Guiding my driver in this almost blind environment required all my concentration and consequently I failed to detect the smell of burning until the operator screamed, "We are on fire!" A bedroll was burning on the back of the tank and creating our own smokescreen; it was lying just above the petrol caps. He jumped out and kicked it off. Navigating my way out was no real option either, because even the bright desert sun had difficulty casting a shadow on my sun compass through all that muck.

Instinct took over and I just followed my nose. To date I had lost two tanks, but each time we had all survived and escape to the rear had been possible. Getting out of this cauldron on foot would not be so easy.

Details of the events that followed are extremely vague but I know I left the airfield in a cloud of dust and smoke. At the top of the escarpment visibility was no better and my radio was dead; apparently I had lost the aerial. I missed the squadron completely and was following an infantry group of vehicles. Unfortunately, they would be carrying none of the supplies I required, and we were getting rather short of petrol. Better than being alone, nevertheless.

Groups of vehicles were still milling around in the dust and smoke and a few tanks and lorries passed nearby. That was a more likely source of supply so I joined them and another lost tank tagged on behind me. The column stopped, so I took the opportunity to jump down and run to the tank in front to ask for information. A head popped out of the turret and a voice said "Hello Bob." It was my cousin from the north of Scotland and our first meeting for many years; not exactly an ideal spot for exchanging pleasantries, but it showed how small the world really is. Our next meeting was three years later.

Almost by accident, I found the Regiment, or what was left of it; once again, we were down to half our normal strength. We appeared to have lost contact with our own Brigade and were under the control of another, but the situation was just the same. Battles seemed to be raging all around us, tracer lacing through the air in all directions, and the palls of smoke from burning vehicles were everywhere. I was tired, hungry, my body ached and I was sick of this dreadful carnage all around me. No sooner had we beaten back one attack when another batch of enemy tanks came at us from our flank. This was hell, in the worst possible sense.

The days that followed were chaotic, with German and Allied columns milling around each other, trying to gain the advantage. I lost count of the days or weeks we had been in action. I felt worn out, almost to a state where nothing mattered any more. Fear and exhaustion had almost reached the limit of human endurance and yet with every new order I found some hidden reserve. Someone must have sensed our dilemma; we had two days off to wash, clean up, eat, sleep and re-equip with more tanks and crews. Many new crews and tanks had joined us during the campaign; they had fought and died without leaving even a name to remember.

Eventually, after many skirmishes between the Sidi Rezegh area and the Egyptian border, Tobruk was finally relieved. I never really understood how this was achieved, but historians said that Rommel was not defeated but decided, because of a shortage of ammo and petrol, to withdraw his forces out of Cyrenaica to an area behind the salt marshes at El Ageila. The activities of our Navy and Air Force in the Mediterranean had been very effective in reducing enemy supplies from Italy to a mere trickle.

The enemy withdrew to a prepared defence line stretching south from Gazala on the coast, but our forces in the north were hot on their heels. Rommel hit back with tanks a number of times to allow his a/t rearguard screen to get away, but where did all his tanks keep coming from? According to our Army HQ figures of the casualties we had inflicted, he should have none left. At least for a couple of days it was not our problem; we were given time to get our breath back and moved south into the wilds.

What a lovely feeling it was to take off that balaclava I had worn for many days; it was damned painful though, since the hair on my face had grown through it. A wash and change of clothes brought new life into my weary body and a six-hour undisturbed sleep made the hard desert floor feel like a bed of feathers. My socks had long since become a series of holes held together by strands of wool and removing my boots attracted a cloud of flies. My God, how I must have stunk, but even my best friend didn't tell me. Sleep and cooked food in a relaxed and quiet atmosphere brought back some normality. I could see smiling faces and hear laughter, but deep inside we all knew that within an hour all hell could be let loose again.

As far as the tanks were concerned it was two days of hard work and a chance to see in daylight just how much punishment they had taken. That poor girl of mine had gouge marks in a few places where armour-piercing shells had tried to get in; they must have been long distance shots or hits at an angle, otherwise they would have gone through. In battle, the atmosphere had just been a mass of noise, with bumps, bangs, the scream of shells and the whistle of bullets, mostly unidentified, against a background of constant voices in my earphones and concentration of the mind on the task in hand. As usual, the thin metal lockers along the side of the tank were a bit scarred and the bedrolls had a few tears, but otherwise our luck had held.

An urgent call for briefing brought me back to reality and the dreaded thought of 'here we go again'. This time it was a very dodgy operation; a hundred-mile dash up behind the enemy's Gazala line to cut the road near the coast and force Rommel to withdraw. The whole Brigade was involved and we were in the lead, moving through unknown territory of rocks, cliffs, and dust bowls. In my usual position, probing well ahead, I stopped on a ridge and observed the scene behind me. What a spectacle! The whole Brigade was spread out across the desert, partly obscured by the dust it created and once again I felt proud to be part of it.

It was rough going, even for tanks, and we had to change direction frequently to allow passage for our transport, which was lagging dangerously behind. Remarkably, we saw no enemy until we reached the coast road, when our first contact was a small convoy of lorries, which we destroyed. The light faded and we withdrew for the night, only to discover that only a few of our supply wagons had reached us. The rough conditions had been too much and the bulk of the Brigade was still far behind us.

With a limited amount of fuel and ammo, we turned west and ran slap into an enemy column of tanks spread out across a valley full of transport. Apparently, this was an HQ control area and no way were these tanks going to allow us into it; we lost a few more of our tanks but did as much damage as possible before pulling back south the way we had come. We later heard that our foray had been effective in causing Rommel to abandon the Gazala line and retreat down the coast towards Ageila.

From our position at the south end of the Gazala line, we probed west through the now deserted enemy defences, under orders to drive towards Ajedabea and thereby cut the road south from Benghazi and trap the enemy's retreating forces. In the meantime, a reorganisation had taken place and our regiment became attached to another Brigade while the other two regiments of the 4th Armoured Brigade returned to Egypt for a rest and refit, the lucky devils. Someone remarked that if we had not been so bloody good at the job, we would probably have been sent back. I suppose we all had our cross to bear, but mine was getting a bit too heavy.

Near the old fort at Msus we stopped for the night and in the morning, in an empty desert, the order was for breakfast. no contact had been made with the enemy during our march, but the RAF had paid us a brief visit, just long enough to drop a few bombs and remind us there was a war on. Yes, because of this fluid desert warfare, with movements over large areas, we were bombed by friend and foe alike, and we did throw a bit back, just for spite. However, breakfast was not to be, the appearance of some Honey tanks driving towards us from the north, being chased by a column of enemy tanks, prompted immediate action.

We were caught unprepared, but fortunately the area we retreated through gave us the possibility of partially hiding amongst the hollows and firing down on the enemy tanks as they came up the slopes. From my position on the flank I caught a few side on and saw two start to burn, but with so many shells flying about, anyone could have been responsible for the hits. All along the ridge we were losing tanks and continually forced back until relief came from the other two regiments. It was another hell of a day but we failed to stop Rommel's retreat to the safety of his defences at Ageila.

It was around Xmas and the battlefront was static, with little or no activity. We relaxed, well out of danger, trying to get back some normality into our lives and our Padre was a great help. He had been gone for a few days with a couple of lorries and returned loaded with goodies. There was tinned meat and veg, bacon, soya sausages and all sorts of food we had not seen for months, even bread; I had almost forgotten what it looked like. For Xmas pudding we cooked a real gourmet delight: a slice of bread, coated thick with jam and fried in fat from the bacon until the jam had soaked right through. What a treat that was!

But most important of all came the order to move back to our old camp at Cairo, Beni Yusef. In the eyes of the generals, the battle had been won and Cyrenaica recaptured. I recognised only the weariness of six weeks in action with but 2-3 hours sleep a night, limited rations of bully, biscuits, cheese and jam, and water just sufficient for drinking and radiators. But that was the life to which we were committed and we just had to get on with it.

I suppose in many ways we were lucky. We had our own mobile home for four, complete with kitchen, lounge, dining room and bedroom, a little cramped, perhaps, but it was still home; rations for four delivered to the door, unlimited fuel for cooking, and only a mess tin, mug and spoon to wash up. Breathtaking conducted tours daily in an exotic ancient land of sand, rock and sagebrush. An adventure never to be forgotten. I certainly have never forgotten it.

From sunup to sunset was the longest day, every day. Start up the tanks and spread out, half an hour before daylight; no lights, no fires, no hot drink. If no enemy in sight as the sun rises and no orders to move, then brew up quickly or you may not make it. Breakfast, what a lovely start to the day, unless, of course, you are in the light squadron and sent out on patrol, then it is Hobson's choice, standing in the turret of a bouncing tank, trying to drink a mug of tea without losing too much, directing the driver on the safest route, searching ahead for the unknown, listening to messages in my earphones with the poor wireless Op underneath me, cursing the hot tea spilling down the back of his shirt whilst he tries to prepare a gourmet breakfast of jam and cheese on hard biscuits.

One thing we learned was, if at any time you were given the chance to brew up you should seize the opportunity, there may not be another all day. The routine was organised to perfection whenever we stopped for sufficient time. An empty petrol tin with the top cut out and air holes punched in the sides was half filled with sand, soaked with petrol and lit. When the water boiled, you shaded your face against the three-foot flames and threw in a handful of tea, then removed the dixie quickly before it boiled up and into the fire. Tapping the sides of the pot caused the tealeaves to quickly settle to the bottom, then the black liquid could be poured into the mugs. With sugar and tinned milk it was the nectar of the gods, to be accompanied by the music of screaming engines, rattling tracks and a moaning Wireless Operator.

Flexible meal times, with the blessing of the enemy, allowed you the freedom to eat when you felt like it, with a menu of your choice. You could have biscuits, cheese and jam; biscuits, jam and cheese, or just a hunk of cheese. But, for a real treat, how about a tin of bully all to yourself, opened carefully to prevent the warm fat running down the operator's neck and devoured quickly to ensure your fair share in competition with the flies? Add some grit thrown up by the tracks and you have a perfect balanced diet, grinding the hard biscuits to assist digestion and at the same time scouring the teeth clean. Of course, fresh meat was always available, just like us, the flies loved the sweet things and often paid the penalty. I never could tell the difference in taste.

As the sun sank slowly in the west, one's body sagged gently with relief and one's ears sharpened to the crackling in the earphones, waiting for the order to withdraw, the signal that said we had survived another day, although in the light squadron, doubts would still dwell in your mind. You could be ordered to stay on the battle line to ensure that the Regiment was not followed to the Leaguer area by an enemy patrol.

In that Leaguer, no lights meant NO lights. Fitters struggled to carry out repairs with a torch hidden under a tarpaulin, but everything else was done by starlight or moonlight. Petrol was poured into twin funnels, sixteen gallons at a time and a cloud of volatile high-octane vapour hung in the air. On one occasion a sheet of flame shot out of a tank turret and with it came one of the crew; the idiot had been using a petrol cooker inside the tank. The whole area was lit up and the regiment had to move;

naturally the CO was furious and so were we all at the unnecessary loss of sleep.

At last, with tasks all done, now for that last relaxing cigarette of the day. But what about our infantry outpost guards, with orders to shoot out any lights? No problem. Men wandering around holding a round cigarette tin to their mouth was a curious sight but it was the only way to have a smoke. A cigarette was inside the tin and small holes punched in the lid gave access to the air but showed no light.

But what about a hot meal at night? The ingenuity of man knows no bounds. Tins of food, such as meat and veg, when available, were jammed between the exhaust pipe and the hull of the tank such that they were cooking whilst we were on the move. Through a hole punched in the top, curry powder was blown in with a straw and the smell of curried stew drifting across the battlefield, amidst the stench of exhaust, cordite fumes and burning vehicles, set the taste buds afire. Some clever devils even strapped an oven, made from empty cans, onto the silencer, and a can of water strapped on, added to a drop of concentrated tea, saved during the day, provided a hot drink.

Every triumph has its price, and our dash across the desert meant we had doubled the length of our line of communication, so even just sitting in the desert in a stalemate situation, we were denied the simple things that could make life a little more bearable. Amidst all this gloom and doom there was one ray of sunshine that brightened our lives, the water was actually drinkable. Back in the Tobruk area, during the withdrawal after Wavell's victory, some bright spark had a brilliant idea to salt the wells, thereby creating a problem for the enemy. During our advance, we were the idiots who had to use the damned stuff; drinking it was horrible, but there was no choice. Tea tasted quite grim and the addition of milk made it worse, it just curdled and floated around in sickening blobs. Another problem was washing, normal soap in salt water will not lather, you just end up with a sticky mess and it smells. It was different on board ship, where special saltwater soap was available, but we had none.

Confronting an enemy in this vast desert, where observation and movement was generally not restricted by geological features, battles tended to be flexible, with movement over large distances a part of the strategy. This, of course, created the problem of supply, where all the necessary goods required to conduct that war had to be transported. Petrol, ammunition, food, water and vehicle spares, moved hundreds of miles across terrain that was a driver's nightmare to be delivered to those who required them.

In action, a tank may burn about 50 gallons of petrol a day. Multiply that by 150 tanks, add the requirement for all other vehicles in the Brigade and a measure of the problem is indicated. Considering that only about 50% of the fuel that left base actually arrived, due to leakage from the flimsy four-gallon cans, then the task of organising supplies became a nightmare. Of course the priority was petrol and ammunition, everything else took second place, including food.

Here, the rambling thoughts of some poor soul cut off and locked up in the defence of Tobruk come to mind...

I am an RTR man stationed in Tobruk
And I have a little dugout in the sand,
The fleas they gather round me as I settle down to sleep
In my flea-bound, bug-bound dugout in Tobruk.

The windows they are missing and the doors are four by two
The sandbags let the howling blizzard through,
I can hear those bastard Jerries as they circle overhead
In my flea-bound, bug-bound dugout in Tobruk.

The desert it is strewn with bully and meat roll
The marmalade and jam it is but few,
But we're as happy as a band in this land of shit and sand
In my flea-bound, bug-bound dugout in Tobruk.

I wish I had my sweetheart to sit upon my knee
And relieve me of this mess that I am in,
But the angels up above will tell her that I love her
In my flea-bound, bug-bound dugout in Tobruk.

Now the Jerries they are coming, the Stukas they fly low
The ack-ack shells are bursting overhead,
And I've got to see the dawning of yet another day
In my flea-bound bug-bound dugout in Tobruk.

But now we've left Tobruk and we are on our way
To Derna or Benghazi any day,
But I wonder what's the best or to have a good night's rest
In my flea-bound, bug-bound dugout in Tobruk.

Breakfast in the desert.

Maintenance crew.

~ CHAPTER 12 ~

BACK TO BENI YUSEF

W HAT A PLEASURE IT WAS to see that camp on the hillside, just above the cemetery and to smell the aroma of rotting vegetation, mixed with that of garlic and spicy cooking and, wafting gently in the background, the stench of camel dung. What a wonderful feeling to be back in a civilised world! We had left behind the fear, tension and weariness, but we brought the smells of the battlefield back with us. The stench of rotting corpses had become engraved in our minds and our bodies were saturated with the smell of burning cordite. When a tank gun was fired, the empty cartridge was ejected on the recoil of the weapon and fell into a bag beneath the breech. With it came a red glow and the pungent fumes of cordite, filling the turret and absorbed into the lungs of the crew with every breath. For many days after returning from action, the presence of any tankie who had actively been involved with gunfire could easily be detected; if he passed wind the air would be rich with the smell of cordite.

The top priority in everyone's mind was leave. We had been in that desert a long time and craved a little of what life had to give. Many of us had never been teenagers, we had become old men before our time. It took but a few hours of shellfire and death to turn a boy into a man, the more bitter your experiences the more you aged, and knowledge gave a better chance of survival, so you aged a little more. It was a vicious circle of experience, survival and ageing, but the desire to recapture what had been lost was always present.

My turn for leave came within a couple of weeks and, luckily, two of my best friends had the same period; we could not have planned it better. It was a hotel for us in the centre of Cairo and we all had the same priorities, a long soak in a hot bath, accompanied by a few bottles of ice-cold beer. What a beautiful experience to feel that cool liquid trickle down your throat. Next to a salon for the full treatment: haircut, shampoo, scalp massage, fingernails, toenails and finally, a long slow rub down all over with oil by a girl with soft, gentle hands. Sheer heaven.

We walked out onto the streets of Cairo smelling like a bunch of poofs, and half the flies in Egypt descended upon us.

I should have known better than to gulp down ice cold drinks in a hot climate; within 24 hours I was running to the toilet like a trainee for the Olympics and I occupied it day and night for about three days. The hotel manager did his best, treating me with mint tea and other witchdoctor concoctions, but to no avail. I sat all night long, cold and shivering, watching large brown cockroaches chewing up newspaper on the floor. It was a very poor substitute for a nightclub. Eventually, having lost about a stone in weight and still feeling very weak, I did venture out, but just the smell of food was enough to satisfy my appetite and my route had to be carefully planned around the location of known toilets.

My mates were having a smashing time, but they did refrain from tormenting me with the details of their exploits, although one of them did accidentally involve me in what must have been one of his more dubious escapades. Since I had not been using my nicely-starched khaki drill, he borrowed it for the evening, on the promise that it would be washed and starched for me by next morning. Of course, he forgot, and I had to wear it next day. It was my first venture out onto the streets again and they went with me to ensure I was OK. I noticed my mate Boris (the borrower) was scratching his groin and asked him jokingly if he had crabs.

"Yes, I think so," he said. "They have been driving me mad for a couple of days now."

"You lousy bastard!" I shouted. "I have probably got them now!"

I had. Within a few days I was scratching like mad, but by this time we were back at camp.

That was one spell of leave I shall never forget!

Our doctor, Captain Macmillan, fed me up on arrowroot and other things and helped me get rid of the crabs. I had tried the usual army method without success, that ism to pour a tot of whisky over the pubic hair and rub in sand. It was said they get drunk and stoned each other to death, but it didn't work for me.

By the time we got back from leave, fighting in the desert had erupted once again and our forces were pushed back to a new defence line. This ran from Gazala on the coast to a fort called Bir Hakim, 50 miles south in the desert and occupied by the Free French from Chad. Apparently Rommel, re-equipped with supplies from Italy, had struck at our weakened forces and re-captured a large part of Cyrenaica, including the port of Benghazi, along with its supplies and equipment. This was followed by a few months of stalemate, with both sides licking their wounds and re-building armies for the next onslaught.

In the meantime, back at Beni Yusef, we were re-equipped with a squadron of Honeys and two squadrons of Grants. By now, our experience with the Honeys had shown that although they stood very tall, had only a small 37mm gun and guzzled petrol at an alarming rate, they proved to be mechanically very sound. Our initial doubts about the ability of rubber track plates to survive the destructive desert terrain were partly justified. The rubber did wear out rather quickly, but we stripped the tracks, turned the plates upside down and re-connected them;

it worked very well and many more miles were travelled before replacements were necessary.

The Grant tanks were new to us. They had just arrived from America and looked like big, frightening monsters, even more so than the Honeys. However, they did have a large 75mm sponson gun mounted on the right side of the hull and a 37mm in a separate turret on top, plus a 0.5-inch ack-ack and the usual .300 machine guns. Power was supplied on some by a 9-cylinder air-cooled radial engine, another petrol guzzler, but many others had a rather unusual engine of five 6-cylinder blocks mounted on one crankshaft and located fanwise through 180 degrees. These ex-Chrysler bus engine blocks each had its own ignition system and carburettor. Just imagine trying to tune that lot! There was no Crypton tuning available in those days, just the sound of the engine, the smell of the exhaust and a prayer.

Re-training began in earnest with the arrival and allocation of replacements from base and other regiments. We had lost many good, experienced soldiers in the last campaign, some good friends too but to brood was unhealthy and this was not the time for it. A number of promotions filled some of the vacant spots, but I and four other sergeants who had been commanding troops of tanks seemed to have been left behind. By requesting transfers to other regiments, followed by interviews with irate squadron commanders, we were all promoted. I became a squadron quartermaster and soon afterwards squadron sergeant major, so once again I was back commanding a troop of tanks.

~ CHAPTER 13 ~

'UP THE BLUE' AGAIN

I N MARCH, THE TANKS WERE loaded on a train for Mersa
Matruh and transferred to transporters for the long journey
across the desert. We had a slight delay in setting off by
train, my final task was to check the travelling accommodation
for the squadron personnel and, lo and behold, there in the
corner of one coach sat a 13-year-old girl. She had, apparently,
been bought from her father by one of the men for four pounds
and could not understand why I was throwing her off the train;
to her it was a question of family honour. If I had found the
man who had bought her, I would have reduced his honour to
nil, and his future marriage prospects along with it!

A few more weeks of desert training and we moved forward
to an area near the battlefront, ready to be deployed as the
situation demanded. An occasional recce was ordered and,
being in the light squadron, the job was often ours. It was on
one of these occasions that I drove up to a high mound with a
pile of stones on top, settled down behind it with just the top
of the turret showing and scanned the ground in front of me.
As per normal practice, my troop sergeant's tank was behind
me on the right and the troop corporal's to my left, both hull-
down below the ridge.

The sun was overhead and the desert shimmered in the heat.
Large pools of mirage 'water' changed shape as I scanned the
terrain ahead, but nothing moved on that vast expanse of grit,
sagebrush and rocks; it seemed so quiet and peaceful I could
have nodded off. A sudden screech and a crash followed by a

Jock Watt · *A Tankie's Travels* · **107**

burning wind across my back, threw me into near panic. I dropped into the turret, screaming to the driver to get the hell out of there. He needed no prompting from me; we were already reversing like mad down the slope as a second salvo of 105mm shells dropped on the very spot where we had been.

Below the hill, I ordered a stop. My heart was thumping all over my body, I was shaking with fright and needed to think. I cursed myself for my stupidity; that was a burial ground I had parked on, one of the few points marked on the almost vacant desert maps. It should have been obvious to me that all artillery in the area would be dead reckoned on that spot. This was dangerous. I was getting careless. That was the closest I had been to joining the celestial choir for some time and I knew that with every day of survival the odds of remaining unscathed must be getting shorter. I had not seen the flash of guns or anything else that indicated an enemy presence, but they had been there all right and we had nearly bought it. Idiot!

That near catastrophe had shaken me up quite badly and the crew were not too happy either, so my relief was great, just a few days later, when the order came through to pull back out of the battle area for a few days rest. Obviously, the higher command recognised that in the front line, just waiting for something to happen, searching the desert through binoculars for movement whilst suffering lack of sleep from a dawn stand-to, can create an army of nervous wrecks.

Whatever the reason, the opportunity of a few days relaxation was welcomed by everyone. I had never seen the troop pack up so quickly. The area chosen even had a name on the map, it was called Menphia, although how this flat plain of grit, stones and sagebrush earned such a name is mind-boggling.

However, as we headed towards our haven, in open formation, the order came over the wireless to slow down to a crawl. Oh no, surely we were not going to turn around and drive back again! My heart sank into my boots as I waited for the next message. I was not biting my nails; what was left of them had long since been chewed down to my knuckles. I need not have worried; the next order was for one of the crew of each tank to sit outside on the front and search for tortoises, they were crawling about everywhere, apparently. What the hell was going on now? We eventually stopped and spread out over a large area. Hopefully, this was to be our resting place for a few days. For the first time in weeks, I crawled into my bedroll before midnight.

I feel the heat of the sun on my face and my eyes are closed, what a wonderful world... But wait a minute, something is wrong, the sun is up and I am still in bed. I struggle out of my bedroll in a panic and look around with bleary eyes. The tanks are all spread out and the crews are wandering around as if on holiday. Thank God! I remember now. We have pulled back for a few days rest.

This was the life! To wake up to a steaming cup of hot tea – a benefit of being in charge and blessed with a well-trained crew. Ah well, no time to sit around, there was much to do. No rest for a Sergeant Major with the squadron's welfare to attend to. I also had a problem of my own. Last night, when I had unwrapped my bedroll, it had rolled out like a camouflage net, badly torn by shrapnel, but I was so tired I had hardly noticed the difference. A check on the tank revealed that the mudguard lockers on one side had also been damaged, the ones in which we stored our food. What a bloody mess! A number of tins had been ripped apart, including our last two tins of peaches. We had bought them from the NAAFI only a few weeks ago and now look at them, floating in a lovely sauce of juice, milk, chopped up bully and jam. Amongst the survivors was a tin of streaky bacon. At least we had something for breakfast, and the fat would come in handy later.

The fitters had done their bit with the limited spares available and we, the crew, had completed our tasks of general maintenance, cleaning guns, replenishing ammo and generally making the tank, our home and weaponry, an efficient piece of machinery once again. Apart from the buckled lockers and a few gouge marks from anti-tank shells around the front end, the old girl was in good shape.

Now, at long last, our first opportunity for a little self-indulgence. With more than the usual allowance of water available, a splash of that cool, clean liquid on the face was like a kiss from heaven, but removing many days growth of beard with an old razor blade was a painful and bloody business. Someone said the water came from a well nearby, in which, a few days previously, there had been a dead donkey. So what? He was probably a damned sight cleaner than we were a few days ago!

Now we knew we were back in the land of the living, a change of clothes had been issued. The removal of that smelly shirt, with its wide salt sweat mark up the back, in which I had lived, worked and slept for so long, took with it much of the built-up stress and anxiety. That clean, crisp new shirt, smelling of antiseptic, sliding over my body, prompted memories of a Cairo massage parlour and the feel of a nice, hole-free pair of socks was a tonic to my blistered, aching feet. Mind you, the holes did allow a bit of ventilation and the smell was hardly noticeable amongst all the other pongs. My god, how we must have stunk in that heat, although nobody mentioned it. After all, we all smelt the same.

At last came the most important event of the day, the ration wagon arrived. I wondered what goodies he had, other than bully, biscuits and rice. I hoped he had some salmon, it was our turn to have a tin between the four of us (normally issued one tin between ten). We fared very well, even a tin of soya sausage and, from the Good Lord himself, a loaf of bread; a bit dry and stale, but bread all the same, what a treat. But what to do with it all? Have a damned good stew-up now or leave the best for another day? Of course, we could lose the tank tomorrow and all would be gone, so what the hell, let's live today and enjoy a real treat.

The greatest treat of all was mail from dear old Blighty, letters from home, even a bill for something months out of date but, most welcome of all, a letter from a girlfriend. These were read many times over during the following days and even weeks until the next lot arrived sometime in the distant future. Every word and sentence was absorbed and analysed until it could almost be rewritten from memory. It was the lifeline back to that other life of family, love and caring, almost lost in the mind amongst the noise, stress and fear of war.

Now things were really looking up, someone had dug a toilet and put a box seat over the hole, luxury indeed, a walk across the desert carrying a shovel and newspaper was the usual exercise. Mind you, it could be dangerous first thing in the morning, without checking carefully inside that box. When the sun went down and the desert became freezing cold, the warmth coming up from below attracted scorpions. They are vicious little sods and don't like being trapped inside your shorts when you pull them up. If you do they will soon let you know it!

It was great to be free from the voices and atmospherics in my headphones, from the constant searching the ground ahead for threats to our existence and wishing the day onward to the haven of darkness. Even so, every visit of a staff car or dispatch rider brought new anxieties. What the hell were we in for now? Just a false alarm, but the fear was still there. Ah well, we were not on guard tonight, so at least we should have one good night's sleep. What a way to live!

Once settled here at Menphia that crazy order became clear, the tortoises were to be prepared for 'a day at the races', organised by the padre and once again the ingenuity of man manifested itself.

That day at the races, with the Padre running a tote, was a never to be forgotten, hilarious event. There were races for 'maiden' tortoises (2, 3 and 4 fingers high) and even one for the disabled (with three legs). All entrants were clearly marked by the owners and, at a signal from the padre, were released at the centre of a circle. They raced away in different directions, with some even going round in circles, but the first one over the line on the sand was the winner.

An obstacle race, with a circular trench followed by a circle of bushes, was not so productive. The start was perfect; they struggled over the trench towards the bushes to shouts of encouragement from the audience, sometimes loud and abusive, but then all was silent. In the shade of the bushes they pulled up their legs and went to sleep. We hadn't realised they were just searching for shade and the race was declared 'null and void'.

How about a swimming pool in the desert? Almost as crazy as tortoise-racing, you may think. Well, we *were* crazy and we *did* have a swimming pool. The superstructure was removed from a lorry and a tarpaulin laid inside the body, which was about three feet high, and the four corners jacked up to take the weight off the springs. Filled almost to the brim with water, the squadron took it in turns to have a splash.

It was quite normal procedure to check out any wells in the area marked on a map and we found one just a few miles to the south with plenty of water in it. A hole in the rock about two feet square gave access to a vast cavern beneath and it appeared to contain a large volume of water; here was the seed that inspired the swimming pool. For many years water falling on the nearby hillside had been guided towards this hole in the rock by rows of stones, placed strategically on the slope, probably the work of wandering Bedouins. We hauled the water up in four-gallon cans, tipped it into forty-gallon drums and transported it to camp. What a pleasure it was to see all this water after months of meagre rations. To stand by a well and have four gallons of cool water poured all over you was sheer delight.

Over the next few days other events took place: we played football, snakes and ladders, and organised a bit of 'ant fighting'. Near our tank we selected an active 'black bull ant' nest, fed them on bully for a couple of days then dug them up and picked out twelve of the largest. Another crew would come along with their team, probably sprinkled with flour for identity and both teams were put together in an open top petrol can. The battle that followed, watched through binoculars, helped to relieve the tension built up during the previous months. Money changed hands on the result, based on the last to survive, but the financial aspect meant nothing; where could you spend money in the desert? Barbaric, you may think, yes we were, but that was the product of war, barbarism. Two opposing sides trained and armed to kill each other, that was exactly what we had been just a few days previously, no different from the ants.

The days of rest were not all play; tanks had to be maintained and deficiencies replaced if available, engines serviced, tracks checked for defective pins and guns stripped, cleaned and tested. All was carried out in an environment of glaring sunlight, sweat, sand and swarms of pestering bloody flies. As usual, our "B" Echelon lorries gave an excellent service, plying between the tanks and the "A" Echelon many miles back across the desert, sometimes travelling in a guided convoy, but also as single vehicles.

Those drivers knew more about the problems of desert travel than tank crews, whose tracks ironed out many of the problems presented by this hostile terrain. On the other hand, the route for a lorry had to be carefully selected to avoid being bogged down in soft sand, breaking springs bouncing on bush mounds, or bursting tyres on broken slate. Added to all this, they had to drive with one eye on the desert and the other on the sky; a prowling aircraft would ignore a tank, but a lorry was easy pickings.

They were not issued with compasses for navigation, but that did not stop them from driving individually across the open desert, where no roads existed. They would request someone with a prismatic to line their lorry up on the compass bearing back to the supply area and the mirror bracket was moved into a position where the shadow fell across the bonnet. Two chalk lines were drawn on the bonnet, one along the shadow and another to the right, if travelling east, at an angle dependent on the distance to be travelled. He would start his journey with the shadow lying along the original bearing line and, as he moved towards his target, the shadow would be allowed to move progressively, in relation to time, towards the other line, a quite ingenious and very effective 'sun compass'.

~ CHAPTER 14 ~

HOLDING THE GAZALA LINE

WE HAD A GOOD REST and were beginning to feel like human beings again when the order was given to move back west across the desert once more, this time to an area at the south end of the Gazala line, near the ancient fort of Bir Hakeim. The minefields of the defence line reached down to the fort, which was occupied by the Free French forces from Chad, but to the south beyond it was just open desert, where anything was likely to happen. And it did.

Although information indicated that Rommel was ready to launch an attack, numerous recces failed to produce positive evidence of his intentions. He had two alternatives; punch a hole through the defences in the north or swing south around Bir Hakim and drive north behind our defences. To attack in the south would considerably lengthen his lines of communication, but that was exactly what he did.

Our position at the south end of the line was such that we could block an attack coming from the south or be in support if he attacked the line further to the north. It was planned that if threatened from the south, we would advance to a predetermined defensive position on high ground, overlooking a flat plain to the south of the Fort, and dictate the battle on our terms.

To be stuck down there, many miles from the coast and with hundreds of miles of desert between me and Cairo, was not a happy situation. Still, waiting for the worst to happen is never enjoyable. Once again I was asking myself, how did I get into this bloody mess?

Camped about ten miles from our intended battle positions the daily ritual of pre-dawn stand-to was rigidly observed. We had no intention of being caught at dawn with our trousers down. Drifting into a sense of false security was always a danger, but with our new CO, Pip Roberts, whom we had all very quickly learned to respect, there was no chance of that. This dynamic officer, by words and actions, kept us very much on our toes. He was a small man in stature, but as a Commanding Officer he was a giant.

Standing in the turret in the dark, slowly spreading out from the night's laager and peering into the twilight, searching for anything hostile, yet praying there was nothing, was another nail-biting routine. Suddenly the sun would glow on the horizon but a frantic search with binoculars revealed an empty desert. What a wonderful feeling, the tension disappeared and the body sagged with relief. Spread out around me, the Regiment covered a large area, giving a comfortable protective feeling, and there, at its centre, the CO stood proudly in the turret of his tank, our guiding light and pillar of strength. Feathers of smoke from cooking fires rose into the morning sky and, although tired from lack of sleep, crews dashed around in the hope of having a meal before being ordered to move.

This holiday in the sun came to an abrupt end. We stood down after the usual dawn vigil at about 5am and settled down to breakfast, but the washing up had yet to be done when the order came through to mount and start up. This was the moment we all dreaded, but no one gave any indication of what he felt deep down in the pit of the stomach, they just got on with the job they had to do. Having experienced all this on numerous occasions was no boost to your chances of survival; in fact, the feeling that this was your time to 'cop it' got stronger and more frightening with the passage of time.

Within the half hour we were moving across the desert to take up our battle positions south east of the fort. Information at a quick briefing had indicated that the enemy, in great strength, was moving south around the fort. We in the Honey squadron moved off ahead of the regiment to recce and report on the situation, but had travelled only a couple of miles when contact was made. There, just ahead of us, was a large cloud of dust, coming in our direction. This was it, the whole bloody German Army coming straight for us and here we sat, out in the open, sixteen light tanks with 37mm pop-guns and a hundred enemy tanks charging towards us, hell bent on driving us into the ground! Men appeared to be sitting on the outside, as if on a day's outing, with the driver's flap open and the commander sitting high on the turret; they did not appear to be aware of our presence and I hoped it would stay that way until we got a good chance of burning up a few.

The rest of the Regiment came up behind us, hull down, and as the range closed, the CO's voice came through loud and clear: "Open fire and throw everything you have got at them, including any spare bully!" Our new 75mm guns caused chaos amongst the advancing Panzers; it was almost as if they were unaware of our presence or the power of our guns until a few started to burn. Tanks started milling around, as if out of control, and the infantry took to the ground, but within minutes the enemy column had stopped and sent a salvo of armour-piercing (AP) shells flying in our direction with high-explosive (HE) screaming overhead.

The next order came as a shock. "Start up and advance." I was ordered to move out to the right flank into some broken ground whilst, with all guns blazing, the big Grant tanks drove forward, and by some miracle reached the next ridge. It was with some surprise that I realised that the leading enemy tanks had halted; perhaps the stream of tracer from our guns flying around them like a mass of angry bees had caused them to hesitate (the glow of tracer gave no indication of the size of projectile; it could be a .3 bullet or a 10lb armour-piercing shell). However, movement of more enemy tanks up onto the ridge and the increase in shellfire directed towards us sadly answered the question; they had come with a purpose and we were in the way.

Tanks were burning on both sides and the Regiment, under pressure from this mass of armour, started to withdraw to the next ridge, with the German tanks following. Out on the flank, the enemy were moving broadside-on to us and we could not miss the opportunity of a shot at his tanks thin side-armour. I ordered the troop to open fire and we scored a number of hits. I saw one tank twist round and the crew bale out. We took full advantage of the situation and loosed off rounds as fast as we could select targets. We must have caught them completely by surprise because no shellfire came in our direction.

Movement on my right caught my attention. Dixie, the troop sergeant was waving his arms and pointing to the ridge on my right. I gasped. Bloody hell! There was the front of a tank with a damned great 75mm gun coming up the ridge just 200 yards away. My scream to "get the hell out of here!" must have been heard in Cairo. The driver could see through his visor what was happening and did just that. The other two tanks were already on the move and we all three went hurtling back towards our own lines.

In the meantime, the regiment had pulled back further to the next ridge. This left us about a thousand yards out on their right flank and we went charging towards them, creating a cloud of dust behind us. I found myself crouching lower in the turret with every few yards of progress, the ominous whistling sound of projectiles passing close was increasing and I had no idea whether they were intended for me or the tanks further ahead. I was taking no chances.

However, we were not out of the wood yet. I could hear a voice in my earphones reporting to the CO that enemy tanks were coming in fast on the right flank. I glanced around but could see nothing, and then it hit me; bloody hell, that was no enemy tanks, that was us he was reporting! I had to wait for a gap in transmission before I could butt in and tell them we were not the enemy and every second brought nearer the threat of being knocked out by our own tanks. I could imagine the gunners getting a bead on us, ready to blow our turrets off. Then I sagged with relief, someone must have recognised us, I could hear the report on the radio calling the hounds off.

My God, that was close.

We were still some distance from our tanks when they appeared to be moving back again; burning vehicles were being left behind. Some HE was bursting near us and tracer continued to streak past towards our lines. It was a nail-biting situation, just waiting for that thump on the hull to tell us we had been hit. Just a few more yards to go, with relief creeping back into my body, suddenly there was a bang and the tank shuddered and slewed round to the right. Damn it! We had been hit. I screamed to the driver to keep moving. There was no smoke inside, so we were not on fire, but there was a problem with the tracks. However, this was no place to get out and look.

I waved the other tanks on, but there was no need, they had a job to do and were already streaking past me. My driver was doing his job very well, although down to about 10mph and dragging to the right, we were almost over the ridge. My main fear was that the regiment would move off again before I could make it, but there was no question of abandoning the tank. Beyond the ridge I looked at the damage. A shell had skimmed along the side of the hull, hit a bogie-wheel assembly and pushed it out of alignment. Provided we kept our speed down, we might be able to keep up with the others; if not, the alternative was a frightening prospect.

The battle seemed never-ending and although my contribution was very small I was still very much in the thick of it, struggling from ridge to ridge, barely reaching our tanks before they were on the move again. The few rounds we managed to fire over the rear of our tank were merely a token gesture. The withdrawal continued, with the regiment in almost constant contact with the enemy. It was essential that the enemy advance be delayed as long as possible. The desert behind us was full of transport with little knowledge of what was going on. To the north of us, as we retreated west, were the supply areas for all the forces on the Gazala line, including Divisional and other Command headquarters. They were in a very exposed position, with the possibility of being cut off.

Continuous dialogue on the radio painted a very depressing picture. Most of our tanks left in action, and there were not many of them, were almost out of ammunition and our supply column was pinned down by heavy shellfire and could not reach the rallying point. A new area was signalled further to the northeast and the heavy squadrons headed in that direction. For the Honeys, it was rearguard action once again, and for me it was a case of joining a number of other disabled tanks and crawling back to the rendezvous.

Remarkably, the supply column got through with hardly a scratch, but it was obvious that the drivers were anxious to shed their loads and go. And no wonder. Their position was not an envious one. Sitting on top of 700 gallons of high-octane petrol or a load of high-explosives while shells were bursting all around you, was not a very healthy situation to be in. Amongst our drivers were a number who were over 40 years old and on at least two occasions, to my knowledge, they were sent back to base as being too old for front-line duties. Within a week they were back, god only knows how they fiddled it, but they belonged to a Regiment they were proud of and had no desire to be anywhere else. Thank God we had such men.

Refuelling was carried out in stages, one troop at a time, with the rest of the regiment holding the line, but eventually new orders came through to move back to an area south of Tobruk. Apart from the problem of a crippled tank, the journey was not without its moments of anxiety; the desert was covered to the far horizons with masses of transport, some in small groups others individually just milling around as if devoid of purpose. What a depressing situation, it was later revealed that many hundreds of vehicles were captured by the enemy, complete with their stores and supplies.

~ CHAPTER 15 ~

TWISTS OF FATE

RELIEF CAME WITH THE SETTING of the sun. It was a busy night for all of us who were left, but there was little I could do to repair my tank and the order from the squadron leader was to return to Tobruk in the morning for a replacement. I still had my duties as an SSM, buzzing around the squadron, helping in the re-organising of tanks and crews, but eventually managed to get my head down around midnight. It was about 2am when the SSM from another squadron woke me; the orders were that I was to take over his tank and he would take mine back to Tobruk. The bloody creep! I wonder how he fiddled that? My policy was, and always had been, 'never volunteer', but I always carried out orders, whatever they may be. So there I was, in the middle of the night, checking over another tank and preparing for action next day. My crew cursed when they heard the news, so I asked them what they wanted to do. There was no answer, but I understood. They had been through a rough time. I sent them back to Tobruk in the disabled tank.

At this point, it is interesting to note that the part played by fate in the direction of your life is as unpredictable as life itself. Here was I, once again directed towards the gates of hell, while my former crew, with a new commander, would be chugging happily along towards a more peaceful and secure existence. That was how it appeared at the time, but it didn't work out that way. While I was huddled down inside the turret of my new tank, they were crawling along a desert track, miles behind the lines, somewhere near Tobruk, with the crew comfortably relaxed inside and the SSM sitting outside on top of the turret. Out of nowhere, a Messerschmitt suddenly dived and raked the tank with machine-gun fire. The tank survived, and so did the crew inside, but the poor SSM was not so lucky; he finished up in hospital with bullet splinters in his kidneys. Ah... what a shame.

Fate continued to play its cruel games; the tank of my troop corporal, Jim Jolly, was also disabled that day and had to return to Tobruk. They were driving through a minefield, within a few miles of their destination, when they pulled off the track to give passage to an ambulance. Of all the bad luck, they ran over an Italian box mine, which blew a hole in the bottom of the tank, smashed one of the driver's legs, and Jim Jolly lost his eyesight. That was a very sad day for me; he was the best support tank commander I ever had, always in the position where he should be, and had a smile that gave us light in our darkest moments. It was some considerable time later, in Stoke Mandeville Hospital in England, that I met the Matron from St Dunstan's. She assured me that Jim, Jolly by name and jolly by nature, although blind, was in excellent health and spirits. I felt proud to have known him.

The days that followed found us chasing small groups of enemy vehicles, mostly just anti-tank guns, although they were sometimes escorted by tanks. It was on such an occasion that I topped a ridge and gasped in surprise at the sight of a German staff car, just a few hundred yards away, with someone standing up, peering through binoculars. This was a well-known tactic used by Rommel, to see for himself just what was going on. We gave him a few bursts of machine gun as he sped off across the desert. In the excitement of this unexpected situation, we probably missed him by a mile.

Our role in the Honey squadron was generally limited to scouting ahead of the regiment, giving flank protection or shooting up transport, but very often the enemy had other ideas and we took a pounding. The appearance of 88mm anti-tank guns or Mk4 tanks sent us scurrying for cover; there was no sense in taking on those large guns with our limited armament. A Mk4 could knock us out at 1,500 yards but the 88mm, now that was really something. At 2,000 yards that baby could punch a hole through the front and the engine and disappear out through the back as if nothing had impeded its progress. To get that gun from its towing position into action took a little time, but with its range-finding telescope and very high velocity projectile, it seldom missed its target. Those guns were feared and hated by all tankies; to mention the number 88 was taboo. At one transit camp we visited, the site for tent number 88 was just a black patch on the ground. Another Tank Regiment had been there before us.

At this stage, information on the overall battle situation was very limited and, since we were moving around all points of the compass to contact the enemy, I wondered just what sort of a mess we were in. Today started much like any other; stand-to at dawn, spread out as the sun rose and grab a quick breakfast whilst awaiting orders from above. A light wind was blowing and it felt warmer than usual. This was a bad omen. It was the time of year for the *khamsin*, a hot wind that blows from the south. It dried the throat and you wanted to drink, but too much water made you sick; often a severe headache came with it. Not a pleasant time of year to be in the desert. And it could get worse; if the wind increased and picked up the dry dust, then you would get the bonus of a dreaded sandstorm.

As those thoughts ran through my mind, orders came through to move south and block possible enemy movement to the east in that area. As we moved off, ahead of the regiment, the wind was increasing and the dust swirling, with visibility reduced to just a few hundred yards. With every mile the wind became stronger and the dust thicker, pounding the face and burning the eyes, grit grinding between the teeth and the throat rough and dry. Goggles were not much help, they soon became grit blasted and obscured your vision, and a scarf across the nose failed to stop the dust entering the lungs. It got worse as we struggled on, our speed dropped to about 5mph and the tanks closed in to just a few yards apart. Even then, a few strayed and it took time to get them back into line.

Tension mounted with every yard of progress; somewhere out there, a line of anti-tank guns could be sitting, ready for action, the gunners tense, fingers on triggers, listening to our track plates clanking towards them and waiting for us to appear out of the dust. It was madness, advancing under these conditions, this dust storm could go on for days or stop at any minute, leaving us exposed to god knows what. What I wouldn't have given for a cup of tea at that moment.

Suddenly the wind abated, the dust gradually cleared and a vast wall of rock appeared, just a few hundred yards ahead. We quickly spread out and scanned the area, but there was no sign of the enemy. Thank God. It could have been disastrous with all those vehicles crammed closely together, a huddled-up mass of tanks, artillery and lorries. Orders came to get up that escarpment and spread out. We in the light tanks had little difficulty and started to move west along the top. We just pushed on in the hope that the Grants and artillery would make it too and provide backup.

I was near the edge of the cliff, moving forward with caution, and the feeling of being watched was very strong. It was amazing how this sense was roused when needed most. I stopped and searched the far ridge. Sure enough, there they were, coming up onto the skyline, a number of enemy tanks that must have been sitting there, hull down and out of view. The shellfire came screaming towards us, so we dropped back into a gully as the

Grants opened fire and attracted their attention. A barrage of HE shells fell amongst the enemy from a battery of our artillery, which had reached the top and gone into action. More tanks appeared on the ridge before us, about a thousand yards distant, definitely too close for comfort. The enemy column must have been in this area when we emerged from the dust. I thanked god for its protection.

The battle raged on and our tanks were running out of ammo. The CO had a grim situation on his hands. It was late afternoon and to pull back down the escarpment could be a very dangerous manoeuvre, but to delay would mean being stuck up there all night. We were ordered to pull back and I don't know how the others managed it, but I do remember my own frantic efforts to get away from the shellfire and find a route down that cliff. Questions, answers and orders were flying through the airwaves in a constant stream, with the voice of my old friend from our Greek escapades, Jock Stewart, coming through loud and clear. He reported knocking out two German tanks as if he had just burst a balloon at the fairground with an airgun pellet. Left behind on top of the escarpment, as rearguard, he, as usual, put up an excellent performance.

For some unknown reason, the enemy failed to follow up our retreat; perhaps he was out of ammo too. Although we had suffered a few casualties ourselves, from the number of enemy vehicles burning up there, he definitely had the worst of it.

~ CHAPTER 16 ~

THE DEVIL'S CAULDRON

WHILST 3RTR, OR WHAT WAS left of it, was involved in those sporadic actions, battles had been taking place in other areas of the Gazala/Hacheim line. In one such area, fighting had been so fierce and the ground changed hands so often it became known as 'The Devil's Cauldron'. Both sides had eventually withdrawn and one day we were ordered to recce the area and establish contact with the enemy.

I carefully approached the ridge above the cauldron, signalled my other two tanks to stay turret-down, and approached to a position of observation. I scanned the area carefully and observed no movement. The air was so quiet and deathly still it gave me the creeps. Accustomed as I was to battlefield wreckage, I was shocked at what I saw. This was, indeed, a Devil's Cauldron. The valley in front of me, really just a dip in the sand approximately 400 yards wide, vanished to the horizon to the north and south and was littered with an unimaginable mass of debris. The whole area was a confusion of burned-out vehicles, trenches, barbed wire, clothing and equipment, with a few bodies lying around like bundles of discarded rags. What a pathetic shambles. In the heat of the desert sun, a cold hand gripped my body and I shuddered.

The shimmering heat haze distorted shapes, but I identified a German half-track, silhouetted against the skyline on the other side of the valley. Through my binoculars, I could see a large hole in the side of the armour plate, so considered it to be out of action and a possible source of useful information. I signalled my other two tanks to stay put and ordered my driver to reverse below the ridge, count to twenty, then drive straight over the top. This was a tactic I used frequently in these uncertain conditions, where an anti-tank gunner may have us in his sights and be waiting for the whole tank to appear and give him a better target. My hope was that he would give up when the tank disappeared and search for another target.

Leaving the other tanks behind the ridge, my driver moved carefully across the valley floor to a position where, with the minimum of delay, we could get out again quickly. He stopped about 100 yards from our target and switched the engine off. The view through binoculars was much clearer without engine vibration. It was not a very comfortable situation and I took a long time to decide my next move, but having got this far, I just had to go through with it, or my image with the troop would never be the same again.

I jumped to the ground with a tommy-gun under my arm and moved slowly up the slope. Only the buzzing of flies and the crunching of grit under my feet disturbed the deathly silence. My heart was thumping like mad under my sweat-sodden shirt. With a sense of death all around me, and the possibility of mines under my feet, only my stupid pride stopped me from running back to the protection of the tank. With every step, I nervously scanned the ground ahead. Nothing moved, but I could feel the eyes of my operator burning into the back of my neck; he probably had the microphone in his hand, ready to start up and move out... with or without me.

It was as I suspected; the halftrack had been knocked out and through the hole in the side I could see bodies lying around, with a mass of filthy flies all over them. The stench of rotting flesh was overpowering and maggots were crawling everywhere. A fire extinguisher emptied through the hole helped disperse or kill most of the flies and I climbed over the side, keeping my body as low as possible inside the vehicle.

Breathing in the heavy concentration of carbon tetrachloride from the fire extinguisher had me gasping for fresh air. I quickly found the driver's logbook and grabbed a map and papers, but was delayed by the position of one body. He was an officer, crouched down behind the driver's seat, which was empty. His head was hanging over the back of the seat, with his chest resting against the back plate. There were papers in his shirt pocket, which I could not reach, but having come this far, I was not going without them. I had already delayed too long in this dangerous situation. I had a quick look around to make sure I was still alone, grabbed hold of his shoulders and pulled...

As I did so a most unearthly, hideous gurgling sound issued from his body; it broke the deathly silence of this cauldron like a protest from hell and prompted a panic reaction. This was indeed the last straw for my over-stressed nervous system and I cleared the side of that six-foot high vehicle like an Olympic hurdler. I was probably half way down the hill before my feet touched the ground, with my heart thumping like mad as I raced towards the tank. I slowed to a walking pace as common sense prevailed. The driver had seen my hair-raising acrobatics and had started the engine, ready to move.

"What's up?" the operator called, with a nervous tremor in his voice. My hurried departure from the scene had probably prompted a vision in his mind of a mass of German armour about to appear and blast us all to kingdom come.

Of course, I had to lie.

"Just came back for my gauntlets. There are dead bodies up there and we need their documents."

Reluctantly, I trudged back up the slope. I had left my tommy-gun up there and I still had a job to do. As an afterthought, I realised that the officer had probably been knocked unconscious by the blast and was asphyxiated, with his neck resting on the seat's back-plate. My action had opened up his lungs and sucked in air, creating the most unearthly sound I have ever heard.

Once again, I scanned the area. Everything was uncomfortably quiet, but the job had to be done. Unfortunately, the body had not moved back sufficiently for me to remove the papers, so there was no choice, I had to go through it all again. This time I was prepared for any reaction and, for good measure, I liberated his watch and binoculars.

By now, the stench and moving mass of maggots was a little too much for my stomach and I began to feel sick. We had been active since about 5am and breakfast had been a hard biscuit coated with jam, gulped down on the move, not exactly an adequate preparation for this scene of death and decay.

I hurriedly collected his papers, maps and driver's logbook (always a good source of information), shouldered my gun and strolled down the hill.

With a feeling of relief that I had completed the gruesome task, the nervous tension gradually left me. Casually but cautiously, with eyes searching the area, I walked back towards the tank. The heat, as usual, was unbearable and the deathly stillness broken only by the movement of pebbles under my feet. The barbed wire, burnt out vehicles and other battle debris stood around like silent monuments, each telling its own story of the dreadful events that had occurred. I was but 50 yards from my haven when I detected movement on the left. I signalled the operator and indicated the direction. The turret swung round to cover me as I moved amongst the debris. An arm was sticking out of a shallow trench and it moved slowly as I approached. There, in the trench, was a wounded Asian soldier, his uniform at the waistline tattered and bloodstained. A mass of filthy, greedy flies filled the air, hell-bent on getting their share of whatever this poor devil had left to give.

There was nothing I could do to help him. I reported his state and position and hoped that the ambulance service would do the rest. How long had this poor devil lain there? It must have been at least two days since our forces had left that area. Someone must have known he was wounded, but perhaps they had died before reporting it.

A knocked-out German tank in the desert.

~ CHAPTER 17 ~

A Night in the Desert

DAYS OF MOBILE ACTIVITY FOLLOWED, when orders from Brigade would send us scurrying off to a new map reference. We would spend most of the day crouched in the turret, searching the horizon until sunset, then withdraw to a safe area for the night. If contact with the enemy had taken place, a single tank or troop would be left behind on the ridge as a rearguard, watching for any activity that may indicate the regiment was being followed. That commander would then have the unenviable task of withdrawing in the dark, navigating to a given map reference and rejoining the company, a simple task that could turn into a nightmare. On many occasions I was 'Joe Muggins', probably because I had been a lucky survivor for so long. But I did not like it one bit.

During daylight navigation was not too difficult; a sun-compass, backed up by a hand-held prismatic, gave adequate accuracy, but at night the magnetic prismatic was your only guide. With the tank lined up on a given bearing, a star low on the horizon in line with some fixture on the turret was a fairly good guide, and the distance recorded on the mileometer supplied the other vital factor. But this value generally had a limitation of anything up to 25%, depending on the surface condition of the desert; loose sand allowed considerable track-slip, which was roughly determined by the amount of dust thrown up behind. The whole thing was very much a matter of 'guesstimation'.

There was always a moment of anxiety and sadness as I watched the other tanks fade into the dusk; being alone was a feeling I dreaded most. The rattle of tracks fading into the night was replaced by a deathly silence. No sound came from the crew below, tired and hungry and struggling to keep awake. Then there was the waiting, watching and listening. Cracking noises from cooling metal disturbed the silence and ghostly flickering flames from a burning vehicle, probably over a mile away, prompted the ridiculous thought that anyone out there must be able to see me in its light. In this situation, with wireless silence ordered, the decision when to pull back and rejoin the regiment was mine alone.

At last, in the dead quiet of night, it was time to pull out. The tank had been turned around earlier and lined up. I picked a star on the horizon and gave the order "Start up, advance." What a wonderful moment that was.

There is something about a tank that becomes part of you. Stationary, with the engine stopped, it is just a hunk of dead metal, but start the engine and the whole tank vibrates; it becomes alive and you become a part of it, almost as if that engine pumped the blood through your veins. But now, struggling in the dark across this rugged terrain became a nightmarish game of trying to identify possible obstructions while keeping that star in the correct position.

We travelled the distance calculated to reach our laager, but there was no sign of life anywhere. I listened with the engine switched off but no sound could be detected, such as the banging of empty cans or the accidental dropping of a heavy engine cover. We had experienced this before and would have to try the 'box procedure', which involved driving around in a half mile square pattern, south, east, north and west, and if nothing was found, another square, west, south, east and north, and so on, to complete a box a mile square. We would make just these four attempts to find the regiment and if we failed then it was a case of mounting a guard and looking after ourselves until dawn. They were usually quite close and could probably hear us driving around in the dark, but no-one would signal, we could have been the enemy.

On this occasion, we heard their engines start up to move out just before dawn. I could have hit the nearest tank with a stone. The regiment was ready to move, but we were not. Having failed to find the laager during the night, our re-supply of petrol, ammo and food had not been available to us.

Now, in daylight, it was panic-stations trying to obtain our requirements. The other vehicles had packed up, ready to move, the drivers anxious not to be left behind, and voices in my earphones were urging me to get up into line.

What a way to live!

CHAPTER 18

No Rest for the Battle-Weary

A T LONG LAST, THE SUN was touching the horizon; it had been a hell of a day, dodging heavy shellfire, getting in with the 37mm when the range permitted. A short break was welcomed, when I pulled the troop back to re-fuel, but sadly the tank had taken quite a bashing and once again the storage lockers down one side had been raked with shrapnel. What a bloody mess. A pity it wasn't the other side, where tools and things were stored. This side was our food storage and just a few days before a lorry had arrived with tinned food, etc, which we had ordered from the NAAFI. Half a dozen tins of bully had been welded together by a piece of shrapnel; it had passed right through all of them, but that was not really so important as the rows of tinned fruit, a very expensive luxury, which we had not seen for many weeks. All that was swilling around in the lockers, amongst jagged pieces of metal. Our bedrolls, tied behind the turret, had rough, jagged holes in them. God knows what we would find when we unwrapped them.

As I said, it had been a hell of a day on the Gazala line, but any moment now we should get a signal to withdraw for a night's rest. What a relief, I had survived another day, but sadly that feeling was short-lived. Instead of settling down to the usual chores of gun cleaning and re-stocking with the necessities of survival, we quickly refuelled and turned south towards the open desert. It was only us, the Honey squadron, we were to take part in a raid behind enemy lines, whilst the remainder of the regiment went back for a night's rest. They certainly deserved it, what was left of them.

We travelled a long way south, guided by armoured cars of the 11th Hussars, well clear of enemy activity, then turned west. By this time, darkness had descended and heralded the most gruelling journey I had ever experienced. For many hours, in the blackness of the night, we struggled on, nose-to-tail, close up to the vehicle in front, an endless sequence of revving and braking, with dust continuously thrown into the driver's face. From the turret, the tank in front was just visible to me through the dark and dust, but I was no help to the driver in these conditions. They were so close that repeated collision was unavoidable. It was just like railway trucks shunting in a goods yard. I imagined the enemy could hear us all the way to Tripoli.

Standing in the turret, I was bounced back and forth with every impact, the forward movement tolerable, but backwards very painful. Just below the turret ring, a two-inch long plunger, which retained the ack-ack gun in a travelling position, protruded into the small of my back. I found it more comfortable travelling outside the turret, holding on to the gun. The journey lasted many hours, guided by that renowned cavalry regiment, just like cowboys on a cattle drive, and we were the cattle. They had a reputation for operating many miles behind enemy lines and in this instance had shadowed a large supply column for many days. Now parked up for the night and feeling quite safe, probably about 20 miles behind their own lines, they were unaware that a very efficient recce unit had them in their sights.

After travelling many miles west, we turned north, driving up behind the enemy's front line and eventually halted in the darkness. With great difficulty, we formed a line abreast along a ridge, each tank in visual contact with the next. With radio silence imposed from the start, the location of the enemy was unknown, but I just assumed, and hoped, that someone knew where the hell we were. A quick briefing put us in the picture, with orders to move forward slowly, keeping noise to a minimum.

That was a laugh. How can you keep a seven-cylinder radial engine quiet or stop the track plates from clattering over the sprockets and bogie wheels? I was convinced that they must have heard us coming for miles, and probably dispersed the column and replaced it with a battery of anti-tank guns, just waiting to blow our bloody heads off.

We stopped on what appeared to be a ridge, peered down into a black void and waited for a sunrise that was surely going to spell disaster for some of us. The waiting was the worst part; that dreaded fear of the unknown. We were all very tired; it was almost 24 hours since we had slept, and the night's battering had added to our weariness. However, one thing guaranteed to keep you on your toes is fear, especially the fear of being trapped behind enemy lines, and here we were, god knows how far inside hostile territory, all lined up in close formation, waiting for sunrise to show us what sort of a mess we had got ourselves into.

Daylight in the desert arrives quickly and today was no exception. Suddenly they appeared in the valley beneath us, long lines of lorries, packed closely together. There must have been a few hundred of them, all neat and tidy, German-style, with no obvious armoured protection, just waiting for the kill. We opened up with everything we had: 37mm and machine-guns and moved down the slope towards our quarry. The Hussars had done a superb recce job, guiding us across the desert and ending up bang on target.

The attack was disastrous for the enemy. Petrol and ammunition lorries started to burn and explode, setting off a chain reaction of destruction. Men were running around aimlessly, adding to the scene of utter chaos, and our machine guns took a heavy toll. Our troop's task, out on the left flank, was to block the rear end of the column and prevent vehicles escaping. One vehicle did try to escape from our end of the column, a cook-house wagon with a chimney sticking out of the top, but my troop sergeant Dixie had no intention of letting it get away. A 37mm shell through the cab decided the argument. Even before the vehicle had stopped rolling, a sack of sugar and a pot of steaming coffee had been transferred to Dixie's tank. He was a bloodthirsty bastard in battle. A trembling bag of nerves before an action, but as soon as the first shot was fired it completely changed his character.

Perhaps we were all a bit like that.

The order came to break off the action and withdraw. At the top of the ridge, I looked back at the mass of destruction we had created, a sad but satisfying scene. Now our own survival was the priority, to get the hell out of it and back to the security of our own lines. But for us it was not that simple. Because of Dixie and his looting chase our troop was at the end of the column, driving south into the desert, and after just a few miles, I was ordered to halt on a small ridge and observe that the Regiment was not being followed by a hostile force. As I watched the tail end of our column disappear in their own dust cloud, the pangs of fear once again tied my stomach in a knot; I felt bitter at once again at being given the dirty end of the stick.

With binoculars glued to the north horizon, I was jolted by rattling on the outside of the hull. A British fighter, probably returning from a sortie without shooting anything, and unaware of our presence in enemy territory, had decided to vent his frustrations on me. I was lucky not to be hit, my body had been half out of the turret. Idiot, I should have expected something like that; after all, we were behind enemy lines. By now the Luftwaffe would have got the message and they too would soon be after our blood.

We settled down to observe the distant horizon. The air was hot and very still and nobody spoke, we were all too tired to waste energy on idle chatter. From experience, we knew that movement generated heat, and to sit still whenever possible had become a way of life. Here, deep in the desert, with practically no vegetation, there were no insects (except for the flies we had brought with us) and no birds, therefore no noise, and these conditions sharpened the sense of hearing to a level above normal. It was an unforgettable experience to sit quietly in this environment, deep in thought, and be distracted by the sound of a few grains of sand trickling down between the stones. As we sat quietly in this atmosphere of false contentment, a crack from the cooling exhaust system jolted us back to reality, only to succumb again to the weariness of the body and drift back to our dream world.

I had been scanning the northern horizon constantly with my binoculars when I was suddenly awoken from this dream-state by the reality of what I was staring at and yet had failed to recognise. A cloud of dust was moving towards us, fast. It was a column of six enemy tanks, obviously with one object in mind, our destruction. I grabbed the microphone, pressed the switch and reported to the CO, but there was no answer. The normal atmospheric hissing was absent from my earphones. Oh God no, not a dead radio. It could not have picked a worse time to go on the blink. I could not even talk to my other two tanks. Without a radio you may as well be blind. During a battle, other vehicles would start moving around and you would have a clue why without radio contact; then the brain would panic, speculating on the worst possible reason. I looked down at the operator to tell him to check the radio and saw his hand was moving to the switch to turn it on. The bloody thing had been switched off! I was stunned and furious at what I had seen and instantly reacted by kicking him in the chest.

The details of the approaching enemy were signalled to HQ and I waited with bated breath for the answer. Thank God, the order came through to withdraw and we turned tail, driving south like the bats out of hell. There was no need to navigate, the tracks left by about 50 tanks stood out like a roadway across the sand. Apart from one enemy plane that dipped its wings to us as it flew over (the pilot certainly would not have won any medals for tank identification) we saw nothing more of the enemy that day.

It was some time later before we saw and caught up with the cloud of dust that was our regiment. What a wonderful feeling to become part of that cloud and to know that we were no longer alone.

Later that night I got the radio operator by himself and tore into him. He eventually admitted that he had been observing events through the front porthole and had seen the approaching tanks but was afraid that if I reported them, we would be ordered to attack. Weary from lack of sleep and with his nervous system near the limit after weeks of battle tension, he had simply had enough.

How could I put him on a charge? I felt the same way myself. Anyway, on a charge he could have opted for a court martial and been sent back to base and I would have been short of a crew-member.

~ CHAPTER 19 ~

OUR C.O. IS INJURED

I T WAS ANOTHER MORNING OF our usual routine: move, spread out and observe. Although gunfire was heard, there was nothing to be seen, we were probably in reserve to one of the other regiments in the brigade. In late afternoon another move, but this time we ran slap into a line of enemy tanks, hull-down on a ridge. We waited in our Honeys for the Grants to come up into line; our orders were to move over and protect the left flank. Heavy shellfire was already coming our way when I withdrew and started to move across behind the Grants, just as they opened fire. I was more than a little nervous at being broadside-on to the enemy with a lot of stuff ploughing up the sand around me. My god, there must be a whole bloody Panzer Division out there!

A large cloud of smoke billowed up from one of the Grants nearby and some of the crew bailed out. I couldn't believe my eyes; one of them appeared to have no clothes on. He was running around aimlessly, waving his arms around like a blind man, his scorched body looking black, even in the bright sunlight. I ordered my driver to turn towards the casualties. Someone helped the naked fellow onto the tank, behind the turret and I jumped out and tried to wrap a coat around him, it seemed the obvious thing to do, but he screamed in horror and I left him as he was. He was shaking violently, suffering severe shock. I felt guilty and inadequate, but there was nothing I could do.

Another member of the stricken tank's crew clambered onto our tank, it was Pip Roberts, our CO. With his tattered clothing and blackened face I hardly recognised him. He took over my radio and talked to the regiment. I ordered the driver to reverse, turn around and head back towards our "B" echelon. This was not a situation I would have chosen, riding outside, unprotected, hanging on behind the turret, my back to the enemy, with bullets and splinters flying through the air, but somehow we got away with it; perhaps the smoke from the disabled Grant had shrouded our activities. Our passengers were dropped off at Brigade HQ and we returned to the regiment on the battle line.

Someone had already moved to the rear of the CO's tank, hitched on a towrope, and was towing it away; I think it was Buck Kite, one of our most outstanding tank commanders and a comrade from pre-war days. The cause of that explosion was never discovered, but the breach of the gun and part of the barrel had blown apart. The gunner was blown to pieces, almost unrecognisable as a human body; it was a very sad moment for me, he was an old friend from away back and so very few of us old ones were left. Just how many had gone was difficult to remember, but with each one, the pangs of fear gnawing at the stomach became stronger. You knew the odds against your own survival must be getting shorter, but acceptance of the inevitable had to be avoided. A 'don't care' attitude could lead to carelessness and someone else may die because of you.

CHAPTER 20

A Couple of Close Shaves

S INCE THIS WAR HAD BEGUN we must have lost at least two regiments in dead, wounded and prisoners of war. Now our CO, Pip Roberts, had been badly wounded and we had lost him too, a man who, in the short time he had been with us, had commanded with discipline and won respect like no other I served under. His calm voice on the radio, with comments such as, "Come on now, don't be shy, get up into line with me," reduced the most frightening situation to a tolerable level. He had the ability to assess and respond to any situation or information with a vigour and enthusiasm that left you gasping.

His absence was indeed a great loss to the Regiment, but happily, and much sooner than we had expected, our prayers were answered and he came bouncing back.

Once again, we felt his eagle-eye watching over us.

Apart from the Honey squadron, it was not 3RTR any more; individual tank troops and even squadrons had been moved around between Regiments, Brigades and even Divisions. Our personnel changed almost daily, with reinforcements of tanks and crews from other units. Information on the general battle situation was practically non-existent, but we knew that a hell of a lot of tanks and other vehicles had been lost. Skirmishes with the enemy were taking place further and further to the east and no crystal ball was needed to tell us that we were on the run.

The days that followed were chaotic: stop and fight here, rush off and support others somewhere else, but at the end of the day it was retreat again to the east. At night, drag your weary body out of the turret, fill up with petrol and ammo, clean the guns, get something to eat, sleep, with only an average of three hours a night. How the hell did we manage to keep going?

It was like this for weeks.

Today had been a rough one, but not as bad as some. At last that lovely moment in the dark had arrived. I picked up the microphone and gave the final order, "Switch off, dismount" and by habit stretched out my left hand for support on the ack-ack gun to push myself up out of the turret. I almost fell over the side; the gun was not there, just a jagged stump of metal sticking up above the cupola. Where the hell had it gone?

I jumped down and checked the back of the tank, but the gun had simply disappeared. I just stood there, numb with the realisation of what must have happened. I suddenly felt very sick and threw up. That gun must have been cut off by a shell, which had missed the top of the cupola by inches. How it had not also removed my head was a mystery. Apart from a few fleeting moments, when necessity demanded, my head and shoulders had been sticking out of the turret all day. Once again, I knew someone was watching over me and wondered for what purpose I had been spared this time.

The thought came to mind of one of our sergeants who, when sent back to base for another tank, had played the 'constipation and runs' game with two doctors on the site. He got away with it for about a week and came back boasting about how he had fiddled a week's rest. He went into action next morning and died within a few hours. The sad, pathetic, instances of those who 'almost made it' would fill a library, but for me the most depressing was one member of a crew who, having survived everything the enemy threw at him, died when on leave in Cairo, while having a nice cool shower, from some kind of brain problem he never even knew about.

It was another day of 'shoot and run', but on this occasion I did not run very far... the tank suddenly rocked sideways, there was a terrific roar and flames shot up behind me. I screamed "bale out!" and the crew practically threw me out in their efforts to get away. Here was the time when drill and training paid off; many were the days during training when I had moaned about the ritual of mount and dismount from tanks by numbers, but today I blessed every movement. It seemed a miracle that, within seconds, all of us were 100 yards away, each carrying specified items necessary for survival and running like hell to a truck that seemed to appear from nowhere.

The journey back to a reinforcement area was bumpy but uneventful, with a number of crews packed into the truck. It was the first time in a battle area when I was not in charge of my own destiny and I did not like it very much. A recently-arrived lieutenant kept moaning about his predicament; he thought he would be missed and should let the regiment know his position. Little did he realise that without a tank he didn't even exist. Poor devil, it had been his first day in action.

As we travelled east, the sounds of battle faded, but the screams of diving aircraft increased. This was something new for me, to be without the protection of my tank, and I had to learn to get out and dive for cover. It was pretty chaotic, with everyone fighting for a piece of the only road to Cairo, and many didn't make it. Their vehicles were left burning by the roadside. We were recognised as tank crews and stopped on a number of occasions, with the suggestion that we should turn around and go back, but I knew that without tanks we were nothing. My information was that our regiment was reassembling in the Alamein area and I ordered the driver accordingly.

What a relief it was to be back amongst old friends and eat a proper meal, without the usual quota of sand. Even the flies, fighting for their share, sounded happier. But most important of all was sleep; I think I slept continuously for about two days. It had been back in May when Rommel had attacked at Bir Hachiem and throughout the battles that followed, including the fall of Tobruk, rest had been confined to brief lulls in the fighting. Now, in the month of July, we were all very tired and battle-weary and welcomed with pleasure and relief the order to move back to the Delta, near the Bitter Lakes, for a complete refit.

Regiment colleagues inspecting a captured German 88mm, the weapon most feared by our tank crews.

~ CHAPTER 21 ~

PROMOTION TO RSM

TEL EL QUABIR WAS A very large camp in the desert, about 20 miles from Ismailia, on the Bitter Lakes of the Suez Canal and was to be our home for the next few weeks. We were accommodated in tents, but there were many huts, occupied by officers, cookhouse, stores, etc and an open-air cinema. It was the usual Shafto's cinema, with wickerwork seats and tables full of blood-sucking bugs, just waiting for the film to start and signal dinner-time. Compared to soldiering in the desert, this was indeed luxury, with the added bonus of a plentiful supply of good, fresh water and regular cooked meals.

Personnel started arriving in small groups, some of the old hands who had been lost and found, others discharged from hospital and many with lovely white knees, including an RSM almost straight off the boat from Blighty. Our previous RSM, Paddy Hehir, had been commissioned to Regimental Quartermaster, which left a vacancy.

Sadly, our new Regimental Sergeant Major did not hit it off with the desert veterans. Although everyone recognised the need for training and discipline, the regimentation level of a recruit-training depot, which he immediately tried to enforce, was not really appropriate. I cannot dwell on the history of this illustrious gentleman, because he did not dwell long amongst us; he went for an evening out in Ismailia and never returned. We heard later that he was in hospital, apparently beaten up by drunken soldiers. I wonder who could have done such a thing?

They say it is an ill wind that blows no one any good, and this one got me promotion to RSM. The Adjutant called me into his office and asked if I would like to take over. I requested time to think about it. Of course, the news spread like wildfire that "Jock Watt has turned down promotion from SSM to RSM". There was nothing like the jungle telegraph for getting things wrong. That night in the Mess, the other sergeant majors, all older than and senior to me, told me in no uncertain terms not to be a bloody fool.

"Take it," they said. And I did. Still, if I had accepted at the first offer I would probably have been called a lousy bastard; the motivation of enemies was simple to understand but of friends, completely unpredictable. Pip Roberts confirmed my promotion with the comment that he had applied for me to be commissioned and my position as RSM would be in my favour.

We soon settled down to a happy routine of fitting out and retraining, but our complacency was shaken when disturbing news took us all by surprise. We lost our CO, Pip Roberts, who was promoted to Brigadier. It was a promotion well-earned and we wished him the very best, but where the hell did that leave us? His replacement was Pete Pyman and the information was that he had never commanded a regiment in action. Stories circulated that during the battles around Bir Hakeim he was staff officer to a divisional commander; they were both captured by the Germans and later escaped. Because of that event, I was to suffer many sleepless nights in the weeks ahead.

During this period all was not well with the British Army in the desert, or what was left of them. The defences at Tobruk were overrun and desperate rearguard actions fought all the way back across Egypt, to within 60 miles of Alexandria. Here, in the vicinity of a tiny railway station called El Alamein, the order was given to stop, dig-in and fight. Thanks to the wisdom and foresight of some army commander, they had embarked on the building of those defences some months previously and the army stopped and defended this line. Minefields and other obstacles had been laid in a 40-mile defence line stretching from the coast to the north end of the Quattara Depression. This impassable desert bog land, 100 miles west of Cairo and stretching far into the southern desert, provided a natural barrier against an enemy thrust to the Nile. It was on this line that the infantry gunners and the few tanks that were left stood their ground and took everything that Rommel threw against them. It must have been hell in those minefields. Fortunately, with long lines of communication all the way back to Benghazi, the German army ran out of steam and stopped to reorganise their forces for the final assault on the Delta.

The race was on, we were also rebuilding our forces and our aim was the destruction of the German Army. At the top, heads rolled and new names were voiced in the messes, with one acclaimed louder than most, Montgomery. But we had seen so many come and go that one more meant very little to us. Our only hope was that with one of these new names there may come better tanks with bigger guns. For far too long we had taken a bashing from an enemy with superior weapons.

Someone, somewhere, must have got the message. The Americans sent us the Sherman tank, with thicker armour and a longer, more powerful 75mm gun, but there were not many of them, so the majority of us were stuck with the old stuff. For example, I had a Crusader, well known for its faulty water pumps and, for that reason, the original thirty-gallon jettison petrol tank was used for water. The half-inch track pins were a constant headache, with replacing breakages almost a daily ritual. This was one thing we had in common with the enemy; the Tiger tank, which eventually appeared in the desert, had the same problem.

The pathetic little two-pounder gun, with its maximum effective range of about 800 yards, was still with us, and I had one. There were six-pounder guns fitted to some Crusaders, but I was not that lucky. However, I did have a modification to my gun, designed to fool the enemy and keep him further away. A cowling, like a stovepipe, the shape and size of a six-pounder gun with a muzzle brake, was clamped to the tapered barrel. From a distance this abortion looked very effective, but the effect was short lived. After firing a few rounds, this diabolical invention became loose and launched off into the air like a torpedo from a destroyer. We replaced it a couple of times but then gave up. Besides, although it may have kept the enemy a little further away, he could still punch a hole in us with ease.

Perhaps the greatest hazard was the driver's access cover, above his head; this was in two parts, with a hinge between them and another hinge attached it to the hull. The idea was to push up and forward and the two pieces would collapse onto the hull, leaving a gap almost two feet square. This worked perfectly with the gun pointing forward and the turret square to the hull, but with the turret turned off-centre, the flap could not be opened. Generally, access was available to the driver backwards into the turret, but again, at a certain position of the turret, one of the drive panels to the base obstructed his exit. Not a happy situation to be in a tank hit and on fire with the driver screaming he can't get out.

~ CHAPTER 22 ~

BACK INTO ACTION

RE-EQUIPPED AND BACK IN THE desert for further training, an attempted breakthrough by Rommel at the north end of the Quattara Depression had us scurrying back into action. My role during training, amongst other duties, was navigating for the regiment. On occasions I was responsible for moving the B1 Echelon, the regiment's supply column, to the area where the night Laager was formed. In this particular action, with the Regiment moving forward to do battle, this was the task I was given.

I commanded this column from an old Buick truck, fitted out with a radio, operator, driver and a couple of replacement crew. It was a little overcrowded, but we managed, and by the end of the days of battle that followed, I was grateful for the extra bodies we had on board. For much of the time, we had to contend with was soft, sandy conditions, and every few yards the wheels just spun and the old truck bellied down. In some areas it was so bad that the vehicles towing the artillery had themselves to be towed by the tanks. It was a case of digging out the rear wheels, dropping in the sand channels, which were carried for this purpose, and pushing the truck, with fingers crossed, only to belly down again at the end of the channel. This was no picnic at temperatures over 100 degrees, and we sweated, pushed and cursed. There could be no turning back; the supplies simply had to get through. Thankfully, in a few days the crisis was over. Rommel's attempt to break through into the delta area failed, with the loss of many of his precious tanks, and we returned to our training area.

We did, eventually, get some of those new American Sherman tanks with the bigger gun and, in spite of their monstrous size, they gave a very impressive performance during training. Being part of the HQ troop I got my Crusader, complete with sun compasses and a P8 magnetic compass fitted between the drivers knees. This instrument was helpful to the driver, but unreliable for precision measurement, as the movement of tools and ammo from one area to another upset the delicate magnetic balance and the values shown could only be used as a general indication of direction.

With the relaxation of training and a gradual movement in stages towards the front line, tension increased with every move. Many of our crew replacements would be going into action for the first time and were excited at the prospect, but for the old hands there was no excitement, just fear. The memories of past battles and near misses were far too deeply engrained in the mind to be ignored at this stage, but pride prevented the revelation of thoughts that could be interpreted by the inexperienced as fear or cowardice.

Each tank was fitted with a camouflage framework, which changed their appearance to lorries, a release cord above the turret allowing the two halves to fall apart. We moved at night and took the places of lorries that had stood there for many days; it was assumed and hoped that enemy recce planes would have photographed the area and would see no change in the disposition of vehicles. In other areas, dummy tanks, built on lorry chassis, were dispersed to appear like regiments and divisions held in reserve. A number of these actually went into the battle line amongst the real tanks. It must have been quite frustrating for an enemy gunner to see his shells disappear into the side of a 'tank' without effect.

~ CHAPTER 23 ~

INTO BATTLE AT EL ALAMEIN

I T WAS ANOTHER HOT, STICKY day, with our movements restricted, on account of our being camouflaged. Too many people out in the open, especially in black berets, would have given the game away and the effect of hiding our true identity would be nullified. We stayed in the shade of our canopies. It was cooler, but the waiting and the persistence of those filthy flies added to the prevailing atmosphere of high nervous tension, and there were harsh words uttered during mild arguments over nothing. As a commander it was prudent to allow these issues to run their course; to stop them could have resulted in brooding to the point of hatred, a very dangerous but natural reaction that would effect the efficiency of the crew.

My thoughts drifted back over the past two years. Just what had I done for myself? There was nothing positive that I could use to promote a new way of life when this was all over. I had even lost my only chance to live the life of a normal young man and was old long before my time. Even boasting of my exploits was denied me, because I belonged to one of the lesser-known tank regiments that had battled against the odds in Calais, Greece, and in the Western Desert. Sadly, our exploits were ignored by the media in favour of the more historic cavalry regiments, and yet we were part of the original Desert Rats, entitled to wear that symbol on our sleeves.

The sun was setting when the order came abruptly: "Prepare to move." We dropped the camouflage and moved off in close formation. Everyone knew that this was 'it'. Even after all this time and numerous similar experiences, the fear was still there and the lump was back in my throat. The crew members were quiet, each absorbed in his own thoughts and no sound emitted from my earphones; radio silence had been ordered. A liaison officer guided us to our staging point behind Springbok Road. We had shed our sheep's clothing and were once again a fighting machine, ready to dispense death and destruction. It was very dark and unusually quiet, almost as if the whole world had stopped, waiting for some dreadful, devastating event. We sat or lay around, snatching some precious moments of rest in the knowledge that it may be many days before we could rest again.

Suddenly, in the darkness, the ground shook beneath us. It felt as if an earthquake was imminent. The sky lit up and metal screamed overhead. Men jumped to their feet, ready to go, with hearts pounding, at first with excitement and then that dreaded fear of the unknown. With every second the intensity of the barrage seemed to increase, it was a sickening message from our artillery to whoever was over the hill amongst the enemy guns and trenches. We trembled in unison with the ground, almost praying for the order that would take us away from this devilish noise.

I wondered what was going on in that minefield in front of us; the Highland Brigade infantry had gone in under the barrage, followed by Sappers clearing a path through the minefield. The Military Police followed the Sappers and marked the path with unidirectional lights; we could do nothing but wait and imagine the worst. This hanging around, waiting for the order to do what we knew was inevitable, was just another form of mental torture, winding you up like a spring ready to be released.

At this stage I was acting as liaison in the CO's Jeep, carrying instructions between our HQ and the squadron commanders. My tank was in the hands of the operator and, when the order was given to move I found myself still in the Jeep, behind the

CO's tank. The HQ Troop followed two of our squadrons into the minefield, with dust from the tracks almost obscuring the guide lights. For myself and the jeep driver, struggling to see through that cloud of muck, it was hell.

Shells screamed overhead and machine gun tracer darted amongst the tanks as enemy posts, bypassed by the infantry, continued to do battle against unknown odds. We seemed to have travelled for hours, frequently stopping for reasons unknown, which did little to calm the fears that all was not well. Sitting in an open jeep, watching the flicker of machine gun fire, well aware of the whistling sound of bullets flying through the air, was not a recipe for self-control. Some years later, in a book written about Alamein, my driver, when questioned about his feelings at that time stated that, driving through the minefield was a very frightening experience but at one stage, with the area lit up by flares, he glanced at the RSM, who appeared to be completely undisturbed. My God, if only he knew just how frightened I was! Perhaps it was as well he didn't.

Events did not appear to be progressing as planned. We were stuck in the minefield practically all night, beneath an umbrella of shells screaming in both directions and bullet tracer darting everywhere. In the light of star shells, I was shocked at the scene that unfolded around us. We were jammed up, nose-to-tail, with no way forward or back, and the enemy took full advantage of the situation. Although our infantry had passed through the area, a number of anti-tank and machine gun positions remained. They proceeded to create havoc by knocking out some of our leading tanks. Near panic resulted as tanks tried to by-pass those disabled and became casualties themselves by driving onto mines and losing tracks.

During the night I returned to the turret of my tank. How relieved I was for the protection of armour plate. With the constant shriek of metal flying through the air, I kept my head well down inside. It seemed like hours, but in fact was probably only minutes, before the shambles up front was finally untangled and we moved out of the minefield and into a dip below a ridge. In the darkness, we spread out and waited for daylight, I with a knot of fear in my stomach and a lump in my throat. The noise of battle continued above the constant crackle in my earphones and my thoughts turned back to the journey through the minefield and those brave men, alone in the darkness, clearing mines and booby traps to create a safe passage for others.

They say truth comes with the dawn, and it certainly showed the harsh reality of our predicament that morning; a mass of tanks and other vehicles crammed into a small dip in the desert between a ridge and the minefield. Because of its shape, this became known as 'Kidney Ridge' and on that day we blessed the RAF, for not a single enemy plane appeared to take advantage of our shambolic predicament.

As light improved, our tanks moved on to the ridge behind the infantry and vehicles of all sorts continued to pack into this narrow strip of desert, just a few hundred yards wide and perhaps half a mile long. Over the ridge in front of us, our infantry were already well dug in, but this was indeed a very dangerous situation. I continued to scan the skies, but not a single enemy plane appeared all day, which was just as well, for only a dozen heavy bombers could have wiped our Armoured Brigade off the face of the earth.

The engineers continued with their mine-clearing operations, to allow the crews of disabled tanks to dismount and carry out repairs. The threat of anti-personnel devices dispersed amongst the anti-tank mines, dictated that the crews were safer in their vehicles until the sappers had cleared the area. These devilish "S" mines, buried beneath the surface, had what appeared to be tiny twigs, sticking up about an inch above the ground. Step on them and a canister full of steel balls and explosives would jump

2 to 8 feet into the air and explode. The shrapnel flew in all directions, tearing through clothing, equipment and human flesh with devastating effect.

As the light improved, another tank regiment from our Brigade moved onto the ridge amongst the infantry, who hated our "tin cans" as they derisively called them. We attracted unhealthy shell-fire, they said, but we also hated being amongst the infantry because they attracted airburst shell-fire, not very funny in an open-top tank with jagged fragments of shrapnel flying around above you.

The tanks stopped and engaged targets, but were not left undisturbed for long. They were sitting too high up on the ridge and an 88mm gun, somewhere on the other side, fired six shots and knocked out five tanks. That regiment, on its first time in action, was given a sharp and very expensive lesson; don't sit on top of a ridge.

Between the ridge and the minefield, the shambles continued throughout the day, with metal screaming through the air in every direction and with little room to manoeuvre. There was no option but to sit tight and take it, with one eye on the sky and the other on the sun, praying for darkness. An order from the CO to join the other tanks on the ridge was welcomed by the crew. The mental strain of just sitting inside a metal box, listening to the crunch of explosions and unable to see what was happening, merely added to the fear churning in your stomach. I was more fortunate than the rest of the crew; sitting up in the turret, with the freedom to look around, at least my fears were not fuelled by the unknown.

I approached the ridge and stopped, hull-down, to survey the area. A gentle downward slope ran onto a large flat plain strewn with debris and flashing guns. Palls of smoke from burning vehicles added to a large, dark cloud, hanging low in the sky, a grim reminder of the morning's disastrous events. The number of tanks burning along our ridge presented a depressing spectacle; we appeared to have fared much worse than the enemy. His anti-tank guns, especially the 88s, dug in with the barrel almost at ground level, had carried out their task of destruction with devastating accuracy.

On that ridge, in my low-profile Crusader, I could remain hull-down almost completely hidden and still play an active part. Standing in the turret, directing the crew and scanning the enemy through binoculars, the babble of voices was constantly in my ears, but one voice stood out clearly above all others, that of the CO, the voice we had learned to trust and obey like the word of God. Much has been said and written of generals who boosted the morale of their troops and spurred them on to victory. What rubbish! That reaction came from the voice you recognised and trusted and motivation came from your personal pride. To turn around and run the other way was always an instinct deep in the mind, but pride and discipline prevented such a course of action.

Amidst all this noise and clamour of battle, a flash nearby attracted my attention; a tank was burning. Flames shot out of the turret, ammunition exploded like a firework display and black smoke belched up into the sky, almost blotting out the sun. There was no sign of the crew. They could have got out unseen, but I doubted it, there hardly seemed enough time between the flash and the flames. A surge of relief passed through my body; we could have been the target instead of them. What a dreadful cross to bear for the rest of my life, to think that someone may have just died for me and not even know his identity.

The fierce activity of battle faded as darkness shrouded the vast plain before us, but the memory of that frightening day was kept alive by the flickering flames of dying vehicles. We pulled back from the ridge and looked forward to the chance to replenish supplies, eat and sleep, what a lovely thought that was, it sent a surge of new life through my body. I could not remember the last time we had slept. Sadly, the feeling of elation was short-lived; orders were given for the Brigade to advance through the minefield in the dark when gaps for the three Regiments had been cleared. Our gap, at the southern end of the ridge, was never completed, an enemy patrol stumbled on the sappers as they lifted the mines and practically wiped them out. In those first few days we lost almost 80% of our engineers.

Our orders were changed. We were to follow the Regiment on our right and pass through their gap. My instructions from the CO were quite specific; I was to lead the Regiment north and contact the tail end of their infantry column. It was not a difficult task in bright moonlight and in this congested area the distance travelled was but a few hundred yards. I reported contact to the CO but he was not satisfied, confirmation of the name of the captain in command had to be obtained and this involved me leaving my tank and walking past a double line of trucks and Bren-gun carriers to the head of their column.

Some of the troops were standing around chatting, others were stretched out, trying to snatch a few minutes sleep. The flames from vehicles on the ridge, casualties of the day's battle, had died to a flicker. An occasional flare lit up the sky, adding to the moonlight and prompted the feeling that my hideaway had been exposed. There was no problem reaching the head of that column and, with the name of the captain confirmed, I returned to my chariot and reported to his lordship. He seemed satisfied with the information and issued orders that "under no circumstances was I to loose contact with that column."

Within minutes that order was nullified by a sudden, disastrous event. I had instructed the operator to keep watch whilst I tried to snatch a few minutes sleep, but my eyes had barely closed when the tank heaved, as if moved by an earthquake.

Amidst a series of violent explosions, the sky glowed red and the stench of burning penetrated the turret. I looked out and gasped at the scene in front of me; the whole column of trucks and Bren-gun carriers was ablaze. Fireballs shot into the air as ammunition exploded and the whole valley was lit up as bright as day. Infantrymen dashed around, pulling their comrades from burning vehicles, with complete disregard to the danger from fire and exploding ammunition. It was a horrific, disastrous spectacle, never to be forgotten.

From the enemy side of the ridge the fireball showed a column of our tanks, standing out clearly against the glow, and he grasped the opportunity with deadly results. Within minutes, a number of tanks, waiting in close formation to pass through the minefield, were hit and burning; the resulting chaos was indescribable. The orderly columns ahead of us simply disintegrated, with everyone trying to get out of the light and into the security of darkness. Packed in nose-to-tail along the valley, our regiment was very exposed and we were ordered to break column and disperse. Almost in a state of panic, vehicles spread out, away from the revealing glow of the flames, in search of somewhere to hide. A number of tanks, including mine, drove into the minefield without mishap. Truth came with the dawn; we had got ourselves in but dared not move until the Sappers cleared a path.

The cause of that disaster was extensively debated, but never really identified. Was it a lucky salvo of shells or a very accurate bomb run? It was even suggested that someone had recognised the silhouette of a Wellington Bomber. Whatever the cause, to those whose bodies and burned up remains littered the ground, it was of no further interest.

CHAPTER 24

BREAKOUT AT EL AQQAQIR

I T TOOK ANOTHER BARRAGE AND another attack by the infantry to get us out of that disastrous hellhole of Kidney Ridge, but we finally cleared the minefields and spread out on to the flat plane of El Aqqaqir. As far as the eye could see, the blackened hulls of burned-out vehicles stood out clearly against the desert background. These silent sentinels were all that remained as evidence of the previous day's conflict, when two opposing forces had struggled so desperately to destroy each other.

Today the battle was more vicious; our tanks moved across open ground with little protection, trying desperately to dislodge the enemy from prepared positions. His tanks, supported by anti-tank guns, put up a fierce resistance and casualties on both sides were tremendous. As navigator I was with the HQ Troop at the rear of the squadrons in the battle line and it was not an enviable position, sitting in a small Crusader amongst the much larger and less vulnerable Sherman tanks. Anti-tank guns, out of range to the thick armour of the Shermans, considered me fair game, resulting in the necessity to keep moving. Fortunately, my driver, an ex-sergeant, demoted by request to be relieved of his responsibility for others, was very capable and required little guidance from me.

The need for my constant presence near the CO when on the move was due to his fear of getting lost. He had been captured once by the enemy and escaped and he was determined not to get caught again. This fear caused me many problems. On this day we had moved only hundreds of yards from our starting point and yet I was called to his tank to mark our position on his map almost every half hour. Not a very happy situation, given that it required me to get off my tank, run about two hundred yards through shellfire, climb onto his, mark his map, and run back again.

We continued to move back and forth for hours, simply to disturb the enemy artillery calculation of our range. They got uncomfortably close on a number of occasions, but my driver was too clever for them. Generally, my line of movement oscillated between a destroyed bunker and a shell-hole. A number of bodies of infantrymen lay around the area and it was naturally assumed that the wounded had been attended to by their own medics during the advance. It was therefore a shock to see a body lying in the hole, like a bundle of bloodied rags, that was clearly alive.

His steel helmet had slipped to the back of his head, dust-covered face turned towards the sky, with glaring eyes staring straight back at me. As I looked down, petrified by indecision, a hand moved from the side of his body and slowly reached up towards me. My God, what the hell should I do now? The decision was taken from me by HQ moving forward a few hundred yards and I had to move with them. It was difficult to concentrate on the tasks I must perform because in my ears a voice kept repeating my callsign, "MOPE, MOPE, come to me and give me my position". Oh God, not again! We had only moved a few yards. This time I ignored his calls on the pretext that my radio was out of order, but he just kept on and on. My head had been throbbing for hours, probably due to lack of sleep and that persistent nagging voice in my ears was making it worse. I slipped the earphones down around my neck and the voice faded to a whisper.

With our move came more shellfire and I had no desire to run that gauntlet again, but the decision was taken from me when our doctor, Captain MacMillan MC, appeared in his Dingo scout car, came close alongside and, with a grin, touched his earphones, pointing to the CO's tank. That was it; I had been rumbled. I jumped down and ran those two hundred yards to his tank like the bats out of hell. He screamed abuse at me as I climbed onto the back and, with a few foul words of my own, marked his map with a large cross that must have covered about two square miles. I jumped off again and ran for the cover of my tank, the whistle of bullets passing uncomfortably close spurring me on.

What a relief to reach my tank and climb on to the back. Just a quick hop and jump and I would be safe inside the turret, but it happened very much faster than I had anticipated. With just half my body inside, a shell exploded on the side of the turret and blasted me down on top of the operator. The gunner turned around to help me, uttered an oath, and started to unwrap a shell dressing. I could feel the blood running down under my shirt.

"Oh well," I thought, "this must be it."

The instinct of survival took over. The tank had to be moved before the gunner that had us in his sights fired again. I stood up and grabbed the microphone, but it was not necessary, the driver was already in reverse and moved quite fast to a new position. Doc MacMillan, somewhere behind us, had witnessed the incident and came alongside. I jumped onto the Dingo and was whisked back to a hidden hollow, where, with an occasional giggle of pleasure, he proceeded to scratch and scrape pieces of shrapnel from the back of my neck. When questioned how bad it was, he jokingly asked what I would do if I cut myself when shaving.

"Stick a piece of cotton wool on it," I answered.

"That is what I shall do with your ear," he replied. "The lobe is hanging off and the blood is pouring down your neck."

What an anti-climax! I was not going to die. I was not even bad enough to have a few days out of the line. Within half an hour I was dumped back on the tank with a large pad of cotton wool on the back of my head and a bandage holding it in place. 'There must be something about those old remedies of blood letting,' I thought; my headache had completely disappeared.

The plight of the wounded infantryman had been reported to the doctor and I had done my duty, but the question remained in my mind to this very day, should or could I have helped him myself or did my responsibility as a tank commander forbid it? Whatever the answer, the pleading look in that soldier's eyes and his outstretched hand begging for help will always be with me.

The battle for El Aqqaqir went on from dawn to dusk and relaxation did not come with the darkness, with each side anxiously waiting for the other to mount a night attack. The glowing hulks of the day's casualties brought fear of impending disaster. How could we possibly suffer such high losses and still win? The enemy had also suffered, but seemed immovable from his entrenched position.

With the rising of the sun, the ferocity of the battle increased. We were all so weary, there was little energy left for worry. Most of my night had been spent with the CO, ferrying him back to Brigade HQ for briefing. His fear of getting lost cost me many sleepless nights.

Almost as suddenly as it started, the volume of shellfire decreased. We started to move forward and continued to press on throughout the day, with only minor skirmishes to slow our advance. What a fantastic situation, yesterday the depth of depression, today high elation. The enemy defences had collapsed, he was in full retreat and we were now the sole occupiers of a graveyard strewn with burned-out tanks and lorries, smashed guns and defences manned only by the dead.

Pursuit of the fleeing forces was conducted with extreme caution; we had suffered in the past from his clever defensive tactics. His method of screening tank withdrawal with dug in anti-tank guns holding us for a time then leap-frogging back through another line of guns was very effective. But now, in desperation, his tactics had changed and we paid the price. Guns appeared to be abandoned and our advance continued, but at a very short range a crew would appear from holes in the ground, knock out a couple of our tanks and then stand up, with hands in the air. That was simply unacceptable and con-centrated machine gun fire eliminated the obstacle.

We drove west throughout the day and in the darkness turned north towards the sea; our target was an area on the coast road called Galal. The plan was to cut off the German armour facing the Australians at the north end of the Alamein line and trap them with their backs to the sea. As we topped the ridge in daylight the scene beneath us was utter chaos. The road and the flat parts of the desert on either side were jammed with lorries guns and a few tanks, all crawling westwards. The tanks were disposed of first and then we settled down to what could only be described as a pigeon shoot. In reality, it was a sickening orgy of death and destruction that gave us great satisfaction. Such is war.

A vast tract of land between the road and the sea, obviously a supply storage area, was alive with lorries attempting to load up and get out. Very few escaped the trap, but the object of our overnight advance was a failure, the bulk of Rommel's armour had escaped. However, all was not lost; from that day on our CO became known as 'Pyman of Galal' and he was very proud of that.

At that time, I felt that the grand Montgomery plan to destroy the German Army at Alamein was a failure. The chaotic and near disaster situations that frequently occurred during the battle were countered only by the skill and tenacious attitude of our commanders in the field. We know the enemy lost large numbers of tanks and guns but, at about three to one, our losses were very much higher. The enemy's long lines of communication probably contributed more to his downfall; our supply route was almost at our back door.

We followed the coast road west towards Mersa Matruh, with frequent stops for many reasons, mostly road blockages associated with mines and delaying rearguard actions by the enemy. To further add to our problems, the rain came and turned the desert into a quagmire, with vehicles slipping and sliding all over the place. These conditions held us up for days, often in areas recently vacated by the enemy, which produced additional problems, especially for the less experienced crew members. The urge to search amongst abandoned stores and equipment was something new and exciting for them and the warnings of danger from mines and booby-traps seemed to go unheeded. The old hands had seen some of the devastating results of such follies and were reluctant to risk their life for a handful of souvenirs; when you lost a tank, all the loot went with it anyway, so why bother?

At one point, where all traffic was stopped, tank crews, relieved and relaxed at the break from action, grabbed the chance to escape from the cramped conditions and heat of the turret and travelled on the outside. The CO considered this to be a dangerous practice showing lack of discipline; he instructed me to drive up the column in his jeep and record the names of all men riding on the outside. Instead, I pulled onto the desert, clear of the column and, when obscured from the HQ Troop, fired a few short bursts from a Bren-gun into the air. That had the desired effect; the crews, fearful of an air attack, dived back inside. There were no names to book and the CO was furious. Later, when challenged by the Adjutant to explain my action, I pointed out that, when charged with an offence it is a soldier's right to elect a trial by Court Martial. In those circumstances, I enquired, who would be available to man his tanks?

~ CHAPTER 25 ~

THE CHASE IS ON

PURSUIT OF THE ENEMY CONTINUED across Cyrenaica, but our Brigade, having flogged its guts out at El Alamein, was ordered to rest and re-equip near Mersa Matruh. What a paradise that was! Spread out along the coast, with no dust bombarding your face, just a pleasant cool breeze caressing the skin and a sky devoid of enemy aircraft, regular cooked meals, eaten without haste, a mug of tea whenever the need dictated and, most important of all, a good night's sleep.

Once again, for the third time in as many years, the enemy stopped and defended his positions south of Benghazi, on those memorable Salt Flats of El Agheila. This was familiar territory to the Eighth Army, since we had been there twice before, and it looked as if we would have to do it all over again. This time, for the 500-mile journey across the open desert, we were to be carried part way on tank transporters. Now we were being pampered, at least, that is what I thought...

Well, you can't always be right. Each trailer had three rows of eight wheels, mounted in pairs, the tractor had another two and a ten-ton lorry loaded with spare wheels followed each squadron. I wondered why, but it became perfectly clear on the first day, pieces of slate trapped between a pair of tyres generally burst both. In many instances, depending on the location of the punctured wheels, the tank had to be unloaded to effect the change. Carry out this exercise two or three times in a day at 120 degrees in the shade and all that lovely water you had soaked in on the coast was sweated out forever.

The journey took about a week, partly on reasonable desert tracks, the remainder across rough terrain strewn with stones and sagebrush mounds. Those areas reduced our speed considerably and the need to hang on to this rolling bouncing chariot with both hands was a boring and tiring experience.

Thankfully, about a hundred miles from Agheila, we unloaded, settled down in open leaguer, and prepared once again for battle.

New crews had to be trained, not only in the art of war but just as important in the art of survival. To stop and refill with petrol in a hurry and check the outside of a tank required the precise cooperation of the whole crew. But the body too required sustenance and to produce a mug of tea, as described earlier in this narrative, on a petrol fire, required real skill. Ridiculous as it may sound, the art of making tea in record time was just as important as loading shells in the breach of a gun; each had its own place in the pattern of survival.

As usual, in open leaguer, the tanks had to be camouflaged and toilets dug out, but when we were on the move the tank commander usually 'slopped out' the water pots (empty shell-cases saved for this purpose). Anything else had to be suppressed for a suitable opportunity to walk over the hill with a shovel and a newspaper. On many occasions in action someone with a stomach bug who could not wait had to crouch down behind the tank in the hope that, in the meantime, the regiment did not move. What a pathetic sight to see a lone soldier left sitting in the desert unable to move and hoping to be picked up later by our transport column.

Water shortage dictated a strict pattern of daily life, for example no washing of plates, they were scoured with grit and sand and the last mouthful of tea in a mug was used for teeth cleaning, that is, if you still had a brush, it may have been blown off the tank with the rest if your gear. A shirt washed in petrol and dried in the sun may smell for a day or two, but there was no problem with fleas or lice. With feet enclosed in rubber-soled desert boots, sometimes twenty hours a day, smelly socks were a big problem. Walking in bare feet whenever possible helped dry the skin and harden the soles.

In this hostile environment of heat, food, dead bodies and hordes of filthy flies, stomach bugs were a problem and an additional drain on water supplies. On one occasion my crew were quietly playing cards in the shade of the tank when suddenly the gunner jumped up and ran towards the toilet. He got just about half way to our desert toilet, stopped and walked very slowly – a frequent sad story of 'too much too late'. Travel 50 miles deep into the desert and there is nothing, no vegetation no insects no birds no noise. But open a tin of bully beef and flies would descend by the thousand to devour every last fibre; where the hell did they come from?

Since rations were issued to each tank separately, the opportunity to use your culinary skills was unlimited. 'Sausages' made from a mixture of crushed-up biscuits and bully, were very popular, that is, if there was fat to fry them in. On very special occasions, a tin of fatty streaky bacon was cooked to death just for the fat and we could have our sausages. For me, a Scot, my special delicacy came from the issue of wholemeal biscuits. Just half an hour smashing them up in a tin with a hammer and I had my plate of 'porridge', although I must admit a lot of imagination went into it. On one occasion we picked up plain flour from a deserted Italian bakery, not much good by itself, but we were lucky, our driver had stomach problems and a visit to the doctor resulted in a handful of bicarbonate tablets... A stew of bully, biscuits, soya sausages and anything else you could beg borrow or steal was absolutely delicious, but the ultimate delicacy was rich, sickly sweet, rice pudding; that really put the final touch to a gourmet banquet!

Someone must have got the message that we were settling down very comfortably in this peaceful part of the desert and the order came through to pack up and move. I navigated from the front with a recce troop ahead of me, but it was a task made difficult by a number of officers, who considered that with their superior rank came superior knowledge. Throughout the journey, frequent suggestions to the CO informed him we should be travelling so many degrees to the north or south, whichever took their fancy. The CO instructed me accordingly, and I passed the order to my driver to turn to the new bearing. However, navigating by dead reckoning, using a sun compass on a tank sliding sideways on sandy slopes, and judging distance from the tacho mileage, less track slip on soft sand, is not an easy task, as I described earlier. This could only be achieved by confidence in one's judgement therefore, after passing on the CO's orders to the driver, I added my own instructions to swing back to our original course over the next half mile.

Often, in the absence of the sun, navigation was confined to a hand-held prismatic, backed up by the driver's P8, but, move some tools or ammo and the P8 lost its accuracy. Fortunately, on this journey we had a star-gazing major who carried a theodolite; he would shoot the stars at night and calculate our true position to within a few yards on the ground. He could tell me precisely where we were, but sadly, according to my map, that was not always where we should be, but we were never very far adrift.

After the Wavell campaign, an Army survey team produced new maps of Cyrenaica with numbered reference points marked and identified on the ground. Empty forty-gallon drums, filled with sand and erected on mounds, carried the reference number of that location. That was a very clever aid to navigation until we retreated and pushed the enemy back again, he had very cleverly changed all the drums around and we were lost again.

The last leg of our journey took us to the defence line at Agheila, where we were to support an infantry brigade of the Highland Division. When we arrived, they were already dug in, about a mile to the north of our calculated position. Of course, the argument that ensued between our colonel and the infantry brigadier was won by the brigadier, he being the senior rank. Our CO was left with no option but to order us north to a position behind the infantry. However, this was later reversed, when our brigadier, Pip Roberts, arrived and informed us we were in the wrong position. Those poor bloody infantry had to pack up, move south in daylight and dig in again. The enemy took full advantage of the situation and shelled them all the way. We were not very popular with them; in their eyes, it was all our fault, of course.

Back at Agheila, the fears and doubts started all over again; would Rommel once again pull a trump card out of the bag and push us all the way back to Egypt? I don't think any of us 'old hands' had the stomach for another defeat like that. Like me, most of them felt, I am sure, that the odds in favour of their personal survival must be fast running out. On waking up in the morning my first thought always was, 'Good, I have got another day … but roll on the sunset!'

Although a bit of tit-for-tat shelling took place, I have no memory of a battle, but as usual we waited for the worst to happen. It was late in the day and the recce squadron was reporting activity in the hills behind the salt flats. Pillars of smoke were rising from the gullies behind the enemy lines and one patrol reported that a general exodus appeared to be in progress. Rommel was pulling out. From then on, a gradual withdrawal continued all the way back to Tripoli, although his clever rearguard tactics continued to take their toll of our forces. We were involved in numerous skirmishes, but there were no all-out battles like that at El Alamein. Nevertheless, for a tank crew in action it was still a battle for survival; death was always just around the corner.

By now, our tank numbers were sadly depleted, and replacements were slow to catch up with the speed of our advance. Our role, supported by an Infantry Brigade, was to harass the enemy in the southern part of the desert, with an occasional 'right hook' towards the coast, to cut off his rearguard. We travelled along tracks and minor roads, parallel to the coast, frequently held up by mines and enemy activity.

At one point we turned north, towards a road through the mountains in the region of Tarhuna. From the top of a ridge, across a wide, cultivated valley, we could see the road running from east to west, disappearing into the hills on our left flank. There was no obvious sign of activity but it was just too quiet for comfort; our presence in that area must have been reported, so where the hell was the enemy? A farmhouse with a walled-in area around it lay mid-way between us and the road and another building stood by the roadside further to the left. There should have been something moving on this large area of farmland, but there was nothing, and it gave me the creeps. Even the radio was silent, which indicated that all eyes were busy searching but could see nothing to report.

The light squadron was ordered to advance. I was with them and headed straight for the farmhouse, across the open valley. We were almost there when anti-tank guns opened fire, sending shells screaming past us. Voices in my earphones from our Shermans on the ridge reported guns firing from the corner of a house. My God, that must be the house just ahead of me! I was almost at the farmhouse, near a gateway in the wall, and screamed an order to the driver to drive through into the walled garden. My original intention had been to break through the wall and approach from the other side, but a structure built onto the wall on the inside put the mockers on that idea.

Attempts to turn around and get out again were frustrated by a hail of HE shells from the Shermans on the ridge. We collected a lot of bricks and mortar on the outside of the tank and in the turret, but were otherwise undamaged. It was the wrong house they were shelling, the enemy guns were located at the other house, by the roadside. I later discovered that the salvo crashing around me was laid down by my old friend from Greece, Jock Stewart, and I had a feeling he knew I was there. Some joke!

The gun was quickly dealt with and we pushed along the road into the mountains until shellfire stopped the troop of tanks in front of me. A bridge had been blown and the enemy were defending from the other side. There was no room to turn around and reversing back down this narrow road, which had a sheer drop on one side and a cliff on the other, was the only alternative.

A troop of our artillery had set up in a dip at a bend in the road and started to lob HE at the hills around the bridge. I was concentrating on guiding my driver in reverse while at the same time worrying about shells that seemed to be screaming ever closer to my head, and I failed to notice that we were reversing onto the muzzles of our 25-pounders. The shells were almost shaving my hair off. The bend in the road saved us; if the range had been dropped before we reached it, they may well have had my bloody head off. I suppose it would have been an end to my problems.

Since being caught by that shell-blast at Alamein, I had suffered the recurring problem of small boils on my back and neck; they would come to a head quite quickly and throw out tiny pieces of black debris, but now, a boil on my neck, almost a week old, was growing larger each day. I was suffering from the cold and wearing an Army greatcoat with the collar turned up, plus having a pair of binoculars hanging around the collar, was not exactly a soothing situation. My numerous requests for the doctor to do something about it resulted in the usual sympathetic answer: "It is not quite ready yet." At least the persistent agony distracted my mind from other worrying events.

The infantry were given the task of clearing the enemy from these mountains and a temporary bridge was erected. With the assistance of artillery, they did an excellent job, but sadly, once again, it was the end of the trail for many good soldiers. Although this mountain barrier offered a natural defensive position, Rommel seemed reluctant to stand and fight, offering only token resistance to delay our advance. Of course, we were unaware of the success of our forces driving along the coast, which probably had a considerable influence on his decision.

Once clear of the mountains, the race for Tripoli was really on. We were all very tired and the voice in my ears was getting on my nerves: 'Push on! Push on! We are right behind you.' What the hell did he think we were doing? Belting along this black tarmac road in the moonlight, every bush on this flat desert might be an anti-tank gun just waiting for us. My body was rigid with tension, trying, with and without binoculars, to identify objects in this moonlit landscape, just waiting for that flash at the roadside to tell me we had run into an ambush. It was a real nail-biter and the agony of the boil on the back of my neck, rubbing on my coat collar, was not exactly a help.

My main role was still navigation. I drove along with a troop of Crusaders in front and the RE's halftrack behind while the rest of the Regiment followed, what was left of them. According to my map, a bridge over a Wadi should be just ahead and the two tanks in front of me would report it. But what the hell was that? A red glow appeared on the horizon. Probably the bridge being blown, we couldn't be far behind his rearguard. We slowed down a little, peering hard into the night, well aware that he may have left a couple of a/t guns behind just to let us know he had not given up yet. But there was no problem; they had done their dastardly deed and gone. The bridge was completely destroyed and a thick pall of smoke hung over the scene. That was close; we had almost caught up with him.

The old track across the Wadi, alongside the bridge, looked undisturbed and very tempting in the bright moonlight, but it was sure to be mined. Surely they would not be so stupid as to leave us with a clear run across? The tank behind me was in line with the track entrance and was ordered to drive across it. I was surprised, a few minutes later, to hear him signal he was through to the other side. With the words "Push on, push on," ringing in our ears, the next tank moved down onto the track and proceeded across the Wadi. He had just started to climb up the other side when an almighty bang told us a mine had blown his track off. Fortunately, the dirt track was wide enough at that part for other vehicles to pass, but now the whole track would have to be checked for mines.

The CO considered we had already lost too much time, so the order was to clear the mines and get on with it. There were only three REs left from our original ten at Alamein, so I helped by following the sergeant with the sweeper, throwing down his bayonet every second sweep to check that the detector was working. A number of mines were found and disarmed before we cleared the disabled tank and moved on towards the road. The crew standing on the back of the tank asked if it was safe to dismount and join the group which had followed us; the sergeant agreed and we carried on with the sweep.

Almost immediately there was a loud bang and we hit the deck. A black cloud of smoke hung over the scene behind us and bodies were lying around, some groaning, others quite still. My immediate thought was that we had been caught in a trap, but action was necessary and we rushed back to assist in sorting the mess out. I attended to the driver, who was on his side and had a partly smoked cigarette hanging from his lips. His leather belt was broken at the back, cut through by numerous steel balls from an "S" mine. I tore open his shirt and exposed his back; it was covered with small red spots where steel balls had entered and the skin closed again. The Doc looked at him and shook his head; he died as I turned him on his back and removed the cigarette from his mouth.

It would appear that, when sweeping near the tank track, the detector picked up the tank and not the "S" mine; sadly, the driver jumped right onto the damned thing and it exploded behind him. Unfortunately, a number of crews, anxious to stretch their legs, had followed down the track and were caught in the blast and become casualties. Eventually, as Doc McMillan continued to clean up the carnage of that tragic event, we moved away in the moonlight. A dark cloud of smoke still hung over the bridge and a heavy burden of guilt pressed me down into the turret; damn Pyman and his "Push on, push on."

It was almost dawn when we finally moved on again. The shambles at the Wadi had changed our travelling order, there were now two troops of tanks ahead of me, but that did little to quell the fear of an ambush. Sure enough, it came in daylight as we entered a small village of white houses, where, just a few hundred yards further, a T-junction in the road would take us north to Tripoli. However, an enemy 88 crew positioned at the junction had other ideas. There was a loud bang and a shell came screaming down the road. How the hell they missed all those tanks at such a short range was a miracle; they had probably not expected our arrival so early and fired in a panic. They did not get a second chance; we all turned off the road and disappeared amongst the houses. That was just about enough for me; feeling tired and weary I gave the order to the crew "brew up". The Artillery behind us quickly got into action and, with one of our tanks directing the fire, the enemy gunners were soon persuaded to pack up and leave.

It took some time for the CO to assess the situation, re-assemble on the road and for the column to move off once again; in the meantime, the short rest and breakfast worked wonders and, apart from that bloody boil on my neck, I felt almost human again. During breakfast the CO kept calling me on the wireless, but he had been a long way behind me on the road and I had no intention of wandering about trying to find him so his calls were ignored; there are none so deaf as those who have no wish to hear.

There was no opposition to our advance north to Castel Benito, the location of an aerodrome just a few miles south of Tripoli, but outside the village we were stopped by anti-tank guns and dispersed into an orchard. The enemy could not possibly see us amongst the trees, but he continued to send shells screaming through the woods just to make us keep our heads down, and we did. One man, while running between two tanks, was hit by something and fell to the ground; we dashed across to give assistance as he lay on his side with the lower half of his face a sickening mess of jawbone and flesh just lying on his shoulder. The medics arrived and took him away. Remarkably, he lived and information from the hospital at a later date stated that his jaw had been put back in place and a lump of flesh grafted from his hip stuck on for a chin.

At night the order was given for a final dash to Tripoli. I was pleased that the task of leading this advance was not mine; no one could guess what waited for us on that road. However, when driving through the streets of the village, an unusual hazard was present; the stench of partly-brewed beer hung heavy in the air. The local brewery had been hit and the mash was running down the gutter. What a waste!

We knew that the Highland Division was advancing along the coast road, but their actual location was unknown. More important was our lack of knowledge of the enemy's intentions; would he defend or withdraw?

As it happened, there was nothing to stop us, it was plain sailing all the way to within a few miles of Tripoli, when we were stopped and ordered to pull off the road into a field. The 11th Hussars armoured cars passed us and entered the town and we wondered why; perhaps it was considered too dangerous for tanks to be moving through narrow streets in the dark. All was later revealed. They had been given the honour of being the first British troops to enter Tripoli, an honour they richly deserved.

I was also delighted that within minutes of parking the Doc appeared and dragged me off to his ambulance. He took a look at my neck and I felt a searing pain as he lanced the boil. My body sagged with pleasure and relief. I wandered slowly back to the tank with cotton wool and bandage around my neck; a mug of hot, steaming tea awaited me. I drank it and fell asleep.

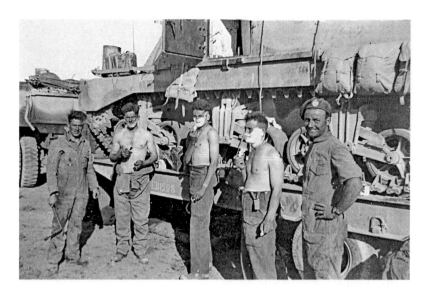

Another close shave.

Essential supplies.

~ CHAPTER 26 ~

THE RACE FOR TUNIS

SECURED BY THE INFANTRY WITHOUT a battle, the town of Tripoli was ours. The loss of this capital of Libya, the pride and joy of Mussolini's African conquests, must have been a shattering blow to the morale of the Italian people. We had come 1,500 miles through hell just to knock that pompous dictator off his pedestal and there was no going back.

In the morning our tank column drove through the streets of Tripoli. This was a new and very exciting experience. Since leaving the battlefield at El Alamein this was the largest collection of buildings we had seen and as if to highlight the occasion the sun was bright and the sky a brilliant blue. At the approaches to the town, small white-painted bungalows with gardens containing flowers and fruit trees lined the roadside. I remember thinking how lucky these people were that they had not suffered the devastation of war. But moving slowly along the narrow streets towards the centre and harbour area the houses were smaller and less attractive and the effect of air raids became evident.

Around the harbour was a scene of destruction: sunken ships, twisted metal, the remains of cranes and other structures and the rubble of shattered buildings. A large concrete warehouse on the quayside about 100 feet tall had escaped unscathed, but an AA gun on the flat roof lay on its side near the parapet and the top half of a body hung over the edge. Strangely, the old fort near the harbour and its enclosing wall appeared to have escaped the wrath of the RAF, as if this ancient, historic building had been worthy of preservation.

The highlight of the day was at a crossroads near the centre. There, standing on a pedestal at the centre of the road, was a policeman directing traffic. Not unusual, you may think, but there stood the enemy, immaculately dressed in a spotless white uniform and highly polished boots, directing the movement of an untidy, weary, victorious army. It was incredible, he stood there commanding the movements of the British Army with a superior air and the precision of a mechanical man that any RSM would have been proud of.

At the eastern end of the harbour, an attractive, small hotel called the Del Mahari had a double tier of rooms, built in the form of a square, which enclosed an open-air lounge. A restaurant on the beach had access from the Hotel via a tunnel under the road. Further along this seashore, a row of white bungalows stretched away to the east; their gardens looked neat and tidy, as did the buildings, giving the impression of a high-class area.

Beginning in the harbour area, a wide, impressive boulevard, running west, parallel to the coast, separated the ancient from the modern. In front of the old fort, the road was wider, allowing a more extensive view of this historic building. The waving palms lining the road that disappeared into farmland in the west added a final touch of Middle Eastern character. On the western outskirts, a barracks, surrounded by a high wall, stood empty, obviously deserted in a hurry, with rubbish lying everywhere. It was not our scene to occupy such a filthy building; we formed a leaguer in the open countryside nearby.

It was just a few days later that I drove into town and stopped to look at a long queue of soldiers that stretched away in the distance towards the castle and every fifty yards an upturned forty-gallon drum supported a gambling game of some sort. This was the first time I had seen such an open display of contempt for Army regulations and there were MPs walking about ignoring it all; in fact, they appeared to be controlling the queue, but what in heavens name were they all waiting for? The answer came as quite a shock. Someone had authorised the opening of brothels, but I doubted very much if it was Montgomery; not with his high moral and religious principles. They did not stay open for long; those in high places apparently considered it an affront to the British People and they were closed down. But what in hell did they know about soldiers living and fighting for years in a stinking desert far away, while they enjoyed all the comforts of home?

At first, the local Italian inhabitants seemed reluctant and frightened to show their faces, but gradually the need to eat overpowered their shyness. Driven by a searching for fresh vegetables and the desire to satisfy my natural curiosity, I visited a number of farms and communicated with the occupants. It gradually emerged that these people had been informed that we were vicious animals who would murder the men, rape the women and loot all of their possessions. One young girl on a farm had even got herself pregnant, believing that no one would rape her in that condition. They could not understand that we were just normal people.

Besides, in the British Army, looting and rape were punishable by death and this was reiterated by the High Command when we entered Tripoli.

However, looting of former enemy supplies, generally in search of food and other survival necessities, was common practice. For example, the Germans were issued with dehydrated vegetables, onions, carrots, etc and to us these in a stew was a delicacy. But the German Army also had food problems, their tinned meat was revolting stuff, including blood vessels tendons and anything else you care to imagine. As a result, they loved our tins of bully beef, evident by the piles of empty tins we found when we chased them out of an area.

Then there were dark, rich-looking blocks of food rather like Xmas cake without the icing. They looked very tempting and tasted sweet at first, but that soon disappeared and you were left with a mouthful of what can only be described as sawdust. The biggest con were long, fat cigars that were not the smoking pleasure I expected. When unravelled the reason was revealed; sheets of brown paper were interleaved with the tobacco. No wonder the Germans had gruff voices.

It was about this time the the famous 'Pete Pyman of Galal' left us. He must have impressed someone, because they moved him on to better things. For me it was a double blessing. Now I could have a reasonable night's sleep like everyone else, instead of nursing the CO in case he got lost. Secondly, a surprise order had me on a plane at Castel Benito aerodrome and flying back across the desert to Cairo; apparently our old CO, Pip Roberts, prior to leaving the Regiment, had applied for me to be commissioned, but Pyman, in his wisdom (or whatever), had suppressed it. However, our second in command, Major George Upcot-Gill, obviously aware of my situation, immediately upon taking command ratified the order and I was on my way...

The journey by plane was a nerve-racking experience; it was an old Dakota, with seats replacing the bomb-racks and as we bumped along the runway, with bomb craters temporarily filled, I am sure we left half the plane on the ground. There were thirteen on board, not a good omen for a superstitious Scot, but there were also other things to worry about. We sat in fours, facing each other, knees touching, as air pockets tossed the plane all over the place. The face of the chap opposite me kept changing colour from tan to ashen grey; I could not take my eyes off him. He was going to be sick and I was in the firing line.

I kept thinking over and over again 'he is going to be sic, he is going to be sick' but then I was ... all over him.

What a marvellous thing aviation is! It had taken us months of hard slogging over unfriendly terrain to reach Tripoli and in just a few hours we completed the return journey. It was good to be back in Cairo again but this was no pleasure trip; the Officers Selection Board, at a camp just outside the city, could not be kept waiting. By this time I was having doubts about becoming an officer, perhaps it was fear of failing. As an RSM I was king of the castle amongst the other ranks; why chuck that up for the unknown?

With doubts in my mind, I entered the arena of interviews, questions and tests, with the watchful eyes of unknown observers assessing your behaviour everywhere and listening to every word you uttered. The probing and sometimes insulting questions from psychiatrists, the sudden orders to stand up and lecture on unknown topics and a series of initiative tests left me mentally drained but unruffled. Perhaps because I was not particularly bothered, just acted quite naturally, did not mouth off in the bar and ate with a knife and fork, I was considered acceptable to join the ranks of the Army elite. I was commissioned as a Lieutenant, the salary of which was less than that of an RSM, so I was paid the salary of a Captain.

A week of hard slogging at an Officer's Training College in Palestine was no real problem; most of the technical stuff I had already been taught, thanks to Major Carey and his cosy coaches. Back at an Alexandria Transit Camp I waited for movement orders to 3rd RTR; apparently they had applied for my return immediately I left, thanks to George Upcot-Gill, our 2nd in command (2.I.C.). Although the social life of Alexandria was great and the cool beer in the Stanley Hotel trickled down with sheer delight, I was not really happy there; deep down, I craved for a speedy return home, not to England, but to the only family

I had known these past few years, my Regiment. How confusing the contradictions in the human mind can be, wasting hours of life cursing and praying to be somewhere else, then wishing to be back in the mess you got out of. We never learn...

The decision was made for me; I was ordered to deliver half a million pounds in notes to the Field Cashier in Tripoli. An escort of four sergeants was provided, their task being to keep an eagle eye on the forty packing cases until they reached their destination. With great relief, I watched the last box lowered into the hold of the cargo boat *Everley* and a few hundred tons of cargo piled on top. We were due to leave in convoy the next day, but we sailed no further than anchorage in the outer harbour; apparently under pressure from the crew, the ship's captain refused to sail without his fresh meat and it had failed to arrive on time from Cairo.

Almost a week later we joined another convoy; there were five ships escorted by four destroyers. The size of the escort worried me; it was an indication of impending trouble. In the knowledge that the best cure for fear is to be occupied, I arranged with the first officer that we take over the AA guns located on the wings of the bridge and the watch was split between the five of us.

It was late one evening that I stood by the gun, elbows resting on the rail, watching for any movement on the moonlit sea and whistling softly to myself. A violent blow to the side of my head provoked an instant reaction; I ducked and turned, prepared to kill. The ship's captain stood before me with a violent expression on his face. "How dare you whistle on my bridge!" he screamed, then he abruptly turned and walked away. I drew a deep breath and calmed myself down, there was nothing I could do. On a ship the Captain is God and I was unaware that whistling on the bridge is thought to bring bad luck.

Apart from frequent instances when one of the escorts would swan around and drop depth charges, the journey was almost uneventful. A deck cargo of potatoes had rotted and was thrown overboard; a week in the hot sun in Alexandria harbour plus days at sea was just too much for the poor old spuds. I felt sad and annoyed at this waste; the lads up in the desert would have enjoyed them. So much for that bloody ship's crew and their fresh meat!

As we approached Tripoli harbour, enemy fighter/bombers screamed towards us, low on the water. We were not the target, but our guns gave them a good blasting as they roared past. All hell seemed to erupt around the harbour, with the rattle of AA gunfire, exploding bombs, flames from targets hit, and a pall of smoke hung over the area. Not a very pleasant welcome... and there was no band to greet us either.

We eventually docked just before dark, with instructions to be ready for unloading at the crack of dawn. At the appointed time our motley crew of sergeants was on deck, waiting, but apart from the officers there was no sign of the ship's crew. A Military Police Captain appeared and questioned why we were not unloading; the answer was that the crew, having spent the night ashore in Tripoli, had got boozed up and were reluctant to turn out. The MP Captain stormed down into the crew's quarters and informed them that this was a Military Port, he was in command and in five minutes they would either be on deck or in a Military Prison.

Work started within minutes and our small team lent a hand. We stripped off three of the hatches while the crew managed the other two, so much for Army training. A company of Sudanese were the dockers; they worked like slaves and enjoyed it. The MPs kept an eye on the ship's crew and we kept an eye on the dockers in the hold. It was common knowledge that if an unrecognised box appeared they would burst one open to see what was in it. I had no intention of losing a box full of money.

In the event, there was no problem. We loaded a truck and drove off to deliver our charge. At the dock gates we were stopped by the MPs, a stack of broken boxes piled high behind them; all contained tinned food and other necessities. They asked if there was anything we wanted, a simple way to minimise pilfering. With our cargo checked at the Field Cashier in a commandeered bank, papers signed and a receipt carefully stowed in my gear, I felt free once again to head for home.

It would be criminal to leave this dialogue without mentioning the part played by the ship's crew, who, with just minimal protection, sailed the cruel seas. At Alexandria they watched the loading of petrol, counting every can as it came aboard and, at one can over a specified number, they requested, as was their right, an increase in bonus money. The First Officer ordered the removal of a number of cans, which negated the bonus, spoilsport! Throughout the journey the crew complained bitterly about the food. I was unaware of this until a ship's officer, desperate to avoid a battle in the mess between my sergeants and the crew, asked that I restrain my men. Apparently, sick and tired of listening to the complaints about food, my men had told the crew, in no uncertain terms, just how bloody lucky they were compared with what those poor bastards in the desert had to live on. In Tripoli harbour the Military Police Captain, determined to bring this bolshie crew to heel, did a search. When the ship was unloaded, he unearthed a mass of goods pilfered from cargo by some of the crew. There were dozens of pairs of Army desert boots, boxes of toothbrushes and other necessities almost unobtainable in the desert and all probably destined for some black market at home. I did hear later that they eventually got what they deserved.

As a song depicting the Regiment has it, "A tank corps crew, way up the blue, a wearing o' the green…" That was me, back up in the desert, with green flashes on my tunic. How wonderful it was to be home. I joined the light squadron, sitting in the desert with no tanks. What were left after the latest skirmish had been passed on to some other poor sods.

Settling down amongst old acquaintances in my new status as a commissioned officer was much easier than I had anticipated; my uncertainty of what may be expected of me in my relationship with those I had worked with in the past was quickly dispelled by my welcome home. Very old friends, what few there were left, were absolutely marvellous; they smoothed the path for me and I had no embarrassing situations. We were all trained soldiers and acted accordingly.

The order to move came late in the afternoon; we had a feeling all day that something was brewing and a lot of our gear was already packed. A fleet of lorries arrived and moved us back down the line to another assembly area. We were not going back to Cairo, as some of the wishful thinkers had voiced, there was a whole Regiment of tanks just waiting for us to climb aboard and head back up the desert. We worked throughout the night, checking the tanks, cleaning the guns, stowing ammo and getting everything ship-shape, just the way we wanted it. After all, it was our heads that would be on the block.

I have a vague memory of some old armoured cars that we inherited with the rest of the gear which, during the night, had the turrets removed, cut up and the plates welded onto the front and sides. They looked very low on the ground without a turret and the thought of standing in that thing, with most of one's body out in the open, sent a cold shiver down my back. Initially, I was to be involved with these, but thankfully that order was changed and I took command of a tank troop.

We moved off at dawn, ready to do battle. What a fantastic example of military organisation that was. We were very proud of our achievement and it was all done in the dark. However, with a change of equipment and many replacement tank crews, the order was to start retraining for the battles yet to come. Rommel had dug in further along the coast at Medenine and he would have to be removed if we were to link up with the 1st Army, which was driving east from Algeria.

Our training was interrupted to rejoin the 8th Armoured Brigade and move forward to confront Rommel; he had launched a sudden attack in an attempt to drive us back east again. We held our ground and the enemy was driven back once again, with heavy losses of tanks and infantry. It was rather a shock to discover that a number of his tanks destroyed were Shermans, apparently captured from the Americans in their defeat at the Kasserine pass in Algeria. He retired and set up shop again behind heavily fortified defences at Mareth, so, with a heavy heart, we knew it would all have to be done again.

Monty decided that another Alamein-style attack would have to be carried out and, at the same time, send another force around his right flank to attack his rear. We came under the command of the New Zealanders and set off on this 150-mile trek, deep into the desert, with the tanks mounted on transporters to preserve the efficiency of our vehicles. It was one hell of a journey, travelling mostly by night, with swirling dust over very rough terrain. Eventually it became too much for our transporters; we unloaded and moved on our tracks to an assembly area near an old Roman wall west of Gabes, to the north of Mareth on the main road.

We moved forward to reconnoitre the defensive position he had set up in the mountains northwest of the Mareth line and decided it was a formidable obstruction. I know we had done it all before, but after such a long, tiring campaign of confrontation and survival, there was little stomach left for what was to come. To reach our objective on the coast and cut off the Mareth line we would have to drive along a valley, with hills either side that appeared to be bristling with tanks and anti-tank guns in prepared positions. We would have to drive through infantry dug in on the valley floor and no doubt supported by artillery and other guns. There could be only one answer; a repeat of the charge of the Light Brigade, and that is exactly what we were ordered to do.

Preparations were carried out in an area out of sight of the enemy, with tanks and other vehicles formed up in line abreast, just like cavalry. In my tank, we primed a box of hand-grenades to supplement our machine guns, which were of little use once amongst the infantry, and behind the turret sat four NZ infantrymen. Our orders were to stop for nothing; that was, of course, if the tank could still move with the tracks still on and not burning fiercely. As I briefed the troop on the part we were to play, I hoped they failed to detect the tremor of fear in my voice.

As we came out into the open and moved forward in line it was my first real look at the battlefield. The hills on the left looked hazy and threatening, but to my right, the spectacle of a mass of our tanks stretching to the far hills gave my sagging morale a welcome boost. In front of me, a cloud of dust created by our movement and mixed with the smoke and dust of shellfire, was blown ahead of us towards the enemy positions and for the first few hundred yards they seemed unaware of our presence.

I waited for the torrent of welcoming shellfire, but it did not arrive. With the dust in his face and the sun in his eyes, the enemy was caught with his trousers down. My relief was short-lived, however, as the guns on the hills, with an unrestricted view, opened up with everything they had and everyone else joined in. God, how I wished it was all a dream.

For the first time in memory, cooperation with the Air Force was superb, with radio controllers on the ground directing aircraft onto targets. They came in droves, low over my head, flight after flight of bombers, tankbusters and fighters, bombing and strafing the enemy tanks, guns and infantry. The worrying thought did cross my mind as to the tankbuster crews' knowledge of tank recognition. Recent stories had been circulating that some tankbusters had knocked out friendly vehicles; just a rumour, I hoped...

For the enemy, it was already too late, we were in amongst his infantry. The New Zealanders dropped off the back and I was tossing out hand grenades as fast as pins could be pulled. It was all happening so fast; the gunner, with freedom to find his own targets, was ripping off five hundred rounds a minute, as fast as boxes of ammo could be replaced. The situation came close to panic, but fear played no part, it was buried under a continuous string of events that demanded immediate attention: guiding the driver through obstacles, searching for suitable targets, watching incoming shellfire, controlling the troop and reporting information. A continuous stream of voices was buzzing in my ears and yet, amidst that constant dialogue, my brain selected messages specifically directed at me.

Even with my ears covered by earphones the noise and clamour of gunfire was deafening but the impact of shells on the hull indicated that someone was picking on us, but so far we were still moving and nothing had entered the turret. A nagging thought kept telling me that with every yard we advanced the more exposed we would be to enemy anti-tank guns on the hills to our left. I hoped and prayed someone else was taking care of them.

The order to halt and take up hull-down positions was quite a surprise. Apparently, we had reached our target and yet in all the excitement we did not appear to have travelled very far. I looked behind to survey the battlefield; a cloud of dust covered the area and was moving towards us, it was created by columns of tanks, which passed through our lines. Another Armoured Brigade had taken over and, with a feeling of relief, we watched them disappear into the dust smoke and shellfire. I wished them the best of British.

As the battle moved up the valley we remained on the ridge in open formation, still part of the action, but in reserve and keeping a wary eye on those hills; there was still a lot of activity going on up there. With the light fading fast and our advance threatening to cut off his forces at Mareth, Rommel's position was sufficiently grave to warrant a counter-attack. We sat in the dark and watched and listened throughout the night. We took it in turns to mount guard and snatch a few hours sleep, God how tired we all were. During my spell on duty I had to frequently get off, walk around, and get back on again, just to avoid falling asleep in the turret.

In the early morning light we surveyed the outside of our chariot for damage. It was a depressing sight. The poor girl had taken quite a bashing, with deep gouge marks in the front of the hull and turret. One particular mark made me shudder, it was on the corner of the hull and must have come from a gun on the left; just a fraction to the right and that gunner would have burned us up. What was left of our gear behind the turret was in tatters but, fortunately, we had no need of it in the night and now, thank God, we had the bonus of another day.

Ahead of us, up the valley, the battle was still raging and around and behind us the sickening devastation of the battlefield stood out clearly in the sunshine. There were bodies everywhere, mostly the enemy, but too many of our New Zealanders lay amongst them. The Brigade had lost many tanks, but the enemy did not escape unscathed, the battlefield was littered with his burned-out vehicles, smashed guns and long columns of prisoners were winding away towards the east. We had won another of Monty's left-hook victories; the frontal attack at Mareth had failed to break through, and the price we paid lay rotting in the desert.

For myself, I had long since ceased to absorb in detail the death and destruction of this bloody war. In the early days, the memories of names struck off the list lingered for a while, but as the casualties mounted and the lists lengthened, the memory faded. It was not a lack of feeling for my fellow man, but the tragic loss of so many close friends brought with it the revelation that, with each one, the chances of my own survival must be getting less. The acceptance of this fact brought added caution, feeding on all the skills and lessons learned from near disasters, as a desperate means of survival. Even to this day, my first thought in the morning is: 'I am still here. Good. I have another day.'

Rommel and what remained of his Army continued to withdraw in a series of rearguard actions up the coast towards Tunis. He was called back to Germany and General Messe appointed in his place. Finally the great army that had supported the legend of the indestructible Rommel, was defeated south of Tunis, in an attack by the combined forces of the 1st and 8th Armies. After the battle to cut off his forces at Mareth, I have only faint recollections of involvement in the skirmishes that followed. However, it took many days for the truth to sink in, incredible as it seemed, the war in Africa was really over.

In October 1942 we had launched an attack at El Alamein to destroy the Axis armies here at the gateway to Cairo. It took seven months battling across 2,000 miles of desert to finish the job. Many hours were spent reliving events since our arrival in Egypt; had I gone through all that and survived – or was it just a bad dream? A search amongst the debris of men that remained, for familiar faces, confirmed it was no dream. Of my close friends in pre-war days there were none and of the regulars I had served with, a mere handful remained. We talked and laughed at the jokes, antics and happy times we had shared with those no longer here; there were no tears. Deep inside, they were still with us.

~ CHAPTER 27 ~

A Welcome Respite

O N A BEACH OF BEAUTIFUL golden sands, edged by a
turquoise blue sea, glittering in the warm sunshine,
we pitched our tents and started to unwind. Lorries
went to Tunis with all the money we could spare and returned
with casks of the finest Tunisian wine. Well, that was what we
believed but even if it had been rough, unfermented plonk, it
still played a key role in our recipe for recovery. We had one big
ball of a party; our Officers Mess, built with whatever we could
find and shaded with palm leaves, was practically wrecked on
the night of its christening.

However, we were not left to our own devices for long; the
Army demanded that we keep fit and were ready for whatever
devilish plan they had in mind. First order of the day was PT or
a long swim, which I preferred, it being the easy option; just
fall out of bed, drop my briefs on the sand, stagger thirty yards
to the water and stagger back to bed without opening my eyes.
Sleeping was not so easy with the sand for a bed and land crabs,
working twenty-four hour shifts, digging tunnels beneath you,
but the Tunisian plonk played a very important part as a substitute for sleeping pills. Many other mental and physical tasks
occupied our day, but we were old soldiers and took it all in our
stride.

Eventually, without tanks and with very few transports, movement out of the area was very limited, but we did have a water
truck. With Willy Macfarlane at the wheel and three of us sitting
each side, with feet dangling, a mad dash to Tripoli was a hair-

raising experience. At the Del Mahari Hotel, we took it in turns to occupy a room booked exclusively for our squadron. How wonderful it was to sleep on a bed.

There was one unregistered form of transport available, a German Army BMW motorbike and sidecar; with Willy riding the bike and me perched in the sidecar, holding on for dear life, a circuit of the Tripoli Grand Prix racetrack was a most traumatic experience. The concrete track, neglected for years, was badly broken up and relegated the drive to a cross between the Isle of Man and scrambling; that mad Scot simply revelled in it.

Again on the move, a few weeks later, we were back in Cairo at that old camp behind the Pyramids, Beni Yusef. It brought back many memories of the good times in Cairo, but also a worrying thought, 'where the hell are we off to this time?' After all, this had been the jumping-off-point for many of our bloodiest experiences. However, on our doorstep was the nightlife of Cairo and we were not about to kick a gift horse in the mouth.

My God, how it had changed. I had forgotten that the American Army was now in residence and with all the money they had to flash around, we were relegated to second-class citizens; the poor bloody British Army. That drawling American accent dominated the bars and nightclubs and a favourite evening entertainment of just walking around the street of brothels, admiring the scenery, had gone forever. The brothels, which had been part of the character of that city for so many years, were closed. They were an arrogant lot, those American servicemen, probably embarrassed at the presence of so many old diehards whilst they had never seen a shot fired in anger. We just ignored them.

Opera Square looked just the same, the Continental Hotel on one side, with its wide marble staircase leading up to the entrance, miniature palms on a tabled terrace and wide glass doors leading into the foyer. On the pavement outside, numerous beggars were looking for a soft-touch like me, to follow upstairs into the foyer wailing *"ana muskien, mafi flous"* (I am very poor, I have no money), knowing that, feeling embarrassed, I would give them money to get rid of them. The doormen, in their smart uniforms and the police outside did nothing to deter this blatant blackmail. I wonder what their cut was?

On the other side of the square stood the Opera House night-club, scene of many a rabble-rousing night. We kept out of trouble by occupying a balcony box for six, above a wing of the stage, looking down upon tables laden with food and wine and populated by fat, gorging men with their teenage entertainers. Our table groaned under the more simple necessities of life – beer and a large bowl of peanuts and, with the addition of an elastic band we were ready for our evening's entertainment. (It must be said we were not envious of the ground floor clientele with their rich food and young birds – just seething with sickening jealousy).

Belly dancers and other entertainers, with their wailing form of music, made frequent appearances on the stage and performed their style of floorshow. Different, unusual, sometimes very slow and boring, but with the assistance of an elastic band and peanuts we put new life into their activities. The management were not very impressed, but the girls seemed to enjoy our appreciation of their acts. That was more than could be said for the ground floor hogs, who ignored the show in preference to flirting with the teenagers. It was disgusting and, acting as honest judges of morality, we curtailed their activities of a wandering hand sliding up a naked leg with a well-aimed peanut on the back of a fat neck. I know, bloody spoilsports!

In contrast to our previous visits to Beni Yusef the atmosphere this time was very different. With no tanks or other equipment to maintain, life reverted to a mild form of Army barrack routine and, for the first time, I had to carry out the Regimental form of Orderly Officer of the day. Mounting the guard, censoring mail (that was a dreadful task, reading private letters and cutting out military information), which, if you were lucky, took just a couple of hours. Attending the men's dining room at meal times, along with the Orderly Sergeant, calling for any complaints, was the most frightening ordeal for me. Having served in the ranks with many of these men, I knew they would do their best to make it difficult for me, if just for a giggle, and the Orderly Sergeant, a very old friend of mine, confirmed my worst fears.

It was breakfast time and we walked into the dining room where the sergeant called "any complaints?". I knew all the old moaners and sure enough one of them stuck his hand in the air and said 'the food was not fit for human beings'. I asked him to move over, sat down, and very slowly and deliberately, commenting on every morsel, ate every crumb of his breakfast and drank his tea. By the time I had finished the food had been cleared from the counter and he had to dash off to get on parade; he had no breakfast that morning and I had no more complaints. We all had a good giggle about it.

The gift shops in Cairo were well stocked and most of us took the opportunity, based purely on wishful thinking, that now was the time to buy presents for our loved-ones at home. Some bought jewellery for wives, mothers and girlfriends, hoping, in the case of the latter, that they would still be waiting, and toys for children who, in some cases, the fathers had never seen and knew only from a tattered photograph, frequently studied with warmth and pride. At this time, many of the men's thoughts turned to home, family and their dreams for the future; I read much of it in their letters and frequently offered a silent prayer that their aspirations would become a reality. However, as 'request hour officer' (when an officer was on duty and any soldier could discuss his problems off the record) I heard of a number of the dreaded 'Dear John' letters, which dealt a devastating blow to many who had already suffered so much.

Letters from home, our only real link with the past, so far away, infrequent as they were, sometimes months old, were pounced upon and reread a dozen times over. Unlike the fantasies written in the national press, letters represented reality, from the antics of the children to Aunt Gertie's ulcers, written in a familiar style and words which, for just a moment, brought that other world so much closer.

CHAPTER 28

GOODBYE NORTH AFRICA

"As the sun sinks slowly in the west we say farewell
To this wonderful panorama of ancient Egypt,
Land of the Pyramids and the sun;
The wog's paradise, the soldiers hell,
Land of bastards fare ye well..."

A VOICE ON THE ship's Tannoy, loud and clear, said it for us all in the language of the day. We sailed from Alexandria in a troopship named the *New Holland*, destination unknown, but with a prayer in everyone's mind that we would be going HOME. For years this word had been just a dream but now, with the war in Africa over, it could be for real. In the desert, we knew that it was simply wishful thinking, but that did not stop frequent rumours circulating among the men and causing unrest. As an RSM I had to keep my ear to the ground and stifle these stories before they got out of hand. On many occasions the Adjutant would ask,

"What is the latest rumour?"

My answer was usually, "Home on the first, Sir."

"On the first of what?"

"On the first bloody opportunity Sir."

That pretty much said it all.

On board ship, a contingent of about eighty nurses occupied an area of deck cabins; a most welcome indication that gave credence to the rumours that we were going home. How comfortable they were in their cabins was difficult to assess; a twenty-four hour guard was placed on their quarters, supposedly to keep the troops out. But the problem, in fact, was keeping the girls in. With hundreds of troops and just a few girls in such a confined space it was a difficult situation. After just a few days at sea an order was given: 'Double rugging on the upper decks will cease forthwith.' Very difficult for the Orderly Officer to enforce on a ship blacked out against air raids.

Our accommodation as junior officers was on a par with the other ranks, although in some ways they were better off, with hammocks swung in a large open area below deck. We were eight in a cabin, with just sufficient space to squeeze between four double bunks. It was not simply a question of whose turn is it to move, but whose turn to breathe and because no portholes could be opened due to submarine activity, it was worse than in a tank with the hatches battened down. Of course, there is usually some form of bonus and we had one; an officer who used a sickly sweet smelling anti-perspirant. His presence was a blessing; that sweet smell dampened the stench of body odour and sweaty feet.

Two of our residents were dedicated classical music lovers and had an old wind-up gramophone, a worn needle and six played-to-death records. I have always enjoyed the classics, but how about the 'Emperor' six times a day, screeching through the octaves like someone treading on a ferret's tail, followed by a post-mortem on the quality of presentation? Sadly, after days of mental saturation, it got broken. Someone accidentally put their foot on it getting out of bed. What a shame.

The food was definitely an improvement on tank rations, but sadly it was a dry ship – no alcohol in any form. However, there was a stimulant of sorts, we could have a chat with the opposite sex during dinner or in the lounge, but for me, a man of twenty four, most of them were a little too old. Like us, they had played their part in the desert war and earned the gratitude of many a wounded soldier, but some had been in the sun just a little too long and it showed. Mind you, they probably thought the same about me. These nurses were members of the Queen Anne's Imperial Military Nursing Service (QAIMNS). Some joker suggested that the letters stood for 'Queer And Impossible, Mostly Not Sane'.

Sailing through the Mediterranean in the warm sunshine, undisturbed by the enemy, was a tonic; sitting on deck with eyes closed, the warm sun caressing your skin and the gentle rhythm of water lapping the hull was just the right medicine for a return to sanity. It was a dream world and we soaked up every beautiful moment. But, alas, no heaven on earth for us for long. A Mountain appeared in the morning sun, sitting in the middle of the ocean, getting larger and more menacing as we sailed towards it. A pall of smoke hanging over its peak gave us a clue. It was Mount Etna. Now all was revealed; we were sailing to Sicily.

What the hell were we going there for? The island had already been captured by British and American Armies and landings on the mainland must be well in hand. Surely they had no need of a bunch of battered old desert rats like us? Speculation was rife and morale sagged a little as the convoy sailed past a minesweeper that had opened the entrance boom and we entered the harbour of Port Augustus. A number of wrecks lay around, probably the result of RAF activity, but the remains of a couple of our landing craft, lying on the seashore, indicated that the landings had been no picnic.

The memory of that minesweeper suddenly jolted me back to reality. My brother was captain of one of those. I dashed around find a pair of binoculars and searched for the number on its side. Yes, there it was, HMT *Karerra* T.200. What a stroke of luck! I had searched for that ship at every port I had visited; it was more than three years since we had last met and now, quite suddenly, there he was. I eventually found the adjutant, who took me to the ship's officer on duty and obtained permission for the signalman to send a message to T.200. All this took time. Standing on the bridge, we searched the harbour in the fading light, but it was too late, the ship had gone. Messages between the ship and Naval Control confirmed that he had been ordered up the coast on some other task. So near and yet so far.

The rumour was we would sail next day so it was up with the sun for a run round the deck and a last look at Sicily. Ignoring the Naval and Military presence, I scanned the gentle hills, covered in neat rows of fruit trees and vines. It looked a lovely, peaceful island now that the war had left it behind. Just a final look at the harbour, then breakfast; it looked peaceful enough, but suddenly my heart missed a beat. There, lying at anchor just a few hundred yards away, was the T.200. What a wonderful surprise. Breakfast was forgotten in a mad rush to get that signal sent again.

About an hour later, a rowing boat with a single occupant approached the ship's gangway and an untidy-looking seaman in baggy blue trousers, fisherman's jersey and peaked cap staggered up the steps with a mailbag on his back. The ship's officer of the day, an immaculate example of the Senior Service, responsible for the security of our ship, at first barred this unsavoury-looking character from stepping on deck. An explanation that he was, in fact, the captain of the battered minesweeper across the bay, resulted in salutes and embarrassed apologies.

Having said our hello's I dragged him off to a secluded spot, anxious to discover if that mailbag was full of loot or just his dirty laundry (and that would not have surprised me, knowing him). But it was definitely loot: a bottle of whisky, brandy, half a dozen bottles of beer and about five hundred good quality cigarettes. I had my doubts about where all that stuff had come from. He explained that having to clear the mines ahead of Landing Craft they were first on the scene and thus the first free to search for whatever needed to be 'liberated'. He must have done a lot of liberating, bless him!

The sun and providence continued to shine on us and throughout the remaining days of our journey to Britain we saw nothing of Hitler's air force or submarines, thank God. The inner glow provided by our small oasis of alcohol on board this driest of ships, added the final ingredient to a recipe for contentment. Even in the Atlantic we carried the warm sunshine with us almost to the coast of Ireland, where our khaki drill was finally exchanged for normal uniform.

We sailed up the Clyde in the early morning mist, standing on deck in our heavy winter clothes, shivering with cold, or was it apprehension?

We waited patiently for daylight to brighten the shoreline and show us the land we had fought so hard for and prayed so hard to return to. As the light dawned, white, frost-covered roofs appeared through gaps in the mist and straight rows of drab-looking houses lined the long, dark streets.

It was three years since we had sailed from Liverpool and this was not exactly a warm, welcoming scene, but we didn't care.

This was our land and we were home.

~ CHAPTER 29 ~

HOME ON LEAVE

W E DISEMBARKED, CARRYING OUR LIGHT equipment, into railway coaches waiting on the quayside. Our heavy baggage was to follow by goods train to a destination as yet unknown. It was a long, cold journey, travelling south throughout the night, across England to a camp in the vicinity of that famous racing town, Newmarket. Not very impressive on a cold, frosty, foggy morning, but a comfortable solid bed with room to spread your gear around was heaven compared to that cramped, stuffy cabin. It took a couple of days to settle in and become familiar, once again, with habits long forgotten. Just to walk into a bar and order a pint of cool, refreshing beer was almost an adventure, but foremost in the minds of all was that urgent need, the ultimate in pleasure: Home Leave.

The thought of leave brought back the memory of those last few days in Cairo, when many of the troops, believing or just hoping they were going home, bought and showed off presents for those they had left behind; perhaps jewellery for a wife or girlfriend or toys for children many had never seen, yet boasted of proudly. Such thoughts turned to dismay and anger when the goods train with our heavy gear arrived at Newmarket and a working party was detailed to unload it. The doors rolled open and a shambles was revealed. It was a sad shattering blow; many of the kitbags and cases had been ripped open and presents and souvenirs for friends and families had been stolen. Never have I seen so many men with murder in their eyes! What sort of animal would steal from these proud soldiers, who had suffered so much and given the best years of their lives, depriving them of a smile on the face of a child or a hug of pleasure from a loved one? As one soldier put it, "may the lousy bastards rot in hell!" I recalled moving the cargo on that tank ship and finding all those empty boxes, prompting me to add my own lifetime curse on all thieving dockers.

Whilst waiting for our turn to go on leave, the nightlife of Newmarket was worth investigating, with one pub in particular being worthy of our custom. On our first visit, a few of us stood at one end of the bar and Bennett, a dapper little officer with a frightful accent, stood at the other end, chatting up a bird. It was just a joke to start with, but turned out to be a very useful ploy. We ordered a round of drinks and quite casually added, "and give Lord Chumley up there a beer". The Publican's eyes popped out of his head and he served his Lordship first. From that day on, we could drink in that pub for hours after it had closed and 'Lord Chumley' carried on with his act. Of course, it cost us a bomb, because his Lordship threatened to blow the gaff unless we continued to buy his beer. And I thought he was a mate of ours.

At last, it was my turn for leave, but that journey through the night to the north of Scotland was a nightmare. Still hardly daring to believe it was for real and not just a dream, the night was spent counting the miles and checking every station. I kept awake, fearful that the train may miss my destination, even though I knew that the train started in London and terminated at Aberdeen. Although I had arrived here on numerous occasions in the past, it was never like this. I could barely read the name on the platform board through the tears in my eyes.

It had just passed 7am and the Services Canteen, run by the WVS, was open. I was ready for breakfast: egg, bacon, sausages, fried bread, beans, a couple of butteries and a mug of tea, all for one shilling and ninepence. I knew then I was back in Aberdeen. Waiting for the train to Fraserburgh, just 45 miles away, I almost chewed my nails to the knuckles, but that last couple of miles of the journey home was worth every agonizing moment I had suffered.

The large mounds of sand dunes with tall, waving grasses, appearing and fading between the hills on the golf course, obstructed my view of the beach, but in my mind I could hear the waves breaking on the seashore, drowning the call of the seagulls, and see the water rushing up the sands. At the end of the dunes came the promenade, with its café and changing rooms, then the rocks, stretching round to the harbour breakwater with its eighty-foot lighthouse standing proud at the end. Looking back, a five-mile beach of golden sands formed a crescent around the bay, enclosed in towering dunes, cloaked in a mantle of welcoming waving grass, shining green against the gold of the sand. The old church spire stood out against the skyline, the seagulls screeched as they flew above the harbour and the tang of seaweed hung in the air. now I knew I was home.

I walked slowly through the town, excited at being here and anxious to confirm the memories of how it had been, but in my mile-and-a-half wander through the streets, every turning brought a fresh twinge of sadness. The lighthouse, a prominent and necessary beacon, had guided enemy bombers onto their target. Many buildings had disappeared and only heaps of rubble remained as silent memorials. It was unbelievable. I had never imagined that a small fishing town insignificantly placed in a northeast corner of Scotland could be a target for enemy bombers, and yet I was to learn that there had been eighteen air raids, seven hundred buildings destroyed, forty people had died and many more injured.

I felt guilty at the envious thoughts I had conjured up on numerous occasions in the desert, of friends and relatives living a quiet, peaceful life at home whilst I went through hell. Excitement mounted as I turned into the street where we lived, but I stopped and gasped, trying not to believe what I could see. A string of bombs had straddled the street and the house across from ours had gone.

I hurried indoors to the warmth and sheltering arms of my family and the war outside ceased to exist.

How wonderful to be back. Just to wander aimlessly along the seashore, looking for the seals on the rocks, to stop at the Scorgie and remember the past when, as a boy, I would sit for hours on those rocks with my hook, line and sinker, catching fish. Further along the coast path was Kinnaird lighthouse, with its massive foghorn, bringing back the memory of swimming in a pool below, when one almighty blast frightened me to death and sent us scurrying up the braes. The harbour, with its five basins, appeared much larger than I remembered, but my memory went back to the days when it was full of ships. Today it was comparatively empty. That five miles of long sandy beach was still there, just as it must have been for the past century, washed twice each day by the tide, giving it a clean new face.

I stood still, leaning on the promenade railing, and slowly scanned this beautiful bay to the distant beacon at Cairnbulg. This was my heaven on earth. A cold breeze blew off the sea into my face but I was almost unaware of it. White horses rode the waves and died into froth as the water rushed up the sands. The birds on the shore followed the motion, running up the sand as if afraid of getting their feet wet, then following the water back, searching for any food the sea had brought in.

As I walked towards the water's edge, the seagulls rose and swirled in a noisy cloud and waders feeding in the shallows hurried along ahead of me, complaining at my invasion of their privacy. This was their sea, that mighty provider for all. The line of debris left by the receding tide turned my casual stroll into a search for treasures from the deep and within minutes I had once again become a fanatical beachcomber. Lost in the excitement of the search, my aching legs finally urged restraint; I was unaware of the wandering miles I had covered and the sun was setting. Weary, but happy and contented, I headed for home.

Despite my fond memories of the past and the fact that the town looked the same, apart from a few scars, I felt almost a stranger. My old friends were not around any more, most had joined the forces, many were fishing from ports around the coast, and the whole area was overrun by soldiers from a Polish Division. Here, in this small community in the far north of Scotland, the winds of change were blowing and I felt it would never be the same again. Once again, although very happy and contented with my family, I found myself yearning for my other home, the Regiment, but my leave was not yet over and my girlfriend at Kettering in the Midlands was demanding my presence. We had met briefly, before my homage north to God's country, but to realise the dreams we had created in words on paper over a period of three years would take a lot of time and patience. The war was not yet over and I had no illusions that the worst was yet to come. I felt it would be unfair to commit myself to anyone with my chances of survival being so slim.

The streets and buildings of the country town of Kettering, Northants were just as I remembered, but here again the winds of change had touched the people and altered their way of life. American servicemen now crowded the footpaths and their military vehicles roared through the streets, but they were welcomed and tolerated by the local people as allies in our fight against Hitler and also, of course, as the bearers of goodwill and lots of lovely money. They had cigarettes for Papa, chocolate for the children and God knows what for Mama!

My girlfriend was now a corporal in the WAAF, stationed at a base nearby and living a regimented lifestyle in barracks. We were determined to make the rest of my leave an event to remember and visit all the places with fond memories of our past. In an attempt to get her some leave, I visited her base for an interview with her commander. It was lunchtime and I wandered through empty offices without being challenged by the many staff wandering around the base. I was disgusted at the lack of discipline and security; here I was, an Army officer in khaki uniform, wearing a black beret, and no one appeared to notice. I waited in the CO's office until she returned and pointed out this dangerous lack of security; needless to say, I had no problem in obtaining seven days compassionate leave for Corporal Robinson.

Our first night out on the town was almost a disaster. Our favourite bar was packed with Yanks, perhaps a little drunk, but certainly loudmouthed and arrogant. We sat quietly at a table, drinking and chatting, but it was obviously not our night; our table was repeatedly nudged by everyone who passed, deliberately spilling our drinks to prompt a reaction. My girlfriend was very frightened and frankly so was I; there was only me and about thirty of them and it was obvious we were not welcome in 'their' bar. Everywhere we visited was just the same, although we did manage a dance, of sorts, in a hotel ballroom, but even that was limited by the flying legs of the jitterbuggers.

Despite its shortcomings, I did enjoy that leave and added a stone to my weight. There was no doubt that it was wonderful to be back in this land of ours, even if it would never be the same again.

~ CHAPTER 30 ~

HOSPITALISED FOR D-DAY

A T LONG LAST FITTED OUT with new tanks and equipment and brought up to strength with a large number of replacements, we were on the move again, this time north to the seaside town of Bridlington. The replacements were quite a joke, but not a funny one; due to some directive issued prior to our departure from Egypt, we had left behind a large number of our experienced crews and now required new ones. Officers, NCOs and men came to us from all kinds of depots and regiments, but many brought problems with them. It was immediately obvious when scanning the records of some of these men, that their former units had jumped at the opportunity to weed out a number of their less desirable characters.

In our squadron, the major commanding, a captain 2IC and myself were, to the best of my knowledge, the only original officers; the remaining five were all new and inexperienced. We all sat in on the task of interviewing, assessing and placing the new intake into the different tank troops, according to their skills and past record, and for me it was a disastrous day. I finished up with twenty of the worst; all those with difficulties in training who had scorned discipline or done time in the Glasshouse were allocated to me. Once again, as often in the past, I got the dirty end of the stick, this time with the comment: 'Being an old hand, Jock, you are better able to handle that bolshie shower!' That, however, was a gross overstatement. I was sick of war and weary of ordering people about, but there was no alternative and so we knuckled down to the task of training and preparing our tanks for whatever the powers-that-be had in store for us.

Bridlington is a lovely peaceful seaside town, set in a bay of golden sand and edged by a long promenade. The Yacht Club, at one end, with a long glass frontage, provided the members with a panoramic view of the sea and midway the tall structure of the Spa Ballroom stood out against the sky. Although, at times, the northeast winds blew cold and wet, the fresh tang of the sea was a welcome change and certainly healthier than the damp, foggy atmosphere of the Newmarket wetlands.

Our tanks were parked under trees in a residential part of the town and the crews billeted in houses and other empty buildings. We, the squadron's officers, occupied half of a large four-storey building just a few yards from the Promenade; the other half was occupied by a group of WAAFS. Very nice too, you may think, and those were exactly my thoughts when I heard the news, but next morning when I pulled the curtains and looked down upon the back garden my dreams of the good life were shattered; there, hanging on the clothes-line next door, was a long row of 'passion killers' – RAF-issue, long-legged, blue bloomers. From that moment on the sight of a WAAF in uniform, with the exception of my girlfriend in Kettering, of course, prompted the shuddering thought of days gone by, when parents locked their daughters up in chastity belts.

Life in that town was pleasant and peaceful and the local residents treated us with warmth and affection, ever ready with tea, coffee and cake, when we were working on our tanks. They even assisted in arranging a Regimental Dance in the Spa Ball-room and, although restricted by food rationing, supplied much of the buffet consumed that night. I was involved, with others, in organising this event and spent much of my free time scour-ing the local farms for black-market food, although, sadly, I did not get to taste the fruits of my labours; on the night of the Dance I was under orders to attend another event.

A number of all ranks in the Regiment received a Royal Summons to attend an investiture at the Palace and unfortunately the dates clashed. It was a most memorable experience, waiting in a long line, in order of merit, to walk up to the rostrum, shake hands with the King, who uttered words of congratulation, then rejoin friends and relatives, who were invited to be present. My Father had travelled from the north of Scotland, at the expense of the Army, to witness the event; he looked proud and excited, wearing his World War 1 medals as if he had just been presented with them. The event was followed by a fantastic celebration that went on well into the night. I remember my father had more than his share and was not so bright next morning; a few of the party made a proper meal of it and went absent for a couple of days.

Back at the Regiment, life returned to normal, stores and supplies for the tanks arrived almost daily and the task of issuing and recording occupied much of the day. An order for all officers to meet the brigadier at our HQ on the promenade disrupted the daily routine and I hurried along the seafront with a load of problems on my mind. A voice from behind called "Stop." I turned and saw a staff car at the kerb and a captain running towards me; it was the Brigadier's Aide.

"Why did you not salute the Brigadier?" he demanded.

"Because I never saw him," was my answer.

Apparently, he had driven past me and thought he was being ignored.

Later in the HQ, he gave us a talk about our role in the war. It was not very impressive, but he did end with one interesting comment: "An officer who fails to see his Brigadier at ten yards could not hope to see an enemy tank at five hundred."

What a pathetic statement that was! I could have answered that a commander who was unaware of the experience of his officers and failed to recognise the significance of the medals they wore, should question his own ability. I was furious, but gulped down my pride and, like a good soldier, said nothing. In later years, reading the memoirs of our Divisional Commander, Pip Roberts, I believe that brigadier was the first to be kicked out.

Sadly, our holiday by the sea was short-lived. Soon we were to pack up, load the tanks on a train and travel south once again, this time to the barracks at Aldershot. This was indeed a change for us, located reasonably near to the nightlife of London, where the bombardment by enemy aircraft had faded considerably. But, for me, the good times would have to wait, because I, along with an old pre-war mate, Sergeant Buck Kite, was dispatched to the Gunnery School at Lulworth, to learn and become familiar with a new gun, the 17-pounder. This gun had appeared briefly as an anti-tank weapon used by the Guards Brigade, towards the end of the Desert campaign, as an answer to the German 88; at long last someone had got the message that we desperately needed a bigger gun in our tanks.

Returning to the ranges at Lulworth was like turning the clock back. This was where I had spent six weeks during my early days of training, learning about guns and how to use them. Back then, what spare time we had, and there was not much of it, had been spent by the beach at Lulworth Cove, especially on a Sunday, when the paddle-steamer from Weymouth would arrive with a boatload of visitors, including lots of lovely girls for us to chat up. But now there were no steamers and very few visitors. Of course, there were plenty of ATS girls, I even had one as a batman, but for me that one was off limits.

The familiar pub at the bottom of the hill was unchanged, packed to the door, as usual, with recruits but they recognised

Buck and I as old hands and respectfully allowed us to the bar for a drink. We, in return, allowed them to buy all the drinks for the girls before offering to escort them home, just to ensure they were not molested on the way. We did enjoy our stay, because much of the course was familiar ground to us and full use was made of our free time. At the end of the week they even threw in a concert in the NAAFI for good measure; Sergeant Arthur English, a gunnery instructor, was one of the entertainers and very good he was too.

At Aldershot I was given a troop of four modified 'Firefly' Shermans with 17-pounders mounted in the turret, that was the Regiments entire allowance. Assisted by one of my troop sergeants, Jim Caswell, who had just completed a waterproofing course, and our motley crew, we got down to the task of water-proofing, in preparation for the invasion of Europe. Within a week my opinion of them changed; they were not easy to handle but they worked very hard and were proud of their achievement. Mind you, if I stopped working, they stopped; I had to wear overalls when all other troop officers wore battledress. Bribery was one of my weapons; if they worked the programme ahead of schedule, we could spend an afternoon driving around the countryside, map-reading. On occasions I carried a bundle of blank passes and dropped the men off in a nearby town with strict instructions to be back by midnight 'or else'. Not one of them ever let me down. I must, on their behalf, point out that they completed the work exactly one week ahead of any other troop in the Regiment.

I must have made some sort of impression on them, but they never really showed any feelings one way or another, that is until the night of a regimental all-ranks dance. I was standing at the bar, having a beer and a friendly argument with a very good friend of mine, another Scot, and nearby, also having a beer, were two of my troop. My friend went off to the toilet and

I took the opportunity to ask the two troopers if they were waiting for me to buy them another drink.

"Certainly not," they said. "We are here to ensure that you don't get hurt if that Scotsman turns nasty."

Bless them, they were looking after me, and I didn't think they cared. Then again, perhaps they were just looking for an excuse to have a fight.

I prefer to think they cared about me.

With the waterproofing completed, we settled down to a daily routine of engine, gun and general maintenance, just waiting for the day when all this work would prove to have been worthwhile. For a number of days, I had been suffering from what I thought to be too much nightlife, a combination of headaches and sickness. I had arranged for my girlfriend to come down for the weekend, but on the day of her arrival I felt unfit to travel and arranged for someone else to escort her from St Pancras. Who better than my devoted batman? He did an excellent job, protecting her every inch of the way.

Within a week, my health had deteriorated to such an extent that I was unable to lift myself out of the tank turret. My other troop sergeant, Sgt Sumpter, insisted that I must see the Doc and escorted me to the surgery. Doc took one look at me and pronounced jaundice; apparently he had noticed in the mess that I was not eating and already knew I had that problem. When I asked why he did not tell me sooner he just laughed and said, "If you choose to walk around feeling sick all the time, that's your problem!" Such a generous soul, our Doc Macmillan!

An hour later I was tucked up in bed in Aldershot Military Hospital, being denied any fatty food and milk products, gulping down doses of capsules and looking as yellow as a daffodil. The worst thing about the treatment was the boiled fish diet, especially on a Monday morning, when the nurse could just whistle and the smell would carry it down the ward by itself.

Just a few days later the nurses and other staff started rushing around, moving patients out to other wards or unknown destinations, cramming more empty beds into the ward and generally creating an air of mystery and uneasiness. With this chaotic activity came a mix up in diet sheets and I got a plateful of lovely fatty fish and chips. Naturally, being a believer in the unquestionable efficiency of the medical profession, I assumed the meal had been prescribed for me and scoffed the lot. By God I did enjoy that! The mistake was recognised by the young nurse who had issued the meals and came to collect the dirty plates. She looked at the empty, fatty, plate, stared at my record sheet, went ashen white and wet her knickers. Poor girl, she just stood there in a puddle, mouth wide open, wondering what to do next. But it was too late; I was already beginning to feel sick and threw it all up.

According to the doctor, that little blunder set my recovery back several weeks. By morning I felt very sick and was a deeper shade of yellow than I when I had started. Either as a result of that episode or due to the general reorganisation, by mid-day an ambulance had whisked me off and dropped me at another hospital. The last twenty-four hours had been hell, feeling very sick and unable to sleep due to all the noise of movement and continuous dialogue from the moaners, who wanted to know why they were being disturbed. I was surprised they bothered to ask; it was obvious that the hospital was being cleared to make room for an expected influx of casualties and that could only mean only one thing: 'D'-Day must be imminent.

Although I was very much aware that the extensive training and waterproofing of equipment was in preparation for the invasion of Europe, the news of a landing in Normandy came as quite a shock. I felt sick and deeply disturbed, but not by symptoms associated with jaundice. My Regiment had gone into action and I was not with them. All that sweat and worry

I had put into my Tank Troop had been for nothing. How could they have gone without me? At first I professed to being annoyed and deeply hurt, but deep down inside, pangs of shame were twisting in my stomach. What would my troop and others be thinking about me? Perhaps they were whispering to each other: 'Do you think Jock Watt fiddled the jaundice to get out of the invasion?' That thought was unbearable and I began to feel very sorry for myself.

It was during the next few days that my morale reached an all-time low. I felt weak from repeated sickness and lack of nourishment and the ward they had dumped me in was full of soldiers who had lost limbs or had other physical disabilities. Although I had seen bodies lying about like bundles of bloodied rags throughout the battlefields of Europe and Africa, this was something very different. Here was the reality of this sickening war, the remnants of human beings, blown to pieces and put back together again by skilful, dedicated surgeons and given the opportunity to try and recapture some of the life they had almost lost.

My God how they tried! One had lost both legs in a minefield and was struggling to overcome the problems of trying to walk on two artificial ones; I will always remember him, leaning on a frame and dragging one foot past the other, sweat pouring down a face twisted in agony but with a steely determination reserved for personal conflict. Another had only stumps where his hand had once been and was struggling with even the simple things in life, but he would often make the joking comment, 'how's that for a bloke with no hands!' if he managed to hold a mug of tea, perhaps precariously, by himself. An Air Force pilot who had been serving in India had landed his plane and immediately collapsed with polio; he spent all day lying on his back, struggling to pull himself up on two rings suspended above his bed.

All this I watched while lying on my bed, feeling sick but suffering only from the pain of five insulin injections a day. To me this was an embarrassing and disturbing situation. I explained this to the Matron with a request that I be moved. She understood my concern and I was wheeled along the corridor to a special ward for Tropical Diseases. It was laid out in single and double rooms; there were only five patients and during the day five nurses to look after us. I had a single with my own nurse to look after me. What a turn up for the book that was!

Here, in my new surroundings, I started to recover. The sickness had gone and the civilian doctor responsible for me prescribed a special diet to build up my depleted physical condition. In a small dining room at the bottom of the ward we sat down to some excellent meals, all five of us having recovered sufficiently to be allowed freedom of movement. One of the patients, an American Army Lieutenant, took this freedom to the limit by going out for the evening and returning in the middle of the night. He frequently took advantage of our friendship to wake me up in the early hours and let him in by my bedroom window.

Another patient, a Lieutenant in the Royal Engineers, blinded by an exploding mine, had the added benefit of his wife to assist him in his recovery. A secretary at the War Office, she had been given special leave to be with her husband and assisted him in everything from eating and drinking to combing his hair. She even corrected all his mistakes for him.

That situation was changed suddenly by the arrival of a Matron from St Dunstons. It took her just three minutes to realise what was happening and immediately ordered the wife to leave. The argument that followed was ended abruptly by the Matron who threatened to request the termination of her leave on the basis that her activities were detrimental to her husband's recovery. We all enjoyed the heated exchange because none of us liked her and the nurses hated the interference with their duties; even her husband seemed to enjoy fending for himself and rectifying his own mistakes, the matron left us with strict instructions not to help him.

She was certainly no Dragon, as that woman had suggested, and the blind patients in that hospital worshipped her. She nightly escorted half a dozen of them to the local pub and we would listen to them singing their heads off as they marched down the hospital drive a couple of hours later, arm-in-arm, with Matron in the middle. The hospital authorities complained about her disturbing other patients but she was adamant, her patients, who would be blind for the rest of their lives, were going to enjoy every minute she could afford to give them.

Discharged from hospital, with three weeks sick leave to complete my recovery, I retired to the peace and tranquillity of Fraserburgh, where a loving Mother fed and nourished her youngest and favourite son. Here was my recipe for a speedy return to normal health – combing the shoreline with the sharp tang of sea air in my nostrils, the thunder of waves breaking on the beach and the scream of seagulls whirling and diving overhead. To rest on the sand dunes, surrounded by a continuous ballet of moving grasses swaying in the wind and dream to the music of their rustling fronds was contentment indeed.

~ CHAPTER 31 ~

OFF TO NORMANDY

THE POSTMAN CHANGED ALL THAT. He brought a letter with movement orders to report to a Replacement Unit at Newmarket. Back to the wetlands, fog in the morning and beer at night. No longer did I crave for the Regiment that had left me behind, nor did I suffer from guilt at being safely tucked up in bed whilst the troops were dying on the Normandy beaches. I had come to accept that my contribution to this bloody war had been more than adequate and that by some strange quirk of fate I had survived the death and destruction that had been all around me. Whatever new assignment was ordered I, as a soldier, would accept, but under no circumstances would I volunteer to put my head on the block again.

Once again, I was given a new lease of life. The CO, recognising my experience with tank gunnery, instructed me to set up a gunnery training programme. In his opinion, many of the replacement crews lacked adequate training and, after brief discussions with the men, I agreed with him.

When I looked upon these innocent faces, the memory of an incident in the desert, involving one replacement loader / operator, brought back a shudder of horror. We had collected a recovered, refitted Honey with a blued breechblock fitted in its 37mm gun; it had been salvaged from another burned-out tank and I was determined to test it before leaving the depot. We drove out into the desert and fired off about a dozen rounds. One of them was a misfire and I assumed the proper procedure had been followed.

We were about to turn around and drive back when the loader asked me what he should do with the misfire. The bloody fool had put it back in the rack, where the shock of any of the following explosions could have set the damned thing off. There was no time to order 'bale out'; the rest of the crew had already done so and I was there with them. It took some time to pluck up enough courage to get back inside, ease the offending shell out of the rack and pass it gingerly to the crew outside. They handled it like the professionals they were, with a stream of comments about strap-hanging untrained recruits and some very positive suggestions about what I should do with the shell.

Allocated to me as my assistant was none other than Sergeant Arthur English, that character I had met at Lulworth; a very knowledgeable gunnery instructor with a presentation that was as impressive for its jokes as it was for its technical content. He was a natural born comedian who brightened the lives of all around him with his personal brand of wit. Once we included him in a darts match at the local pub and it was a disaster; it took an hour and a half to play one game.

When the British Army had finally dislodged the German Panzers from their defences at Falaise we moved across the channel to Normandy and set up shop amongst the devastated villages of that battle-torn peninsula. My god, what a shock that was. I had become accustomed to war in the desert, where only soldiers and their machines were exposed to the destruction of conflict, but here every living thing and habitat had become part of the struggle for superiority and survival. Entire villages that had once housed generations of families had been reduced to piles of rubble, deserted, silent and with the smell of death hanging in the air. This was indeed the tragic, depressing face of war. Here the local inhabitants, although predominantly farming communities and therefore better placed to feed and fend for themselves than city dwellers, had suffered badly during the years of occupation. Most of their livestock and possessions had been appropriated by the Nazis and now the final blow to their meagre existence had been struck by the destruction of their homes, in many cases in an act of spite by a retreating enemy. But even from the depths of despair, the resilience of these people was already at work, sifting the debris and fitting together the pieces of this vast, tragic jigsaw puzzle.

Freedom from this depressing environment was occasionally achieved with the assistance of that well-known Normandy delight, Calvados, an apple brandy distilled from local cider. Sipped with strong coffee, it was guaranteed to sweep away the doom and gloom of war, at the tolerable price of a thick head and queasy stomach. However, an accidental witnessing of the manufacturing process was to put me off the stuff...

My office was above a cowshed, reached by stone stairs on the outside of the building and a wide door at the bottom gave access to a cider-making room. Inside, a large stone wheel was dragged by a horse round a stone trough. Apples brought in from the orchard were shovelled into the trough, crushed by the wheel and the juices collected in a cellar beneath. The stench floating up the stairs was unbearable so I went to investigate. As the horse trudged around in a monotonous circle, apples were crushed under his metal-clad hoofs and as I watched he messed on the floor; it was all shovelled into the trough, adding a final delicate ingredient to the character of the mash. For me, that was it, Calvados and cider lost their appeal.

As our armies advanced to the borders of Germany, we moved forward to a village near Hasselt in the north of Belgium and, although information was limited, we knew by the demand for replacement crews that tank losses were high. Redirected men from Armoured Corps sources had slowed to a trickle and to make up the shortfall, men from rear echelon units such as lorry drivers and pen-pushers had volunteered to man the tanks, probably keen for a slice of the action before the war ended.

I moved with my staff to moorland near Bourg Leopold and set up a shooting range. Derelict farm buildings became our quarters and within a couple of weeks the permanent staff had turned this shambles of wood and masonry into a home from home. Once again, the ingenuity of man worked miracles, holes were knocked in walls to be filled with frames, complete with glass and a door, a brick oven appeared in the yard, made from new bricks and a forty-gallon drum, and an old barn was floored with the steel platforms from two burned-out lorries. I never dared to ask where all these materials had come from, but I did recognise that within any group of men a wide range of skills lay dormant until necessity demanded. For example, an Insurance Agent who had done nothing but push a pen for most of his life built the oven and the two men who knocked the holes in the walls had no knowledge of buildings. By a miracle, it did not collapse.

Here in our humble abode, remote from the daily routine and discipline of the unit, we settled down to a very pleasant and peaceful existence, with outside interference limited to the regular arrival of rations and trainees.

We were somewhat puzzled when packages of food mysteriously started to appear on our doorstep during the night. Although, on occasions, we had been disturbed in the early hours by the barking of our dog, which we inherited with the farm, he always appeared to be barking at nothing. We set up booby traps of parachute flares around the area, but only one was ever fired and the dog did that. Eventually, a few whispered remarks by one of the locals solved the mystery. Our range lay across an old smugglers route, which was currently in use, and the smugglers had no desire to be shot at by our guards. Their gifts of meat, fruit, vegetables and drink were very welcome, and in return we saw nothing.

An occasional violent explosion nearby jolted us back to the reality that there was still a war on. I took a tank to an area where smoke was still rising and discovered a damned great hole with lots of metal debris lying around. It was the remains of a V2 rocket, but why here, in the middle of nowhere? From then on, we watched the sky to the west and saw the smoke trails of the rockets being launched, directed at London or Antwerp. Ours must have been a dud that came straight down. It was quite a shock to realise the front line was so near.

A further jolt to our complacency came with the news of a German counter-attack in the Ardennes, just south of our location. We were ordered to be in a state of readiness to move at short notice. This information shattered my dream world of peace and security. Being remote from enemy activity for so long, I had shed the mantle of constant nervous tension and the feeling that my luck was running out. I had become lulled into a false sense of security but now, once again, that deep feeling of foreboding returned. I had no desire to become involved in active warfare again and the churning sickness of fear in my stomach told me so.

The enemy had infiltrated the front line in many areas, using specialist troops dressed in Allied uniforms and our area, with its remote moorland farms, was a perfect hiding place. We mounted patrols to search farms and other remote buildings, often moving in at first light in an attempt to catch the unwary, but always in company with members of the local police, who handled the language and legal side of the operation. It was known to the police that many local girls had fraternized with the enemy and may be tempted to continue a relationship with an old boyfriend by hiding and feeding him; what could be more natural? Special attention was given to the areas where they lived.

It all developed into an exciting game of 'hide and seek', but although we found two recently-used hideaways in the woods, the birds had flown. We stumbled across many unexpected finds in those tumbledown barns, such as illicit stills, hidden amongst stacks of corn and other debris, and on one farm a cache of stolen Army food, which took four 3-ton lorries to remove. The police were very interested in those finds, but did not appear to be surprised. I wondered why. We carried out our own investigation, in cooperation with a captain from field security, and a number of Army personnel, including one of our own cooks, finished up in the cooler. No wonder the troops were complaining about poor rations; a lot of their tinned food was being secretly shipped out of camp in the swill bins.

With the defeat of the German forces in the Battle of the Bulge, the war moved on, leaving us far behind, but we continued to turn out a constant supply of human fodder necessary to keep those churning tank tracks moving ever forward. Their departure was just another stage in the training schedule. I had given them the benefit of my experience and long since ceased to shoulder the burden of the possible destiny of those noble soldiers. As they climbed aboard the trucks, destination unknown, I knew, by their loudmouthed jokes and banter and the tremor in their voices, that the show of bravado was just an act to hide the fear of uncertainty churning in their stomachs.

As I waved them off and wished them well, I wondered how long it would be before they asked themselves, "What the hell am I doing here?"

~ CHAPTER 32 ~

HOSTILITIES END

ROM A CONFUSION OF DISJOINTED scraps of information, the news gradually filtered through that the German High Command had surrendered. Even then, the killing continued for some days before hostilities by the more fanatical enemy units finally ceased and the announcement could be made that "The War in Europe is over." Just a few simple words, but the impact of their meaning reverberated throughout the whole continent. People danced in the streets, prayed in the churches and wept silently over graves. It was the signal for happiness, thankfulness, sorrow, and new hope for the future. For me, the surge of relief that passed through my body left me drained and confused. I found a quiet corner and wept.

With no more demand for replacement tank crews, the unit was eventually wound down and staff dispersed amongst the regiments. I was posted back to my old regiment, 3rd RTR, and once again felt excited at the prospect of returning to the tanks, guns, transport and men that had been my home and haven for so many years. But although I yearned to be amongst my old friends and comrades once again, I was fearful that because of my absence from their battles across France and Germany, they would treat me with cool indifference. My fears were totally unjustified. What was left of them, and there were not many, welcomed me as a long-lost brother. I realised that they had no knowledge of my activities since D-Day and accepted me as the person they remembered. The dog, which had been my constant companion since those days on the farm, and used to ride on top of my tank turret, was officially accepted and became an honourable member of the regiment. He most certainly fed better than I did.

As the days passed, grim details of their struggle across Europe gradually unfolded: the hammering they had taken around Caen and Falaise, the mad dash to Antwerp... As usual, they had been pushed in to clear up many of the dodgy situations that arose, and it had cost a lot of good men and tanks. They had been part of 11th Armoured Division, commanded by our former CO Pip Roberts, and I could well imagine him using them to the full, the Regiment he knew and trusted. Sadly, without a recognised name, like the historic cavalry regiments, their gallant deeds passed largely unnoticed.

By comparison, my contribution to the war in Europe was negligible, and I knew that they were bound to find out about it sooner or later, so I reluctantly told the story, just as it happened. Their reaction was rather surprising; they demanded to know all the gory details of the life of luxury I had been living and, at the end of it there was just one comment:

"You Jammy Bastard!"

The words of true friends.

At some point after the war had ended, I was ordered to take a convoy of about a dozen tanks on transporters to a German experimental area on the moors between Fallingbostel and Belsen. Most bridges across the Rhine had been destroyed and although pontoons had been erected, the only bridge capable of carrying the load of my convoy was a Bailey Bridge, built on stilts, at Wesel. Although the autobahns were in good condition, the transporters were not; they had been in constant use during the advance across France and Germany and now the effects of poor maintenance were beginning to show. It took two long days of breakdowns and punctures to reach the bridge. Everyone had become irritable at the slow progress and now, at the ramp of the bridge, an RE captain in charge stopped us with the words, "You are not taking those bloody great things over this bridge."

That was the last straw and a near riot situation could be imminent. However, after an exchange of heated pleasantries (we were both tired and hot-headed Scots) he explained that, because a barge had collided with one of the stilt pontoons during the night, the bridge had been downgraded and my tanks on transporters were far too heavy. The arguments were getting into second gear when a staff car, flying an impressive pennant, stopped to allow a smartly-dressed brigadier to approach us with the question.

"What is the problem?" We both saluted smartly and the captain started to explain why he was holding up the tanks, but before he had completed his report the Brigadier butted in with the comment, "Yes, yes, I have read the report, but it is perfectly safe take the tanks across." He then jumped into his car and drove off across the bridge.

You could have knocked me down with a feather. That poor bloody captain just stood there, red in the face. I thought he was going to explode. I certainly would have blown my top. He eventually found just two words, "Bloody Idiot!" We discussed the problem and decided to unload the tanks and drive them across individually, allowing only one vehicle on the bridge at a time. I rode across on one of our motorcycles, stood up on the parapet and watched the first tank drive across. My heart was in my mouth; the centre of the bridge oscillated, with a swing of about six feet.

The captain had been was right; to have driven across in convoy would have been disastrous. With the last vehicle across and the convoy ready to move, I thanked the captain for his assistance and we headed east once more. The drivers and crews seemed to have recovered from the depression of the previous two days and the temporary hold up at the bridge; I think the relief at having crossed the Rhine instead of the prospect of wandering up and down the river, searching for a crossing, made us all feel much better.

Fallingbostel was a small, pleasant, peaceful town by the river, but also the location of a Prisoner of War camp, Stalag 11b, now used by the Allies as accommodation for Displaced Persons. Not many miles to the south, the dreaded Belsen Concentration Camp was located on moorland, a perfect setting for the mass graves of thousands of inmates who perished there. Many of the survivors still occupied the camp, but it was now under new management.

We took up residence in a tented camp on a field outside the town; it was a very unpleasant mud patch, ploughed up by the constant movement of vehicles, but in a village nearby, the defeated Germans lived warm and comfortable in their houses and cottages. It took a little time, but eventually someone decided the boot was on the wrong foot and it was time for a change. With a troop of men, backed up by German police, we descended on the village, selected the properties we required and gave the occupants 24 hours to leave. They were not very happy and complained bitterly. I reminded them of Belsen, just down the road, and of those whose voices would never be heard again. Of course, they protested, 'it was not us, it was the Nazis' but to me they were all the same. We moved in 24 hours later.

On the gunnery ranges nearby we discovered many fascinating pieces of experimental equipment, including a telescope capable of ranging on targets in the dark. Modified tanks with bigger guns and thicker armour were shipped back to England for investigation. We took particular interest in the Jagdpanther tank-destroyer; it had no turret, just a flat front plate, four inches thick, set at an angle, with a souped-up 88mm gun of limited traverse mounted in the centre. We tested the penetration powers of our 17-pounder on this monster at a range of about 1,500 yards. We registered over seventy hits, but our shells simply bounced off. The gun mounting was shattered, the welds connecting the front plate to the hull had failed and the whole front slid down to the ground, but no hole through that armour plate could be found. On the other side of the coin, at the same range that souped-up 88mm gun could punch a hole clean through the front of anything we had. And if the night vision telescope had been perfected and fitted to that gun...? My God, what a shuddering thought.

Throughout the whole bloody war, the British armoured regiments had battled against an enemy whose tanks had the advantage of more powerful guns and thicker armour. When we had 37mm guns, they had 50 and 75mm; by the time our 75mm guns came along, they had the dreaded 88, and their armour was always just that much thicker, giving them better protection, boosting their confidence, and making them a more dangerous enemy. Much of the credit for victory must go to the crews who manned our tanks who, even in the knowledge that the odds were stacked against them, and often devastated by losses two or three times that of the enemy, doggedly battled on in the midst of all the death and destruction around them.

With the non-fraternisation ban imposed, life in Germany was tolerable for a time, especially while feelings about this nation, which had created such devastation all over Europe were laced with bitterness and hatred. But the British, as a nation, are always champions of the underdog, and who could be lower than the people of a nation totally defeated in war? Behind the scenes, the political and industrial bigwigs, recognising the wealth of brainpower and materials now dormant in this defeated land, were keen to get their grubby hands on the lion's share. Not easy when one side is not even talking to the other. The propaganda machine that had brainwashed a nation into dying for their country now churned out the theme of 'love thy neighbour' and eventually the frat ban was lifted.

But on the day that war ended, and the order to physically stand down was given, the brain, having tolerated a high stress level for so many years, was not capable of sudden change like switching off a light. Confusion in the mind brought out the worst in many, where men of usually normal behaviour did stupid, unexplainable things, and I certainly did my share. Excessive drinking became the norm, sometimes sitting in the bar until the early hours, without any real purpose.

Perhaps our location had something to do with my state of mind, but I doubt it. We had moved into what was officially described as a Brain Research Establishment in the village of Suchteln, near Krefeld. This was not in any way related to our behaviour, but merely a readily-available group of buildings suitable for winter quarters. The area of large houses, dispersed amongst trees and gardens, had a large frontal block of offices with cellar stores that contained many hundreds of brains, all perfectly preserved in jars of alcohol and presenting a very gruesome spectacle. Each house was self-contained, with its own kitchen, rest room, surgery and about ten bedrooms with double-glazed windows, which kept out the cold, but were probably designed to keep the screams of the patients in. There were still a small number of patients and staff in the area, but they had been moved to a remote part of the plot and fenced off. Some suggested that we had been sent here to join them, but no one attempted to climb the barrier, although I was surprised some of the drunks did not fall over it in the night.

We occupied one house as our Squadron Officer's Quarters and wallowed in the luxury of our surroundings, with frequent drinking parties to occupy the off-duty hours, but for me the novelty soon wore off and finding work for the brain became a serious problem. An officers club had opened in Krefeld, providing an alternative to boredom in the Mess; it gave us a few hours away from the regiment, an opportunity to socialise with other units and the luxury of ordering a meal from a menu, even though the choice was Hobson's (take it or leave it).

Although, in true military style, the Army attempted to return to peacetime soldiering with the posting of orders, parades and daily duties, it quickly turned into a boring charade. The majority of the regiment's personnel had been legally abducted from civilian life, taught the rudiments of war and discipline and dispatched to an environment of nervous tension. Now, having done what was asked of them, they just wanted to go home. Like the proud soldiers we were, we all carried out the orders given to us, but the maintenance and other duties were now just a chore, instead of a necessity for survival.

This situation was fully recognised by the powers-that-be and every effort was applied to occupy the mind as well as the body, and to this end educational courses were run in art, languages and any other subjects that men were prepared to teach. The number of volunteer teachers from all ranks with sufficient knowledge of their subject to be able to teach was unbelievable, especially some individuals who previously had given no indication of knowledge other than what the Army had taught them.

An exhibition from the art group displayed on the walls of the other ranks dining room was based on the theme of well-used Army expressions such as "take your finger out." This was shown as a donkey being pushed from behind by a burly, red-faced sergeant with no thumbs; the donkey, with the usual straw hat over its ears, looked back at the pusher with the words coming from it's mouth. The brushwork was also commendable.

Being a lover of the countryside, I spent much of my spare time wandering amongst the trees, sitting quietly by the river and, with the dog for company, locking out the present and wandering down memory lane. I usually carried a shotgun, for the purpose of adding to the kitchen, but seldom fired a shot, fearful of interrupting the music of the birds and river that filled the air around me. I would take aim at a pheasant or rabbit disturbed by the dog, but invariably let the quarry escape with the excuse that I may hit the dog. After all, he enjoyed chasing them and why should I spoil his fun? On one occasion, however, he chased a rabbit into the woods and I never saw him alive again. Some weeks later, when walking a path behind a cottage, that I saw a number of skins hanging on the wall. His was amongst them, poor devil; he had been eaten. For some time the civilian population had suffered serious food shortages and practically everything in the animal world had been eaten. I saw no cats and the few dogs around were used as beasts of burden.

At the Krefeld Club, the dialogue between officers from different units centred around social and personal life. As we entered the building, war was left outside in the debris that spilled onto the streets from the empty shells of derelict, bombed-out buildings. We also learned the locations of other clubs, both Army and German, which extended our range of evening activities. While the frat-ban was imposed, it was a men-only social event, but a change of scenery from the same old faces in the mess was very welcome. It was on the return journey, in thick fog, from such an outing, with four of us crammed into a jeep, that we collided with a lorry travelling in the opposite direction and finished up in a ditch. By some miracle, three of us stepped out with only cuts from flying glass, but the other officer, sitting next to the driver and on the side of impact, finished up in hospital with a broken leg. By a strange coincidence, he was the only one of us who had suffered no wounds in action. Now, like everyone else, he could boast of his injuries. Sadly, the quirks of fate had not quite finished with him.

We were informed when he was ready for discharge from hospital and drove off in a Staff car to fetch him. He sadly waved those lovely nurses farewell but was pleased to be returning to the fold. I often wondered if there was something wrong with him. I would have been very pleased to stay. However, we all felt this was an occasion for celebration and stopped at a club to christen his leg plaster. The celebration lasted a little longer than anticipated, so dinner was included, followed by a few more toasts to the leg, but the driver, in his wisdom, called 'time gentlemen please' and drove us back to our loony bin. We stopped close to the plaster legged friend's billet, in the narrow track leading to our mess. he stepped out of the front passenger seat, amidst repeated shouts of 'goodnight', slammed the front door, and off we drove to the Mess for a final nightcap.

Within half an hour a visit from the doctor informed us that the plastered leg was already on its way back to hospital in an ambulance, along with its owner. Apparently, unknown to us, as he had waved goodnight, his feet had slipped on the muddy bank, his legs had slid under the car and we ran over him. The driver had found him lying on the track as he drove back from the Mess. He turned out to be a very unsociable character and refused point-blank our offer to collect him when he was discharged some weeks later. You just can't fathom some people, can you?

The non-frat ban caused a lot of trouble for us. A number of other ranks stepped out of line, got caught by the MPs and, sadly, had to be dealt with, but they were not alone. Our squadron officers were also caught and ended up on the carpet. It was during an evening out to a nightclub for all of us, including our squadron commander. We had never been there before and were very surprised, not unpleasantly, to find a number of German girls socialising in the bar and on a dance floor. Of course, being British Army officers and gentlemen we could not rudely turn our back on them, besides, they looked much more attractive face-on, and we were not about to kick a gift horse in the mouth. We were just settling down to this new-found luxury when a Captain MP, whom we all knew and recognised, appeared, looking a bit guilty, but gave the clear impression there was no problem. But unknown to us, the lousy bastard had already been on the phone and within half an hour the place was overrun by MPs and all our names were taken. By a stroke of luck, our major, who had gone to the loo or some cosy corner with a girl, was missed off the list. Needless to say, the brigadier was furious and our very embarrassed major had to discipline us with seven days confined to camp. I can still see him, sitting behind his desk, with all of us lined up before him taking a verbal hiding for misbehaving; I don't know how he managed to keep a straight face. Of course, the other ranks took full advantage of the situation; as we walked around the camp in the evening, as a form of exercise, it was to the strains of the song 'Don't Fence Me In'. I would not have minded so much if it had been 'This is a Lovely Way to Spend an Evening' but you can't always choose your friends.

Total victory by an Army brings with it responsibility for the welfare of the defeated nation. For some considerable time there had been a serious shortage of food and fuel amongst the civilian population, the Nazi War Machine having come first and the civilians having got what was left, if anything. The Allied Commission set up to administer the country did their best, under extremely difficult circumstances, to maintain supplies for the mass of the German people, but added to the problem were the hoards of other nationals wandering aimlessly around the country who had formerly been forced to work for the Reich and now belonged to no one.

Most of our regimental transport was seconded to the task of moving food and fuel around the country, but there was little that we could do to supplement this effort. We were aware of the shortages in our immediate area and did what little we could to help, but others were quick to recognise a shortage and make capital from it. Bicycle tyres and coffee were valued like gold and men on leave would return with as much as they could smuggle, to be traded for watches and anything else that could easily be smuggled back and sold. Many returned to England with a row of watches strapped on each arm, bought with a packet of coffee or a bicycle tyre or tube. I was demobbed without even a watch to tell the time.

On lush, wooded estates nearby, which had been reserved for the elite of the German Army, we hunted game for the locals, but spread amongst the many it was a mere pittance. A wild boar hunt was arranged in the forest, where for years large areas of nettles had been planted and maintained, so that the boar could feed and breed without the need to wander. Since these animals were large and extremely vicious if wounded, the hunt had to be carefully organised, with local gamekeepers in attendance and, because service rifles were used, we could not shoot at the oncoming animals, due to the risk of shooting one of our own beaters.

We spread out along the edge of a firebreak roadway with our backs to the beaters, so that we had no target until the animals had passed us. As I listened to the noise of rustling and grunting behind me, the knowledge that the largest boar shot in that area was almost a metre across the shoulders did little to quell the heart thumping in my boots.

When I walked to the nearest tree and tested the strength of a branch, a major on my left shouted "Coward!"

"Yes!" I answered, and tested the branch again before settling down with my back against a large stump. Fortunately, the grunting sounds moved off to the left, so I practiced my aiming ability on a stag deer about a hundred yards in front, moving amongst the trees. I followed him with my sights trained on his head, with no intention of killing that beautiful animal, but when he stopped, my reaction was instantaneous and I squeezed the trigger. The Venison was much appreciated by the local population.

~ CHAPTER 33 ~

FAREWELL TO THE NUTHOUSE

O NCE AGAIN WE WERE ON the move, this time to the extreme north of Germany, to the town of Flensburg, on the border with Denmark. I never ceased to be amazed at the mental ability of our generals; they appeared to be capable of seeing into the minds of men and always decided to move them just when they had succeeded in moulding themselves into an acceptable pattern of living. That is how it was with me. I had just accepted that my destiny was meant to be within the confines of that nuthouse and here I was, packing up again.

It was a long, tiresome journey and as I eased my aching bones from the cramped confines of a small Daimler scout car, I wondered how many more moves before, like the Israelites, someone would lead us back to our Holy Land. I had returned to England for a short leave and enjoyed the pleasures of familiar surroundings and friends, but my enjoyment was marred by the knowledge that I would soon return to a meaningless existence in Germany. In England, the population appeared to be carving a new life for themselves and I was not yet a part of it.

This time we took over a German army barracks, with all the facilities we needed to maintain our hard-worked transport fleet. The attics above the main building housed row upon row of neatly-stacked ski equipment, indicating that it could have been a base for ski troops, but to us it was a nice warm billet, away from the cold weather outside. An excellent Officer's Club was in operation, with a much more attractive menu than at

Krefeld, and with the frat-ban lifted and a well-populated town just a short walk away, we were ready to enjoy the high life.

I believe that this area had at one time been part of Denmark and consequently a large percentage of the residents were of Danish origin; mind you, I was sure that a proportion of the people who claimed to be Danish and to have hated the Germans were merely using this as a ploy to curry favour. The border with Denmark was just a few miles north of Flensburg and we appeared to be on the main route to Germany. Taken over by Hitler early in the war because of its large agricultural capacity, it was now a convenient breadbasket to help feed Germany's starving population.

This was also the perfect opportunity for the long convoys of lorries, plying between the two countries, to indulge in smuggling food for the black market. At a control post on the frontier set up by our military police, lorries were stopped, loads checked and any illegal goods found unloaded at the roadside. I had been ordered to take over the duties of transport officer, a thankless job in which you carried the can for the filching of goods and the misdemeanours of about fifty drivers. Also under my control was a petrol station which, apart from fuelling our own transport, provided for a number of small units in the area, including the Military Police. This was a very useful connection; the MP captain and I became like old buddies and perks from the goods hoard on the frontier improved our standard of living considerably.

Since the end of hostilities the attitude of many Regular Army officers towards those, like myself, with 'emergency commissions' had changed; the 'comrades in arms' relationship had become one of 'them and us'. For example, one of our officers, commissioned in the field with an outstanding performance in North Africa and decorated for bravery, applied for a regular commission; he did all the right things, answered the questions, passed the tests and the recommendation went to the War Office for their approval. No answer was received. The war continued and in Europe he proved himself a brilliant leader and earned the position of Squadron Commander, but at the end of hostilities, when an answer to his application was again requested, he was told that the exams would have to be taken again. The message was loud and clear: "thank you for your heroic efforts in the defence of our country, but we don't want you in the ranks of the elite, take a slap in the face instead.

It was during our stay at Suchteln that I first noticed a change in attitude, especially from the CO and his close colleagues. On a number of occasions, the CO would ignore my salute when passing. At first I thought perhaps his mind was on some distracting issue and he had failed to notice me, but I began to have my doubts. The message really sunk in when I took over as transport officer at Flensburg. Things had got into a mess, with lorries lost and misdirected, but every blunder was laughed off as a joke when discussed by the CO and his hangers-on during dinner. The captain in charge was a Regular Army officer, a very nice chap, but unfamiliar with the devious methods of deception practiced by some of the drivers. On the other hand, I had served in the ranks, probably practiced many of these tricks myself and had known many of these men for a number of years.

With the aid of a Sergeant Dusty Miller, also an old associate, we lashed the troublemakers into shape, allocated the most valuable loads to the most trustworthy and gradually turned it into a reasonably efficient organisation. Of course, there were mistakes, but unlike my predecessor, they were no joking matter, my errors were practically court martial offences.

However, demob procedures were already operative and the rantings of the elite became less effective.

Life in Flensburg was not all doom and gloom, far from it; we were compelled to be in the mess for dinner one evening a week, as specified by the CO, but that was a normal procedure and apart from that we were free. There were parties in other messes and in the Officers Club and even an occasional dance at the DP camp nearby also, and with the frat-ban lifted there was plenty of scope for everyone.

We also had an occasional treat of a show in the local theatre, put on by a touring company of ENSA; not to be compared with West End musicals, but nevertheless it brought a little light from home. These shows were marred a little for the officers, who were instructed by the CO to attend. He considered it right that we should be there as an example to the men and, in all fairness, he had put a lot of effort in getting the shows to come our way. However, on one occasion his instruction did conflict with arrangements we had already made; we had a hurried dinner at the Club, washed down with a little too much wine, staggered up the street to the hall and occupied the front row of seats, all of us in a troublesome mood. The show was really quite good but we, an ill-mannered lot, disrupted the programme by laughing before the end of every joke. Of course, the audience joined in and laughed their heads off with us. Poor Nellie Wallace, star of the show, never finished a joke, and towards the end she could hardly get a word out for laughing herself.

Unknown to us, the Concert Party had been invited to the Club after the show. What a shock to walk in and see them all standing drinking at one end of the bar and we sensed that the biggest blow was about to descend on us. Napier and I had been the worst culprits and were not really surprised when the Adjutant called us across. Nellie Wallace had requested to meet the two officers who had disrupted her show. It was not the welcome we expected; she shook our hands, laughed her head off and asked if we would come to the next show in Hamburg and get the audience laughing. She was really great and invited us to a party in their hostel the next evening.

What a turn up for the book, even the CO was not invited and we had all those lovely young dancing girls to chat to, what a night! Close up, Nellie looked a little older than we had imagined, but the surprise of the evening came when someone told us her age; how could that girl we had seen prancing around the stage like a gazelle be over seventy years old? She was fantastic and I believe, sadly, she died just a few years later, at seventy four.

Located within the Barracks was a row of stables, complete with a string of beautiful, well-kept horses, a bonus for some of the officers who were ex-cavalry and keen horsemen. They were used on a rota by the CO and others and the spectacle they presented when riding out through the gates, perfectly erect and proper, almost like toy soldiers, brought back just a brief glimpse of Old England. We also rode through the gates sometimes after lunch, but Joe and I were in a jeep, complete with shotguns, off to find a brace of pheasant or duck for dinner. Joe was also an Emergency Commissioned Officer, a redhead with a fiery temper and very outspoken, often at the wrong time and, since he had received his demob date, which incidentally was the same as mine, his remarks had become more abrasive.

For example, we returned from our shoot, dropped our kill at the kitchen and went to the lounge for tea, an afternoon ritual. It was the same familiar atmosphere, there they were in their jodhpurs, sprawled in all the comfortable armchairs, silently buried behind newspapers. We surveyed the scene and Joe was in a mischievous mood.

"What is that funny smell, Jock?" he said.

"I am not sure," I answered.

"I know," said Joe, "horse shit!"

That certainly did not go down well with the colonel's tea and toast and his facial expression told us so.

It may sound as if military discipline was failing, but that was certainly not the case. Although return to civilian life was constantly in mind, the vast majority were good soldiers who carried out their duties in the best traditions of the Regiment. But there were a few who failed to toe the line and one such private was brought back by the Military Police to face charges of desertion and theft and that was a very sad blow for me. Military law gives any soldier the right to choose his own defender, if reasonably available and I, being the only officer he really knew, was chosen and available.

Although I was reasonably well versed in military discipline, the law was something else and I burned the midnight oil for a week, just scratching the surface. I had known this soldier for years and was familiar with his history of promotion and demotion and, personally, I would have locked him up and thrown away the key, but I was duty-bound to defend him to the best of my ability. His story almost brought tears to my eyes.

He was supposed to be picked by a truck after delivery of a vehicle to a depot near Brussels, but it never turned up. He had no idea where the Regiment was and was completely lost. A generous civilian gave him a bed for the night. After a number of weeks of searching he heard the Regiment was near Dusseldorf but he had no transport so, after deliberating his sad situation for another couple of weeks, he borrowed a jeep from an American officer, without his permission. This officer, who was billeted next door and packing up to return to the States, had lost his transport and reported the theft.

At this stage my defendant, who was still living with the generous civilian, decided he could now return to the Regiment. Being the smart-arse he was, his action was probably motivated by the need of a demob date to get back to England. He did not get very far, in fact he was still in Brussels when the MPs picked him up. The day before the Court Martial, a captain arrived from the Judge Advocate Unit with two officers from another regiment to judge this poor innocent soldier whom I, poor devil, was destined to defend. A captain from our regiment was instructed to prosecute and the stage was set for a legal duel.

From that day my luck started to change. The captain from the JA unit was an old friend of mine when in the ranks and we spent much of the evening chatting about old times. Another bonus was the prosecutor, he just happened to be the officer whom I had replaced on transport and his general behaviour was still erratic; whereas I went early to bed and woke up refreshed, he spent a late night in the bar drinking his nerves away and started the day with a hangover.

What a farce that trial was. There were no witnesses to the events. I had demanded that the driver who failed to pick him up be present, but he was already back in civvy street, and neither could the American be returned from the USA to verify the prosecution charge of theft. On a number of occasions prior to the trial, Danny, the prosecutor, had suggested to me that the soldier had no hope of getting off and I did nothing to dissuade him. He consequently did little to prepare his case and just blundered on. My many objections to his statements were upheld by my friend on the judges panel, which did little to bolster his fragile nervous system.

The outcome was a travesty of justice. He was sentenced to three months, having already spent two months inside. I was disgusted; he should have got ten years. He was not a popular soldier and most who knew him would have agreed with my assessment, but to them I was the greatest, I had won a fight for one of their own. However, to the CO, I was the lowest form of humanity, responsible for his loss of face in losing a Court Martial. What a shame... I cried all night.

This new-found fame did me more harm than good, however, because in just a couple of weeks it all blew back in my face. A Brigadier's inspection of the men and barracks resulted in another soldier being charged with illegal possession of enemy arms – a Luger automatic – and he requested that I defend him. It was just a few weeks after an order had been issued that all enemy weapons must be handed in; probably a lot were being smuggled back to England and this had to be stopped. During his round of inspection the Brigadier had stopped at one man ordered him to turn out his kitbag, whereupon the Luger had dropped to the floor. Of all the men in that Barrack Room, he was well known to his mates as the only one who would take such a risk. But why did the Brigadier pick on him? Perhaps as an old soldier himself he had come to recognise the shifty look of a crafty old sweat. The accused was locked in the Guard Room and Court Martial proceedings started all over again. I was not amused; my final return to England was only a month away and this event could hold up my Demob.

But my luck had not completely run out and fate took a hand in the strangest way... After a week of swotting up Military Law again, my batman woke me in the middle of the night with the exciting news that my client had escaped from detention, stolen one of our Police jeeps and scarpered; he even brought me a cup of tea to celebrate the event. I sweated for days, praying that he would not be caught, as news of his escapades, mostly gross exaggerations, began to filter back to the Regiment. One story, verified by the Military Police, was that having parked the jeep in a Military Vehicle Park in Hamburg and gone in search of food, he had returned to collect his vehicle but had lost his ticket and could not retrieve it. Apparently the Park Police allowed him to go to the vehicle for his coat or something, whereupon he drove the jeep to the gates and blasted his way out with a Sten-gun that was in the jeep when he stole it. He wounded a couple of policemen and drove off into the night.

God what a bloody mess he had got himself into! And what a bloody worse mess he had got me into. How could I defend that rat on a possible murder charge? And what about my demob? I could only hope and pray they failed to catch him before I left. My God, how I prayed.

They say 'no news is good news' but the agony of waiting for what I believed to be the inevitable was worse than I had experienced before a battle. However, as the days passed without a glimmer, anxiety gradually receded and the excitement of preparation to leave took over.

Joe and I occupied adjacent rooms. They were quite spartan when we moved in, but that was soon rectified with carpets and furniture liberated from what had been an admiral's house nearby. The carpets were very expensive Persian rugs, too large for the room and went about two feet up the wall on each side. The bed was none too comfortable, but I did have a very large Telefunken radio and a German Army cine-sound with lots of film. Two shotguns – a five-round Browning automatic and a silver-mounted double-barrel 12-bore – stood in the corner, along with a thousand round box of ammo. That was all I needed, and the bathroom was just across the passage.

That Browning did excellent service in maintaining a good stock of rich game hanging in the kitchen, although with its five rounds of rapid fire it did create a certain amount of resentment amongst some of the other officers when out on an organised duck shoot. We had settled down, camouflaged, to wait for the birds to fly in. The usual two scouts flew up and down the river, but someone must have looked up and showed his white face and the usual 100-plus ducks did not arrive. It was quite dark and my feet, with Wellingtons on, dangling in the water, were getting cold. I heard the quack-quack of a duck as it paddled across a light patch of water a few feet away and blasted him out of the water. That mallard was served up for dinner next day but the Colonel refused to eat it. I was in disgrace for shooting a duck on the water. It was just not cricket.

Joe and I enjoyed it, nevertheless...

~ CHAPTER 34 ~

HOME AT LAST

NERVOUS TENSION WAS BUILDING UP. Just a few more days and I would be away across the water and back home, this time for good. We packed our heavy baggage and watched it disappear through the gates; that was the first stage of our demob and at that instant I knew it was for real; there was a strange finality about it. A large lump in my throat was almost choking me as we walked slowly back to our rooms without exchanging a word. It was unusual for Joe to be without comment, but at that moment we shared the same thoughts. Back in my room, Joe gasped with surprise.

"Why is your carpet still here? I packed mine in my bedroll instead of blankets and used them to wrap my photography equipment in those two tea-chests on the truck." Anxious to ensure my own gear was despatched, I had hardly noticed the two large tea-chests, which apparently contained much of the equipment necessary for Joe to set up his own photography business back in England. He had liberated it from a bombed-out film processing factory. The carpet and other furnishings I had gathered around me had most certainly made Army life more tolerable, but I had no desire to retain souvenirs of where and what I had been. I had no need of them, my memory of those past six years would never be lost.

Finally, the time had come to leave. All farewells and other formalities had been dispensed with, we stacked the last of our equipment into the truck, climbed aboard and headed for the railhead at Hamburg. Settled comfortably in a coach for the long journey to the channel, with no real knowledge of how long it would take to reach England, we had gathered around us sufficient supplies for a couple of days. In addition to sandwiches and anything else we could scrounge, I had stored, in the luggage rack, a large Danish Blue cheese, a dozen eggs, carefully packed in a box, and a Thermos full of coffee. A whistle blew, the train gave an almighty jolt and we were off ... and so was everything in the luggage rack. My Thermos and other articles crashed to the floor; what a devastating start to what was supposed to be the most important and exciting journey of my life. The cheese was OK but the flask smashed ... and the eggs? I imagined the worst and avoided the truth until back home in Kettering. In the event there was not even a cracked shell and my mother-in-law-to-be was delighted.

Someone must still be watching over me.

It was a long drag to the Channel across Germany, Holland and Belgium, excited by the knowledge that every clackety-clack of the wheels was a few more yards nearer home. We passed through devastated towns and cities, razed to the ground by bombs and shellfire, with people still searching amongst the rubble for something from the past to help rebuild a future. At long last we were at Calais but it was still dark and we saw nothing that brought back memories of that morale-shattering defeat six years previously. Shunted straight to the docks and aboard a ship with the minimum of formality, we sailed towards that great symbol of England, the White Cliffs of Dover, the gateway to home that to many Luftwaffe pilots during the Battle of Britain had proved the gateway to hell.

The ship disgorged its cargo on to the quayside, everyone pushing and shoving as though in a race to get through customs and away, almost as if they hardly dared to believe they were really home. Many struggled with boxes and packages completely unrelated to Army equipment but appeared to pass through customs unheeded, by comparison, I carried just the basic necessities, my heavy baggage was being handled by dockers. But it was no easy passage for me; I must have had a guilty face. They probed into everything and yet I had nothing to hide. There were some films for my camera at home; they questioned me about where it was, what make it was and did I have a receipt? Eventually they charged me duty on the films.

The message was loud and clear – welcome home.

Joe appeared on the train, looking rather pleased with himself. His tea-chests of photographic equipment were already in the goods van. He had bribed a docker with a fiver to get them on the train without a customs check. The last news I had of him, he had a flourishing business in Bournemouth. We had come a long way from the day when I kicked him between the shoulder blades for switching the wireless off.

At a Demob Dispersion Unit, discharge documents were quickly dealt with, a civvy suit, coat, hat and shoes issued and I was onto a train for home with the minimum of fuss, in the knowledge that my heavy baggage would follow. The organisation was superb, right down to the very last detail of money, travel warrants, etc. The choice of clothes, though not exactly Moss Brothers, was imaginative and adequate. Of course there were some who complained, but probably most of them had spent the war looking for something to complain about anyway and would spend the rest of their lives moaning about anything and everything; perhaps their wives had even blessed the war for providing a little peace and quiet at home.

The memory of my first port of call is vague; Scotland or Kettering? What I do remember very clearly was searching through my wardrobe at Fraserburgh for clothes which I had left behind. I should have known better; my three older brothers had been demobbed and got there before me. They had cleaned out anything worth wearing and left just a few odd socks, worn out shoes and outdated ties. They should have had more respect for me, after all, I was the senior rank in the family.

Back at Kettering, Lilian made me model my suit, marked it up with her tailor's chalk, ripped all the seams apart and stitched it back together again. There was no doubt about it, she was a wizard with a needle, it was her profession. In the WAAF she had been in charge of a Tailoring Department and my suit now fitted perfectly.

Well, that was it. I was back in Civvy Street with a few weeks paid leave to settle in and then what? Things were not the same as I had remembered. People appeared to be more confident, almost to the verge of arrogance, especially the women. They had found a new level in society because of the demand for their services in the absence of men. Due to the years of short-ages and strict rationing, the need to collect, and indeed *demand* your share had become a way of life and this was something I had to get used to.

My first attempt was at the tobacconist's. I joined a long queue for cigarettes and as I moved closer, watching the good brands appear from under the counter, excitement grew at the prospect of a decent smoke. At last it was my turn. I asked for twenty and the assistant produced a pack of American cigarettes from a shelf behind him. Having been compelled to smoke that type of stuff for years, I requested something a little better.

His answer was, to say the least, a bit disturbing.

"That is all I have."

I calmly drew breath and asked if I could have one of those he had been producing from under the counter.

His answer was quite blunt. "They are for my regular customers."

"But I have been out of the country for the best part of six years. Whose regular customer am I?"

"That's your problem, mate," he answered.

Having, with great restraint, denied myself the luxury of knocking him out through the back of his shop, I consulted an Inspector at the local Police Station. He sympathised with my predicament, but there was nothing in law that he could do and he advised me, with a grin, not to do anything 'rash or unlawful'. Ah well, perhaps I was just unlucky there, but I did need a newspaper, so off I went to the newsagent's. This was more encouraging; the counter carried a large selection.

"Daily Mirror please."

"Sorry I don't have any."

"But what about that pile there?"

"They are for my regular customers."

Oh no, not again, this was getting past a joke. I left him without any doubt about his parentage, seething with anger and resentment. Was this what had become of the homeland I had dreamed and prayed for?

But there was more to come. In the pub that night, customers were passing their glasses over my shoulder for a second drink and I was still waiting to be served with my first, but when I complained about this sort of treatment people looked at me as if I had come from another planet.

Perhaps that was the problem. I must have come from somewhere else. I most certainly did not belong here. I had believed I was coming home but this was not the land I had left, fought for, and dreamed about returning to.

This was, indeed, the beginning of a new life, but overshadowed by bitterness and disappointment and the memory of those who would never return. To many, just names inscribed in stone, but to their comrades in arms their faces forever remembered and their voices still loud and clear.

They had died instead of me; how lucky I was to be alive.

War cemeteries in the Western Desert.

I Never Saw a Soldier Cry

The enemy pushed towards Dunkirk, we were ordered to Calais to stand fast,
But when Tanks all gone, we were no help there, so got out amongst the last,
Shelled through streets to the Harbour, full of vehicles and sunken ships,
At the breakwater a lone ship beckoned, come quick for the last of our trips,
I reached the deck as she pulled away with the single hold packed with men,
Shrapnel filled the air, I was stiff with fear, tensed waiting for where and when,
But in that hell hole below was frustration and fear, not a fighting way to die,
Men cursed their luck, caught in a trap, But I never heard a Soldier cry.

Dumped near the mountains in the north of Greece with 52 worn out Tanks,
Just a few of the 60,000 force sent to help stop Hitler's pranks,
But from Yugoslavia he came with a mighty Army and hit us hard on the plain,
We fought for every yard of ground but he drove us south with disdain,
Struggled through the mountains with no place to hide, bombs and bullets ever near,
With nothing to hit back men clawed the ground and cursed with frustration and fear,
They collected the bodies and limbs from the trees and buried them with honour,
No voice told of the sickness felt but grim faces portrayed the horror,
At the end of this land 10,000 were trapped, many asking the question why?
But in all that hell which men went through, I never saw a Soldier cry.

Battled for weeks to relieve Tobruk; at Sidi Rezeigh whole Regiments wiped out,
On to Bengazi, both sides took their toll and victory was always in doubt,
Outgunned by the enemy we paid a high price, burned out vehicles marked our path,
We used them again, pulling back in retreat, when Rommel vented his wrath,
Lost Tobruk, our pride, and land to Alamein; where we stopped to defend our line,
Here, at the gates of Cairo, defeated by the enemy, for no reason we could define,
We had done our best with what we had, it was not good enough; we could not lie,
Fear was high, moral was low, But I never saw a Soldier cry.

The barrage at Alamein was horrific, it brought excitement and feelings of new hope,
Trembling with the ground, metal screamed overhead, I wondered, would we cope,
Through the minefield we passed, the sky glowed red, the patterns of tracer amazed,
But at the break of dawn we were trapped in a hollow, the enemy had not been erased,
Through shellfire and bullets the Infantry pushed on, men falling all around,
But they never stopped, to question the dead, till they captured that vital high ground,
The sacrifice was great, Tanks burned all around, I felt guilty at still being free,
Blood poured down my shirt from a shrapnel blast, but had the others all died for me,
It was often said Soldiers died for each other, the question was always why,
Bodies lay around like bloodied rags, But I never saw a Soldier cry.

On the plains of Tel El Aqqaqir came the final blow and we put the enemy to flight,
The plan to destroy his Armour had failed as they slipped away in the night,
He stood and fought back as defences allowed over 2,000 miles of land,
It took six months of strife, in this God forsaken place, to finally smash his last stand,
The cost had been tremendous; took almost three of our tanks to his every one,
Three Regiments we had lost, 1,500 men, .from Calais until this deed was done,
Now silence prevails and there is time to remember, those comrades that life passed by
But there was no turning back, life moved on, And I never saw a Soldier cry.

Many years have passed but the memory lives on
and bravery of their deeds still sung,
Now I stand among the graves,
And cry and cry for those who died so young.

The Regiment's Battle Honours.